# SCOUNDRELS IN IRAQ

## AN ENGINEER'S ADVENTURES

Kenny Dupar

Don't believe everything you read !

4 AUG 21

# Contents

**Part One:**
**Operation Iraqi Freedom –**
**Baghdad 2003-04**

1 - The World's Biggest Ashtray ................................................. 3

2 - BIAP ..................................................................................... 22

3 - Liaison at Al Kashafa Football Stadium ........................... 44

4 - The White Don King of Baghdad ...................................... 62

5 - Abu Ghraib ........................................................................... 81

6 - Why I Stole a Bulldozer ...................................................... 98

7 - Magical Mobile Mixing Machines ................................... 107

8 - Battle Rhythm .................................................................... 114

9 - The Russian Embassy and the Diaper Rash Miracle ........ 123

10 - Special Operators – Men in Black ................................. 134

11 - Ba'ath Party Bingo .......................................................... 140

12 - Cut Me A Bottle .............................................................. 149

## Part Two:
## McCoy

13 - Medical Hold.................................................................169

14 - Hero to Zero ...............................................................178

15 - The Husky...................................................................187

16 - The Woman with the Purple Finger ............................203

17 - Big Daddy....................................................................210

18 - Allah Akbar.................................................................222

19 - The Call ......................................................................233

## Part Three:
## Retrograde Movement -Tikrit 2010-2011

20 - The Office Jewel..........................................................245

21 - Rock Stars ..................................................................259

22 - Aircraft Simulator at the Gym.....................................273

23 - I saw Santa in Kirkuk.................................................289

24 - Disneyworld................................................................302

25 - Happy Place ...............................................................307

26 - Poison Gas at Halabja ................................................319

27 - Closing Up Shop .........................................................330

28 - ISIS and the Caliphate................................................342

Glossary of US Army Acronyms .........................................347

US Army Rank Structure ...................................................349

# AUTHORS NOTE:

This autobiography portrays my work with the United States Army in Iraq. I tried to have as much fun as I could, while always taking care of soldiers.

When Saddam was in hiding in 2003 the people were scared, and we had our ass in both hands. However, it wasn't long before I realized I could do pretty much whatever I wanted. But first, I had to do my job.

Do NOT get crosswise of Uncle Sugar. He don't play.

# DEDICATION

To the women and men of the United States Army Reserve.

To my daughter: I never planned to become a traveling man. Our loss of time together is my greatest regret.

IN MEMORIUM: JIM FESTER

# DISCLAIMER

Everything in the book is true, except for anything that could eventually lead to my criminal prosecution. Enjoy!

Me ringing the Freedom Bell in honor of
Jim Fester. Capitol Mall. June, 2016
Picture by Bob

Map of Iraq

# PART ONE

# Operation Iraqi Freedom

## Baghdad 2003-04

CHAPTER 1

# The World's Biggest Ashtray

It was like going to war with a gang of thieves and scoundrels. Unless a piece of equipment was screwed down, chained, and guarded, it was obvious to us that no one really wanted it. Even then, bolt cutters became our favorite piece of equipment. We ignored most Army regulations in the lawless state of Iraq, in the summer of 2003. If it could be smoked, we smoked it. If it contained alcohol, we drank it. Within a vague, horny concept of fraternization, the motor pool was the place to go at night if two Army Reserve soldiers wanted to "knock boots."

Members of the 169th Engineer Battalion soon gained the reputation within the military as the most talented builders in Iraq, as well as a criminal organization masquerading as an Army outfit. When we left leadership conferences, other units' officers instinctively checked to see if they still had their wallets. We were given contemptuous stares as if we were outlaws, a reputation we embraced.

I served for the welfare of the soldiers of my unit, Tony, and the President of the United States, in that order.

My name is Kenny.

• • •

The 169th Battalion, headquartered in Dubuque, Iowa, was tasked to support Operation Iraqi Freedom in the second game of a double header, the first having been the Gulf War of 1990-91. We deployed under the control of the 1st Armored Division, which planted their guidon flag in Baghdad after offensive combat operations were successfully completed. The Engineers were sent to build and re-build.

I had seventeen years of service in the Army Reserve and had been working as a union carpenter when Army Personnel Command called me up mid-February, 2003 for the re-match. I was cross-leveled/reassigned to the 169th from another Engineer Combat Heavy Battalion out of Milwaukee. By the end of March, I was in Davenport, Iowa helping to load all of Headquarters' rolling stock (vehicles), the earth-moving equipment (heavy junk), and forty-foot storage containers onto trains bound for a ship at New Orleans. Other companies were placed throughout the State: Iowa City, Cedar Falls, Decorah, and Waterloo.

At that point I was Captain Dupar, so immediately upon arrival at Davenport, as the highest ranking soldier, I was informed that I was now the Detachment Commander. My new assignment was for only two weeks, as the outfit would soon be reunited with our parent unit. Chief Warrant Officer Plummer had been running the detachment for years, so when the local media showed up to interview Commander Plummer, I deferred to him. I wasn't sorry because I was damn lost in process, and it was in fact his outfit. Everyone was a stranger to me. It took a while to start making friends, especially since I outranked everyone there. Happily, Sergeant First Class Hank Molina was a full time Army Reserve soldier working at the unit. He became my battle buddy and friend for life, but it took getting to Iraq before I actually got to know him.

I watched the invasion of Iraq on TV, lying on the bed in my motel room, just prior to convoying to Fort Leonard Wood, Missouri. The infantry boys were kicking ass. And Saddam Hussein's statue was winched down by an armored wrecker. Its brass face was contemptibly beaten with the soles of his countrymen's shoes.

En route to the mobilization station, I finally met the Headquarters Commander, Captain Diana Berry, at a truck stop. I received an old wheat penny with my change from a quick purchase of a bratwurst and a pack of cigarettes. I took that as a good omen. Berry was young, black, tough as nails, super smart, pretty, and experienced. The troopers simply called her "Mom." She didn't leave her Humvee, merely uttering a few syllables to me through the open vinyl window, with a look of distrust towards a fellow captain now stuffing his uniform with a sausage and his lungs with smoke.

All units had to be as close to 100% as possible with personnel before deploying overseas. The Army Reserve had to take soldiers from some units and reassign them, or "cross-level" the Force. When these first mobilizations took place, volunteers for different Military Occupational Specialties (MOS's) were requested. But if an outfit was required to provide, for example, five carpenters, the cream of the crop wasn't offered. Who would you send from your team except those with attendance and attitude problems? That's right—soldiers with borderline personality disorders, the patriotic, those who hated their civilian jobs, and a few with warrants volunteered. The balance were the unlucky, the malingerers, and those who didn't play well with others. Tony and I got caught up in the sweep of the latter group. One third of the 169th Engineers soldiers were cross-leveled, from thirty different states, a cross section of America. Losing military units became shells of their former selves, broken irretrievably. They were combined with others or merely folded up their flags, disbanded and forgotten. Being cross-leveled meant you had no ties to the community, with no allegiance to the gaining outfit, so we became more like free agents on a one-year contract. After the deployment, you'd never see these people again. Conversely, the two-thirds who called Iowa home found temporary compatriots to their own schemes. Lawlessness, in a lawless country, came pretty easily to us.

Soldiers in the 169th were untested, and our battalion was one of the first out of the Army Reserve gate toward the dangerous unknown, or as it is called, "downrange." Downrange was where the bullets flew. At non-automated small arms ranges, soldiers would have to walk forward to score their paper targets. When the line was clear, shooters would walk downrange, in front of the weapons. It was always an exciting feeling. The other side of the world was eerie, dangerous, where there would be live ammunition. Thus the phrase "being downrange."

If we were scared or even apprehensive, as soldiers we didn't say it. It was important to be tough, or appear to be, and stay silent. Nervousness wouldn't help the loves back home. Everything was always "fine" and we complained about something else when at the outdoor phone banks connecting us to parents, kids, wives/husbands, and friends—like how bad the food was. S.O.S. is still shit on a shingle since World War Two.

The Army always gives you a four-day pass just before shipping you off to war. Everybody cries at the airport. My wife saluted me, her face beet red, before I had to turn to walk down the concourse. She held our daughter, almost three. The baby could feel the sadness, too. After a few steps I stopped to grab my handkerchief and gain some composure. I shouldn't have looked back. But I did. They were gone. That was the hardest part of the deployment. In only days I'd be flying over the Atlantic Ocean.

Post-mobilization training lasted for two months at Fort Leonard Wood, Missouri. By the end of May, we finally boarded the chartered 747. In the late afternoon as we were walking across the tarmac in Kuwait City, the 110-degree heat slapped us in the face, windy and dry. It sapped our strength continually, like facing an open blast furnace. Coming down the passenger stairs, our battalion of 500+ soldiers de-planed and crammed into buses with our personnel baggage. Curtains were drawn across the windows for physical security, and I prayed the air conditioning would put a dent in the constricting heat. Many bodies in a confined unventilated space makes the temperature rise fast. The 12-hour flying time from Missouri to Prague to Kuwait City had left us exhausted and on edge. We were a sweaty, stinky mess.

You might ask, did our leaders have our backs? Did they have a plan? Well, our uniforms were woodland camouflage with black boots. The Army Reserve was dressed to kill in Germany against the Russians, not for a counter-insurgency in the deserts and cities of Iraq, where thousands of human beings had died violently in recent months. We were now going forward, not knowing at all when we might be coming home.

At this point I'd like to give the reader a chance to opt out of the book. This account may be too bold and raw for you, so you may want to quit reading. So I'll just answer the most basic question: "How did it feel to be at war in Iraq?" I want you to gather four things from around your home—a shovel, a roll of toilet paper, a flashlight, and some sort of weapon (firearm, steak knife, Louisville Slugger, pepper spray, etc.) Now, the next time you need to poop at night, I want you to gather these items, go out to your back yard and do your business. Try that for a year. The flashlight is actually dual purpose. In Iraq, you only poop in the daytime, as there are no lights inside Port-a-Potties. That's how it feels to be at war in Iraq. Everything is out of place when you go downrange.

• • •

The theater of operations was Southwest Asia. But to get to Iraq you had to go through Kuwait, the world's biggest ashtray.

Sergeants make stuff happen and officers plan and get in the way. The senior Non-Commissioned Officer (NCO) for a company is the First Sergeant, who is responsible for everybody's ass. They do not cry at the airport. The sergeants conduct several head counts, then a by-name roll call, each time the unit leaves for a new destination.

First Sergeant Kringle was getting pissed off, the veins sticking out at his temple as he took another head count to ensure no soldier from the Headquarters' Company had wondered off like Private Snuffy, Chaplain Charlie, or Second Lieutenant Shit-for-Brains.

We boarded a line of buses that eventually swung through Kuwait International Airport's twenty-kilometer boundary, dropping our Heavy Combat Engineer Battalion personnel at Camp Wolf ten minutes later. We were in theater, time to "embrace the suck." We dragged ourselves into large tents that were empty save the plywood floors. But the air conditioning was cranked within closed flaps and the space was clean, as yet unused by thousands of transient American soldiers. We laid on our duffle bags and attempted to rest. Some tried to call home from the phone banks which charged $5/minute to tell Sweetie you're OK, which I did. Ellen was elated I called, but my daughter didn't want to talk into the receiver. She still didn't get the concept of phones. Not talking to her tore me up. It still does, every opportunity lost, to this day.

• • •

The NCOs organized about fifty soldiers from the five companies making up the battalion to help offload the 2000 plus duffle bags and hundreds of M16 rifles from the belly of the plane. When they arrived back at Camp Wolf two hours later, every soldier had to claim four bags. Our equipment, uniforms, and personal clothing were stuffed to the gills in four duffle bags. The desert combat uniforms and desert boots were promised to be waiting overseas. It was the Army's property, but individually signed for. You lose it, you buy it. Going to the desert? The Army makes sure you have cold weather gear, just in case. Going to the frozen tundra of Green Bay? You'll have your mosquito netting. Who knew where the deployment roulette wheel could send you? "Don't worry, it'll be there in theater," the supply sergeants back at Fort Leonard Wood, Missouri had said with a smile. I did not doubt we would be supplied soon, as logistics is one thing at which the United States Army is a master. Killing people and breaking things are two others. The US Military had won a series of tactical victories, but the plan on what to do next was probably written on a cocktail napkin.

Saddam Hussein certainly had chemical weapons and had used them before. He had murdered thousands of people with them. The fear was that he might have had nukes or dirty bombs. In hindsight, his capacity was misrepresented, the intelligence false. Now he was in hiding, someplace. Nuclear, biological, or chemical (NBC) were all weapons of mass destruction. They were stored somewhere, or buried. Nobody knew. We had chemical protective suits in large sealed bags that we took wherever we went. They took up half of a duffle bag or more. They included olive-drab thick charcoal-lined pants and top with boots and rubber gloves, a recipe for sweat. We'd need it to survive a chemical or biological attack. If the alarms sound and you can't get your green weight-reduction suit on fast enough, and you smell the sweet fragrance of fresh-cut grass or almonds even though you're in the desert, it is nerve agent, and you'll be dead in about fifteen seconds. Blister agent or choking agents like mustard gas or chlorine perfected in World War One were a lot scarier. You could be disabled for life, or drown as your lungs filled with fluid. If you lost your protective mask, an immediate and painful response from the chain of command ensued. The entire unit would stop what it was doing until the "sensitive item" was found, with written counseling and great embarrassment to follow.

Although extremely remote, the possibility of an attack was nevertheless real. But the truth was, you were far more likely to be exposed accidently to deadly agents through the destruction of munitions and the whim of the breeze. The Pentagon eventually called this some sort of sickness, but I can't remember the name of it. I never liked to think about it, but I wonder how many soldiers became unofficially disabled. Try and submit that claim to the Veteran's Administration. There are great people helping our vets. And there are providers who can't be easily fired but should be, who prescribe opioids like candy and call it care. In the Army, as in the National Football League, everything is great until you get hurt; then everything changes, for the worse.

The movement to Camp Virginia, Kuwait started five hours after landing. It was evening now, the temperature dropping to a pleasant 80 degrees, the night sky bright and calm. Time for "you're your buddy smile" as we crammed hip-to-hip onto more buses to take the battalion forty miles inland into the unmarked desert. Fencing along every highway appeared to have caught every plastic bag and all garbage that could blow in the wind. White and brown cigarette butts dotted the landscape everywhere. Sergeants soon placed coffee cans in designated smoking areas for ashtrays.

Everything looks like a road in the desert. Floodlights deceive your sense of distance. The line of flatbeds, buses, and admin vehicles serpentined through the ECP and more tents, row upon row, were organized into quads. Thousands of soldiers were stationed there in transit. It was 2:00 a.m. by the time we arrived at Camp Virginia. Time to un-ass, claim your duffle bags again, and drag them into huge tents 100 feet long and 40 feet wide, with the AC blowing low. We plopped down anywhere, exhausted, and tried to sleep. The first order of business in the daylight was to sign for cots. There were plenty of clean Port-a-Potties, thankfully. Three hours later, with a mean headache, I was standing in line to get breakfast. It would take several more days to start feeling like a human being again. For the next two weeks the 169th would acclimate to the blowing grime, camel spiders, the rare scorpion, and getting used to 125-degree heat in the shade. Metal was so hot you had to wear gloves. Our black boots soaked up the sun until our feet felt like they were on fire.

Soon we found the Post Exchange (PX). Yet another line which took about an hour to get in the door. Imagine a small Walgreens with various sundry items like beef jerky, Tylenol, baby wipes, Pepsi, all the basic essentials. I bought a Hot Mamma pickle in a plastic pouch, along with some other stuff I probably didn't need but felt it was wise to have. Having made my purchase, I munched on the pickle outside the PX. It was pretty spicy and I drank the juice it was in, just to be a tough guy in front of other soldiers. I was burning on the outside and now the inside. I'd would soon pay for that bravado.

The next day it was time to get our heavy junk from the port. From the Headquarters Company we had dozers, scrapers, twenty-ton dumps, dozens of Humvees, water distributors, steel wheel vibrators, dozens of forty-foot steel containers, tractors with their low boy trailers, and excavators. There were Magical Mobile Mixing Machines, graders, cranes, generators, air compressors, Vietnam vintage transport trucks general purpose (nicknamed Deuce – shortened from 2 ½ ton cargo), and laser levels. We received our maintenance shops, welders, ambulances, water buffaloes, sheepsfoots, asphalt distributors, and even night vision googles. Included were carpenter, plumbing and electrical kits, along with tentage, camo netting and one mysterious box full of athletic gear, all waiting at the port of Al Zour.

I volunteered to go on the convoy mission, mostly to get off of Camp Virginia for the day, out of curiosity to see more of Kuwait's super highways and blowing garbage, and to help the Battalion Maintenance Officer, Captain Mike Sanchez, with getting our equipment back to Camp Virginia. The heavy junk (said with all affection) was already lined up in rows from ships coming out of the Gulf of Mexico. Other units were receiving equipment, too. Captain Sanchez got started accounting for our stuff when I doubled over. Sixty seconds to launch. I had a tremendous case of the bubble guts and the end was near.

"Hey, Kenny, you OK?" Mike asked.

"No! Is there a Port-a-Pottie around here?"

My future battle buddy, Sergeant First Class Hank Molina, asked me, "Are you sick?" I heard genuine concern in his voice. He put his hands on his knees to get closer to my screwed-up face. A battle buddy is another soldier you can confide anything to. Every soldier is required to have one. If you didn't have one, it meant you must be a first class idiot/asshole. That bastard Tony had a huge grin on his big, fat face. Hank asked again, "Are you OK?" "No! I ate a Hot Mamma pickle yesterday!" Twenty seconds to launch. That made our group of soldiers smile and chuckle at my gurgling stomach. I moved out double quick once the first spasm subsided. It was 9:00 a.m. and already 100 degrees. I wanted to double over and walk but my damn rifle swung on my shoulders wildly. Around one corner, no Port-a-Potties, past another line of vehicles, nothing, and then, there! Shimmering like a mirage at a hundred yards out was a blue box. 10, 9, 8.... Crapping my drawers would have led to never-ending ridicule from the troops. There was even a roll of toilet paper! Sweat was dripping off my nose at two-second intervals inside this tiny oven. My M16 was in one corner of the box, Kevlar helmet and flak jacket in the other, barely room to move. After bolt cutters, baby wipes became another essential piece of equipment, never to go without on mission. I was learning.

Coming out, I felt a breeze, and had a completely different point of view, but was greatly surprised by a smell like that of burning tires. I hadn't noticed the oil refinery, under whose shadow the Army's equipment yard fell. It belched toxins unrestrained. I guess I was focused on other things. But I felt great! Next, I found my comrades to see how I could assist the organization of the convoy serials. I pledged to never again eat a Hot Mama Pickle or try to be a tough guy.

It took hours to get the go ahead to leave the port. Captain Sanchez passed out a strip map he'd gotten from Movement

Control. No scale, no compass directions, no landmarks; just some road names and approximate distances. It was almost worthless, basically crap. Mike took me to one side and said, "Kenny, I need you to take the last serial in the convoy." This was not good. A convoy is divided into manageable segments or serials, usually not more than 15 vehicles each. Being in charge of the last serial meant that I was responsible to pick up soldiers stranded beside anything that broke down. And oh, by the way, the vehicles had been aboard a ship for a month and not maintained. It meant that we would be by ourselves if we had to tow a vehicle, and with a 100% chance of that happening.

"Sure, man. You got it. What vehicles am I going to have?"

"I'll get back to you. Give me fifteen minutes," Mike said.

He, like me, was to lose about 30 pounds over the next year, as we were running our asses off. By the stifling autumn of Iraq 2003, he was promoted to Major. I had to pass two more years after my first deployment before being advanced from Captain.

Mike gave me a little fist bump before he ran off. I didn't see him again until the next day. Hours melted into early evening. Poor Captain Sanchez was running to arrange chaos into some semblance of order. I didn't know when we were supposed to leave. More hours passed. Finally, the tractor trailers started to pull and their gooseneck pintles snapped obediently into place. The serials lurched forward, about 15 vehicles each. Behind the three main serials I had the rear with two wreckers and some Humvees. We crept towards the inevitable, not showing our apprehension, not even to teammates.

Radio communication was sketchy. We had Motorolas with usually pretty fair range, maybe ten miles over flat terrain. I followed out, hearing the chatter between Headquarters personnel, but immediately a Deuce (military cargo truck) broke down. Beloved by the Army, venerable in service, and now a piece of shit, it was only 100 meters outside the gate, its brakes locked up. The mechanics got it going in about 20 minutes. A young soldier gave me the thumbs up when she was done. We could roll again.

"Great," I thought, "just enough time to completely lose contact with the rest of the convoy." We'd already struck out. My radio went dead. The sun was beginning to set. We had eight or nine vehicles in the trail party. The strip map that Movement Control published wasn't to scale and looked like my three-year-old had drawn it. I held it in my lap, using the Humvee's odometer to try and navigate. Less than ten miles in, we found a broken down Humvee near another which had pulled over to help. After the mechanics set up the wrecker we were moving again. More vehicles, more soldiers. Luckily, I found the Kuwait Air Force Base of Ali Al Salem, the last point of civilization prior to driving into the desert. I asked for directions to Camp Virginia. The Kuwaiti Airman spoke some English and followed with wild arm movements, both of which left me baffled.

Now was the worst part, trying to navigate in the desert without commo (communications), maps, or proper signage. It had been about three hours since we left the gate at the port of Al Zour, having traveled some 50 miles. I saw lights in the distance and we drove towards them, but the tracks in the desert kept crisscrossing over each other. I couldn't find the Entry Control Point. We were lost. The soldiers were getting plenty nervous, as was I. Then that same Deuce got mired in soft sand. I decided to leave most of the element there, and proceeded with just two Humvees. I had to find the gate! Soon we were running parallel to the camp perimeter. The berm surrounding it was a dozen feet high with guard towers higher still, placed every 200 meters—probably unmanned, but who knew? Friendly fire was a remote yet still frightening possibility. Keeping the berm

100 meters to our left, we continued to search. Was this installation even Camp Virginia? Another hour had gone by and it was almost midnight now. Eighty degrees started feeling cold against our sweat-soaked green woodland uniforms. We slowed down. Then we noticed small plate-sized discs scattered around us. I told my driver to stop and got out, seeing what I thought was an arming switch on the tops of these discs. Surface laid anti-personnel mines? I had my doubts. My young driver was completely unnerved and refused to move the Humvee. Another soldier suggested we abandon the vehicles and strike out on foot. I guessed that Camp Virginia could be more than a dozen miles all around or more. We backed the vehicles out slowly and turned around. It seemed like another hour went by before we returned to where the Deuce had mired, but no one was there. Now we were truly alone, with no communications.

But then I saw light! We sped toward it. The Entry Control Point was lit up like a vast welcome sign, a quarter of a mile long with serpentines between fighting positions, speed bumps, and floodlights. At the end of it, now "inside the wire," Major Posey and Major Perez sprung out of the last guard shack, slapping us on the backs like prodigal sons and daughters. We were the last in. All accounted for. Mission complete.

Later, I was able to piece together from Camp Virginia's Major Cell that the discs we had seen were probably the storage canister tops from artillery rounds. So much for taking your dunnage/garbage with you so the enemy doesn't know what you were doing or how much equipment and personnel you have. After the previous night, perhaps I shouldn't have been too critical of others' soldiering. I felt pretty sheepish about getting lost. And by the way, those guard towers were manned, but probably at only 25%.

A few days later, around sundown, the sky turned an eerie orange hue. A black wall of cloud was approaching from the west, although the air was calm, not moving at all. I almost bumped into Tony en route to the Port-a-Potties. Pointing to the horizon, I asked, "Is that a sand storm?" He responded, "Dust storm. It's a lot closer than you think. Better hurry and find your goggles. Probably last all night and into tomorrow. This is going to get nasty."

A dust storm spreads a fine talc of whatever has rotted on the desert floor. It moves at a constant 40+ miles per hour. It gets into everything and can last for days. When it hit us, I looked over to a small rise to see four young soldiers mooning the storm. Must have been Iowa boys the way they were screaming and hooting, baring their backsides. Normal soldiers secure ever flap, every possible opening and get into the tent. They're not going anywhere for a while. If you have to use the latrine, you retrieve the humongous googles in the bottom of one of your duffle bags and wrap a bandana over your face. But the grit always gets beneath your clothes, the filthiness taking days to shake out. Better to stay put and swap stories with your battle buddy unless you absolutely have to venture out.

The previous combat operations in Iraq had been wildly successful. The next phase of the strategic plan, Stability Operations, was set to begin. Lieutenant General Franks retired about then after conducting a brilliant operational campaign. I guess no one really had a plan after that. If it had been written upon a cocktail napkin, it hadn't been published. The "Mission Accomplished" banner displayed on the aircraft carrier Abraham Lincoln should have been shoved up some White House staffer's ass. All the self-congratulatory mutual approbation wasn't going to stop the first Combat Heavy Engineer Battalion crossing the berm into Iraq. We knew what to do. We had the Commander's intent: Go build stuff.

I was in the Tactical Operations Center (TOC – pronounced "talk") when I had the opportunity to use a satellite phone to call my wife. Usually, a leader will deny him or herself a luxury not afforded to all, but I still placed the call. Ellen was beside herself, relieved, crying. "This is the best birthday present I've ever gotten!" It was her birthday? I had lost track of the date. But I went with it, saying that of course I'd call her to say I was all right. Very few had called home from Camp Virginia, as AT&T still hadn't made it out into the desert.

Terror in theater exists on many corners. But nothing compares to losing positive control of your weapon. Captain Sanchez and I got a ride to the community center of Camp Virginia after duty hours around twilight. As we got dropped off I turned to grab my rifle, when suddenly the driver revved up. I ran after the vehicle yelling, but lost the Humvee when it turned and turned again. My buddy was gone, too. I was among dozens of other Humvees that all looked the same. This one was from another unit. Career-ending panic rushed over me, as I scurried to find my rifle. They could shut down the entire camp. Seventeen years of service down the tubes. I was sweating despite the cool of the impending night. Then I shuddered, having lost my weapon.

"Nice going, Captain. What's wrong with you? I guess you don't really want to be in the Army!" I imagined the faceless Colonel who ran Camp Virginia sneering. I flung open more than ten vinyl doors. I was shaking like a dog pooping razor blades. Finally, I found it. In the dim light I confirmed the serial number with my little flashlight. Thank you, Jesus! I chain smoked a few butts.

• • •

Captain Diana Berry had a big decision to make. She was the Headquarters Company Commander and I was her Executive Officer (XO). Without Diana, I'd be in charge. And nobody wanted that, especially me. I'd just completed a three-year hitch in Command and couldn't imagine taking on her job. One of her NCOs—a supply sergeant—had gone on a hunger strike. I pleaded with the sergeant to take care of herself, but it was to no avail. Her lack of a family care plan before we deployed became a huge deal, as she tried to claim that she had no one to take care of her two kids. This woman was out there. Maybe bi-polar. Hell, I don't know, but the open rumor was that she'd knock boots with any willing fella. Her steady boyfriend in Fort Leonard Wood was a married man. We lived in a fish bowl, so everybody knew everybody else's business.

As the XO, I had conducted an inventory of all equipment while still at the mobilization station, Fort Leonard Wood, Missouri. I found out she couldn't account for a $15,000 pair of night vision goggles. The promiscuous soldier, who refused to eat when we got to Kuwait, was the full time supply sergeant, and I thought she was going to lose her mind. Captain Berry knew a colonel who was able to grease that issue over. But in the Kuwaiti desert, my sympathy with this recalcitrant soldier was at an end. I recommended to Diana that we take her north.

"She's just going to be a bigger pain in the ass if we take her."

"Yeah, but then everybody will know they can get over on us," I argued.

She shook her head violently, "Oh, no they won't. Not on me." We stared at each other. "Look, Captain Dupar, I've got a chance to kick her ass out right now. She's been a pimple on my butt for years. You just joined us; you don't know."

At first blush it might seem that promiscuity would increase morale. It doesn't. This Sergeant would have continued to play "Queen for a Year," preying on the lonesomeness and stupidity of male solders throughout the deployment. A few times you'd see a female soldier revel in the unabashed attention given to her. Maybe she wasn't the prettiest girl on the block. I observed both genders trying to fill a perceived need, recklessly grasping another body. Sometimes this can become completely destructive. Men taking advantage. Girls just as horny as the guys. Diana sent the supply sergeant home. So, they both got what they wanted.

Just before we departed Camp Virginia each soldier in the battalion received two pairs of desert camouflage boots, trousers, blouses, and several T-shirts. The first stop was the tailor's shop to get our name tapes and rank sewn on our shirts, helmet covers, caps, and boonie hats. The Vietnam era flak jackets were still the woodland pattern. In about six months we'd be resupplied with more uniforms, and receive actual body armor with Kevlar plates.

A rumor started that civilians were throwing children under the tires of military vehicles moving north in order to hinder movement. I didn't know if it was true or not.

"I can't do it, Sir. I'll swerve or stop if I have to." One soldier told me just prior to departure.

"Bullshit!" Several soldiers were listening to me, "A convoy is like a freight train. It don't stop 'til we get where we're going." Pause. "Maintain your speed and following distance, always. And if some asshole shoves a kid under your tires, who killed him? Them or you?" Enough said.

The same idiot who sketched the route from the port Al Zour to Camp Virginia drew the strip map into Iraq—barely a squiggly line showing the 400 plus miles to our objective, Baghdad International Airport (BIAP – pronounced Bi-op). We had military maps and good commo for the tactical convoy. The NCOs and officers organized and rehearsed. We began staging the serials at 2:00 a.m. Start point (SP) was at 5:00 a.m., and the advance party moved out smartly to prepare a new home for the rest of the gang. I made sure I was in the advance party. The rest of the battalion would follow two days later. We were acclimated enough from two weeks' time in the World's Biggest Ashtray. It was time to cross the berm into Iraq.

# CHAPTER 2

# BIAP

Safwan was a shock of living standards. Just over the Kuwait/Iraqi border, the village had a modern highway, and crude apartment buildings. Everything was built from adobe and concrete, devoid of vegetation, an outpost in the desert. Electric lines were strung haphazardly. The 10,000+ Arabs crowded into a few square blocks were quiet. How they survived without arable land was a mystery. However, the few residents moving around at 7:00 a.m. waved, and the kids gave us thumbs up. The town quickly passed into the rear view mirror. Within 100 miles on Route Tampa the highway ended, and we began the arduous portion of the journey through tract destined for future paving. The "road" was dusty and wash-boarded, as we crawled along at twenty miles an hour through southern Iraq. The first fueling point along Route Tampa was called Scania. The "moon dust" was gray, six inches deep, fine like talcum powder, or freshly fallen snow. The heat approached 115 degrees Fahrenheit. We fueled and departed, pitying the soldiers who manned that station.

Then we saw the sand people. From mud brick huts scores of people looking for handouts swarmed our convoy. Sometimes they'd have a wire hooking the home to the electrical grid, just enough to run a radio or hot plate for a few unspecified hours of juice per day. We learned early it was too dangerous to throw water bottles or MREs (Meals Ready to Eat) to them. It would just encourage these people living in the desert waste to come closer to our moving vehicles, and make it harder to begin again if we were stopped by civilians milling about our bumpers. I was surprised at one stop, when a young man came to my zipped-down window (the sides of our Humvees were vinyl.) "Mister, Mister, you look girls, my sister." He added a vulgar hand gesture while holding the pornographic CDs. I wasn't interested. I knew that even in this lawless land, the Army would destroy you for putting porn into a government machine. Anyway, I hadn't been issued a laptop yet. His arm bounced a baggie in front of my face through the window opening: "Hashish, hashish." A true salesman!

"No. I'm sorry. I can't. Sorry," I replied. Maybe the next war. There'd be other opportunities, I supposed, in the immediate future. Too many witnesses, anyway. I looked over at my driver, Sergeant Jim Fester. He shook his head sadly at me. "What?" I hollered at him. Shouldn't I have assumed that the people within a Muslim country smoked the best dope in the world? Shouldn't we respect local traditions? But college had been many years ago. And there's a reason it's called dope. I worried that this war wasn't going to be any fun at all.

"I'm not saying nothing," Jim said. And with that the convoy lurched forward again, at a dreadfully slow pace, bumpity bumpity, kicking up choking clouds of moon dust.

Like an accordion, the line of vehicles curved, sped up, and then violently braked repeatedly for two hours toward BIAP, Baghdad International Airport. It felt like Mad Max at a crawl, heavy metal songs playing in my head while chasing a specter in the Iraqi desert at 20 miles per hour. Our weapons would foul immediately if ambushed, because of the unforgiving dust. The bolt would probably fire a few times if you'd been diligent in cleaning your rifle, but after that? There were no friendly faces to help us if we took a wrong turn, like what happened to Private First Class Jessica Lynch's platoon when they drove through Nasiriyah two months earlier.

Maps could be sketchy in theater, and GPS slow. The point vehicle of PFC Lynch's platoon drove into the city instead of bypassing it. The ambush was a spontaneous orgy of violence. A rocket-propelled grenade (RPG) detonated into PFC Lynch's vehicle. Small arms fire decimated the team of mechanics. Eleven were killed outright, including her battle buddy Sergeant Lori Ann Piestewa. She was the first woman killed during Operation Iraqi Freedom and the first Native American woman in our nation's history to be killed in action overseas. SGT Piestewa left behind two little ones. A year or so later, Squaw Peak Freeway in Phoenix was re-named Piestewa Peak Freeway in her honor.

Six soldiers from the element were eventually rescued. Jessica's torturers were shocked at the sight of an unconscious woman in uniform, and purposely broke her bones in the street. The internal injuries were grotesque. Righteous Muslims rescued her when the fury dimmed. Families in West Virginia brought consolation to the Lynches for the succeeding three weeks until, with the courageous information of good locals, Green Berets, Air Force Para-rescuers, Army Rangers, and a Delta Force raided the hospital where she lay dying. PFC Lynch wasn't their sister. She was a fellow soldier who needed help. The raiders also found the remains of eight soldiers in shallow graves near the hospital. Their bodies were returned to the USA except for three still unaccounted for.

When we were passing Nasiriyah in late May, 2003, no RPGs fired at us, no wrong turns were made. None of our soldiers were left unconscious in the street, stripped naked and abused in the most heinous of ways. But I wasn't aware of that barbarity and her bravery when we left that town behind. I read her book years later while remodeling the exterior of a hotel in Charleston, West Virginia. What would armed men in West Virginia do if an invader wandered into their neighborhood? Defend it? Left solely to their own lusts, listening to evil voices in their heads and the shouts of the crowd, the answer is—anything. What could a newly minted soldier from the Mountaineer State do when savaged and left bleeding in the street? Naturally, Jessica Lynch led, telling the truth about what happened. She was not a hero's hero; she didn't fire her weapon when concussed. But she showed us a grit and determination in years of recovery worthy of the greatest title anyone could have—Soldier.

Our Humvee was a two-seater with a cargo bay, and vinyl covered wood bows capping the bed. The two other soldiers with Jim and me were junior enlisted, and somehow they fell asleep in the back. The grimy dust covered their exposed faces like makeup. The heat was exhausting. It became a blizzard style whiteout. The convoy slowed even more. The young soldiers still racked out in the cargo bed, filthy with dust. The drivers created their own lanes to avoid collision, thus kicking up more dust. The "road" became six vehicles wide; the adrenaline ran higher as the visibility lessened. Jim and I began to talk about the girls who had broken our hearts and our best sex stories. When my meager recollections ended, his were just getting started. I realized much later that to cope with extreme stress men often took to vulgar tales in order to overcome fear. It took my mind off of the present danger that shouldn't exist,

to a girlfriend that never existed at all. I was just storytelling—
not like now.

The commo checks came regularly through the radio. "Hey
you this is me; radio check, over." The vehicle and serial commanders could talk to one another, the more often the better.
But long periods of silence, with nothing to say, would stretch
out until the Convoy Commander had to break the silence and
query the soldiers to see if everyone was still along for the
ride. The convoy was progressing OK. The topography began
to change from desert to barely arable land the closer we traveled within the Euphrates-Tigris plain. Date palms and pista-
chio groves were becoming more frequent. We crossed bridges
and saw small flocks of sheep and farmers with vegetable plots
next to their houses. They lived in simple block buildings with
an electrical wire attached. Chickens were scattered about,
and perhaps the family had a few head of cattle. The highway
started again and immediately we were running at 50 miles
per hour. Armored vehicles and artillery pieces lay bent and
burned along the roadside by the dozens. The famous "Ring
of Death" around Baghdad for the Infantry, Armor and Aviation guys was more like target practice at night. Iraqi forces,
stubborn fellows, ultimately ringed the Capital with their bodies and burnt-out vehicles. It was as if Uncle Sugar had said to
them, "Now don't move. I can see you through our infrared and
night vision. Hide beneath the palm trees if you want to. That's
good. Smile. Click." There are certain things that the American
people can have confidence in: warriors making our enemies
into portions for foxes, dust beneath their feet, their guts into
grease, and politicians gambling with people's lives.

At a big highway interchange we swung wide to the west
of Baghdad. Still en route to Tampa from Kuwait, the road
extended another 300 miles north to the city Mosul. Our convoy

exited after another fifteen minutes, turning east toward Baghdad International Airport. The Alpha Company Executive Officer, Captain Cary Sanchez, was the Convoy Commander for the Advanced Party of seventy-five plus troops and thirty plus vehicles. They did an awesome job that day. Not a missed turn, or scheduled halt, all within the scheduled time hacks.

It was late afternoon, and you could see palaces on hilltops— ornate marble buildings that grew imposingly as we approached. Saddam Hussein Al-Tikriti spent the nation's oil money on elaborate homes for himself. He didn't stay at Best Western when traveling around his fiefdom. European stonemasons built giant structures adorned with Italian marble. Each one was like walking up to the Lincoln Memorial or the West Virginia State Capitol with its golden dome. Having various nationalities creating your electrical grid played havoc with later development. They didn't care about building codes, as long as the chandeliers lit when the President of Iraq showed up.

Entering a field that would become our Life Support Area (LSA), the advanced party halted. We organized, the NCOs taking charge. Each of our Water Buffalo trailers carried 400 gallons of precious water. Placed in lines, our vehicles were our homes for now. MREs were for dinner. Nasty slit trenches for latrines were a few hundred meters away. Piss off First Sergeant Kringle and you'd be adding diesel to the cut-in-half fifty-five gallon drums that caught soldiers' waste, lighting it on fire, and stirring it with a metal paddle. Old school, just like in Vietnam. Call him Santa Claus, as in Kris Kringle and you'd be stirring shit for a week. Merry Christmas! Port-a-Potties soon became the norm, thankfully. Nothing is as refreshing as a just serviced Port-a-Pottie. In the next war maybe there'll be lights inside.

MREs come twelve in a case. Typically soldiers were handed one after waiting in a small line. It was luck of the draw. Each case cost the taxpayers about a hundred bucks. Protocol dictated that you could trade your MRE or give away parts, but you got what you got. Their shelf life is a few decades and there are dozens of varieties, including Mexican Style Chicken Stew, Beef Ravioli in Meat Sauce, Grilled Jalapeno Pepper Jack Beef Patty, Hash Brown Potatoes w/Bacon, Lemon Pepper Tuna, Asian Style Beef Strips w/Vegetables, Chicken Pesto Pasta, etc. A favorite contest required soldiers to eat the two four-inch Saltine crackers that are in every MRE. The winner was the first who could audibly whistle, usually blowing bits of cracker all over his battle buddy. I liked the Saltines with peanut butter and grape jelly. Every MRE had grape or orange beverage powder with a lot of sugar in it, coffee powder, and tiny bottles of Tabasco, creamer, and more sugar. Mixing all these became what is known as "Ranger pudding." I liked all the MREs, which is probably why I'm fat. The Holy Grail was the Jalapeno Cheese Spread—I'd definitely trade for that. You could heat the food with a chemical system provided; just add water and the pouch became hot as hell. I never liked the gum or understood the use for the tiny individual squares of toilet paper.

It got dark quickly. I set up my cot on the hood of my Humvee and crawled into my expensive Army sleeping system, also known as a fart sack. The temperature was now marvelous. The sky was full of stars. I slept like a baby. I always slept great in Iraq. This was one reason my heart condition improved mightily while in Iraq. Work hard and sleep like a king, lonesomeness among dozens be damned. The rest of the Battalion would convoy north the 475 miles from Camp Virginia to BIAP in two days.

The next morning our Battalion Commander, nicknamed Dynamite Dan, wanted a formation to address the Advanced Party. He had arrived in Baghdad ahead of everyone, probably in a Blackhawk helicopter. Dynamite explained our mission to clean up the bomb damage at the airport, and build Life Support Areas both for ourselves and other units. On order, we would begin construction projects in support of the Army's mission to stabilize Baghdad, with its population of more than seven million souls. This with a force in the immediate area of less than 50,000 US military personnel, a ratio of maybe 150 citizens to one American. That comparison would in months get more skewed as active duty units rotated home, replaced by reservists and the National Guard arriving to begin stabilization operations. By the end of the summer, an unexpected insurgency opposed to the American occupation began to plant IEDs on the roads, mortaring bases, and shooting at convoys and aircraft.

Dynamite Dan didn't want to be feared, just loved—a reckless method of leading for any commander in the Theater of Operations. As Machiavelli taught us, it is difficult to be both feared and loved, but if a prince cannot be both, it is far better to be feared than loved. If you are merely loved, then men, in their natural state of selfishness, will pledge their wealth and family until danger comes, but then they will abandon their prince wholesale. But if feared, a leader will be obeyed, as the anticipated consequence of a painful end is always effective. If the prince survived the danger from his frontiers and you hadn't come to his defense, the price would be the destruction of your family and all you possessed. But that was five centuries ago. People must have surely changed since then. Always remember: AUNTIE AND UNCLE SUGAR DON'T PLAY!

Our Battalion Commander told us it was his duty to inform us directly, from the First Armored Division Commander, of a General Order—a set of rules that became known to soldiers as General Order Number One. It listed prohibitions, the violation of which resulted in punishment within the fullest means of the Uniform Code of Military Justice. If you got caught, maybe, and if anybody cared:

1) Destruction of and possession of artifacts, antiquities, and cultural property
2) Gambling and bartering in currency
3) Consuming alcohol or drugs
4) Confiscation of private property
5) Possessing privately owned vehicles
6) Masturbation both real or imagined
7) Photographing human remains
8) Having babies with locals
9) Proselytizing
10) Possession of pornography

Many more prohibitions were laid down, but Dynamite promised he'd talk to Major General Dempsey, First Armored Division Commander, about us being allowed to drink a few barley pops. GO1 made most folks want to move to Vegas and never come back. Tony said it was bullshit; we'd do what we had to do. I'd never seen him that mad before: "Those big bosses back in the States go home every night. Screw them! Come over here and show me what to do, don't tell me what to do. Shit in a hole and eat cold food and cock suckers come over here and tell me to my face what I can and can't do!" Tony's voice echoed soldiers' frustrations. I think the 169th Engineer Battalion violated most of the orders, except for #8, as personnel never had the chance. We lived in a fish bowl and couldn't just leave post. Those beautiful Iraqi women were protected from us. No American orphans would be stranded in this war, to be ostracized and lost forever.

BIAP was in places a bombed-out wreck. The multiple 10,000-foot runways, airport terminals, and the control tower were of course not targeted by American bombs. There were multiple palace complexes, and there was no reason to destroy buildings US forces would need later. Substandard concrete block walls ran around BIAP. They couldn't stop a rifle bullet from going through them. The boundary was immense, over twenty miles. The wall was just a shell. "Engineer Village" was established in the Southwest corner of BIAP. Another Combat Heavy Battalion out of the Army Reserve would join us in a few weeks. A river-crossing Engineer Battalion also showed up later.

Baghdad International Airport complex was like two giant airports side by side, one for civilians on the east side of the control tower, and the other for military aviation on the west side. A road paralleled the military runway for about four miles. The Air Force occupied the side closest to their aircraft, and the Army on the other. These were surrounded by former Iraqi Army and Air Force support structures like hangers, barracks, admin buildings, and maintenance shops, which were now largely blown up. Debris removal from the destruction became a persistent mission during our deployment. Most buildings just had to be bulldozed down. But some could be rebuilt.

One series of barracks that was still mostly stabilized and useable was occupied by the 115th Military Police (MP) Battalion. One super-hot mission for us was to improve camp security for High Value Targets captured by the Coalition. The MPs manned the camp. It was named after Sergeant Kenneth Cropper from the Maryland National Guard, who had been recently killed in action. They made a movie about Camp Cropper a few years later, although I can't remember the plot. The set didn't look anything like what we built initially. Cropper became a lot nicer for the prisoners over time. We had to provide force protection immediately—guard towers, fencing, building stabilization, and larger Entry Control Points. The MP Captains and I became like peas and carrots, besties. I wouldn't have time to be homesick, just work. I'd sweat on my sleeping bag until exhaustion took me away. I tried not to think about my daughter, my wife, and the menagerie of pets. It'd just make me sad.

Getting three-inch crushed stone became priority #1 for us. Used for dust control, the stone was necessary in order to establish sanitary conditions around our battalion's dozens of eight-man tents. The desert hardpan surface was as tough as pavement, having baked in the sun for several centuries. Bulldozer blades skipped across it, so we ripped the earth with our dozer back attachments, but it was a slow process. The attachment was like three curled metal fingers that would rip the earth behind the dozer's tracks. Grading it level was taking forever. Then we placed a layer of broken stone. The unevenness caused many a turned ankle; it was commonplace to hear soldiers cursing while walking between the tents. It was nice to be building again, but we were starting off at a crawl.

Both Sergeant First Class Hank Molina and Tony saw something at the same time. At a nearby compound were two Massy Ferguson tractors and trailers with tilling discs. Unless you've ever looked up www.farmersonly.com/ as a dating site, you couldn't possibly fathom the amount of husk such a thing of beauty could produce (I'm speaking in terms of earth-moving equipment). To break the hard pan earth, we needed those dinner-plate-sized sharpened discs, all mounted in a row, and the tractors that towed them. Otherwise, the blades of dozers would skip, unable to dig. We had to build right now. We had to push dirt now! The word came down and filtered quickly to the boldest of the lot.

"How you guys doing?" Hank asked the young soldiers in a motor pool's guard shack. He jumped out of his hauler. "How freaking hot is it today?" He was alone in the theft.

"I don't know, Sergeant. We're just glad we have some shade."

"No shit, huh," said SFC Molina. He paused to grab three ice cold liter bottles of water out of the cab and handed two to the nub buck soldiers. "This is bullshit," he said as he cracked his own bottle and took a swig. "I have to get the tractors and their tiller attachments to the Direct Service Maintenance Shop today for their quarterly technical inspection or it's my ass. Can you believe it! And oh, by the way do it the middle of the day, too. Dumb ass officers!"

"No shit, right," they agreed. "Hey, thanks for the water. Shit, that's cold."

"Where are the Massey Fergusons anyway? Wait, I see 'em. Shit, only me to load them. Could you guys help real fast? Don't know if I'll get them both today." There wasn't any reason to be in a hurry when it was blistering in the sun.

"Wait, Sergeant. The steering wheel is padlocked. We can't move them."

"No, worries. I brought this." Hank said grinning, holding a bolt cutter above his head.

As promised, my soon to be Platoon Sergeant went back to obtain the other one the next day, of course at the hottest part of the day, when you had to wear gloves to touch metal. The 169th Engineer Battalion put them to good use, breaking ground.

Soon after that, a First Lieutenant noticed that his pieces of equipment were gone. He told the company Commander, who went nuts. When the nub bucks were finally brought before the bench for questioning, the account unfurled.

"What was the name of the NCO that took the tractors?" the Lieutenant asked slowly, trying to keep his voice from shaking.

"He never told us his name."

Between clenched teeth, "What was the name on his uniform?"

The other kid chimed in, "He was only wearing his t-shirt, 'cause it was damn hot."

"What did you just say, Private?"

"Uh. Nothing Sir." The nineteen-year-old was six foot four and still didn't get that he'd been robbed. Why should he care? After all, standing around all day to make sure nothing happened to the equipment in the hottest of hot conditions was bullshit.

"Where did he take them?"

"To the direct maintenance pool. But he said he'd bring them back right away." Everything was cool.

The investigation took about a week. By that time Tony had sweet-talked his way into the Engineer Brigade Headquarters and bygones became bygones. He must have gotten the attention of the Full Bird (Colonel/Brigade Commander). Some deal must have been made to cover the best builders in Iraq. I could imagine the Full Bird telling his boss, "Sir, the transportation unit that found the equipment has no use for it. My guys got those Massey Fergusons breaking ground all day long. Maybe the 169th could owe them a favor?" And that's how things get done in theater, and officers avoid needless prosecutions. It's not like Hank made a profit. The motive was pure, and he was merely appropriating what someone else had stolen. The Transporters couldn't have added the tractors to their property book, since they weren't authorized to have them. The 169th graded and spread gravel over their motor pool and it was called a draw. Not a word was said. Earth was moved. And that was more important than providing a bad precedent for a gang of thieves and scoundrels.

A corporal in the Heavy Equipment Platoon acquired a mini-bike from the vendors by the gate (another infraction) and drove it past the Head Shed during the evening bigwig huddle. Without a muffler, everyone could hear it. The action was another violation of GO1 and Master Sergeant Black made him get rid of it after Dynamite got pissed. Tony grinned; he would have done the same thing. What's wrong with having a hobby? I agreed, but Uncle Sugar was trying to impose some sort of discipline. The Army is supposed to be a team, not a gang.

My future battle buddy, Sergeant First Class Hank Molina, came upon one of his soldiers in the motor pool a few weeks after he "stole" the Massey Fergusons. The soldier was working on a rusted-out Cadillac he had "appropriated."

"Where did you get this?" Hank asked

"I found it running at the PX, Sergeant." Upon opening the trunk, they found several AK-47s and rocket- propelled grenades.

"You dumb shit! You just stole from Special Forces guys." They went back to the PX and apologized for his youthful indiscretion and handed the keys to the real "Men in Black." They didn't seem to mind too much. Nobody was going to ask the Special Forces troops where they got the Caddy either.

• • •

We had three-kilowatt and five-kilowatt generators that we had brought from Iowa. Electrical cords ran like spaghetti to the tents. These General Purpose (GP) canvas tents were treated with diesel fuel, which was a wonderful method to preserve them from the elements for decades, but guaranteed they'd light up like a Roman candle if exposed to a direct flame. We saw the video of a base camp in flames as a caution against utilizing hot plates, curling irons, or Weber grills near our tents. Three-way splitters created more electrical spaghetti running to individual fans pointed toward hundreds of cots. We'd pray to sleep, but usually being tired to the bone, soldiers could bear the dry 80-degree heat at night and rest. Like I said, I always slept great in Iraq. This is where I became heart healthy, with no beer to intervene. Some soldiers forsook sleep and took midnight trips, like moths to a flame, to the motor pool, with a need to knock boots with another soldier.

Building of the Internet Café and shower facilities began immediately. In the Corps of Engineers, we don't believe in suffering. The battalion's café was up and running with twenty computers in about three months. Hot showers followed about that time. Washing machines took six months to procure and plumb.

Master Sergeant Donny Black, whose tent was kitty-corner from mine, was the senior NCO for the Maintenance Platoon and said "wursh" instead of "wash." As in, "I had to go to the Water Buffalo to wursh my clothes."

"Why do you say it like that?" I asked him.

"Like what?" He was usually smoking a cigarette.

"Wursh?" I gave him a dumb ass stare. "How far south are you from? Alabama?"

"No, Waterloo." Donny was 59 and the oldest soldier in the outfit.

"Where's that?"

"Where's that?" He stopped to flick an ash. He was indignant.

They had several Walmarts in Waterloo, Iowa, and even a few rolling hills. "How do they say 'wursh' in Milwaukee?"

"Wash. Don't ya know ja dere hey?" Perhaps the Norwegian immigrants never settled over the Mississippi. Donny looked at me as if I had a penis growing out of my forehead.

"You damn fool." Master Sergeant Black called me that at least once a week for the next year. He owned a bowling alley with his newly-married second wife. His face was wrinkled from spending too much time outside. He wore big-frame "birth control" Army issue glasses and squinted continuously in the sun's glare. Master Sergeant Black's mustache was trimmed to the corner of his mouth in accordance with regulations. He passed away some years ago. Today, I wish I could say "Hey." We looked out for each other. I miss him.

Donny and I were helping to set up the Mobil Kitchen Trailer that we had rail loaded in Missouri and then pulled to Baghdad. A refrigerated trailer was dropped into our new LSA on day four, so we got to work stacking dry goods, building tables, and setting up camouflaged netting for shade, while others graded flat areas for tents. We usually got ice from local vendors at the edges of BIAP. Our bottled water was sometimes ice cold. Rudimentary Entry Control Points had been established. The building and expansion of ECPs would be another huge mission for the battalion, creating half-mile long serpentines with fighting positions, towers, speed bumps, and inspection points. In the middle of the day we still worked. Donny and I passed each other several times when I decided to sneak up behind him and pour some freezing water on the base of his neck. "AAAHH-HHH!" It ran down his spine. He dropped the box he was carrying and his arms spasmed over his head, and then he dropped to his knees. I almost felt bad. He looked behind him to see grinning Captain Kenny and shouted, "You damn fool! Damn near gave me a heart attack." I tried to help him up but he pushed my hand away. He put his sweaty arm around my shoulders and said with a smile, "Don't ever do that again! But it felt good though. Damn fool."

I grinned. "Sorry, Master Sergeant."

A soldier I'd never had the chance to talk with now beamed at me, witnessing my torture of her boss. Michelle considered me, briefly. My knees buckled. Sergeant First Class Michelle Anderson, with her Army issue thick-framed glasses, was pitching in like everybody else. She was a master at ordering equipment parts within the Army systems, receiving them in short order, and hanging them with her crew. Michelle drove the Direct Support Section Maintenance show for the entire Battalion. What the Alpha, Bravo, Charlie, and Delta Company maintenance sections couldn't handle, they sent to her. Playing the standard "Who's the prettiest girl in the outfit" game with my battle buddy, I proclaimed my vote for her. Hank disagreed and put up another name to consider. I told him he was full of shit. Negative. NCO Michelle didn't wear makeup for her own convenience, but frankly, she didn't need to. I was hooked.

As the Executive Officer of the Headquarters and Head-quarters Company (HHC), 169th Battalion, this was as far as I allowed the fantasy to go. Team development was life's blood, straight up. No time for funny business among leaders, since that could only bring the outfit down. Everybody was coming home, hopefully with all their fingers and toes. But she sure was pretty. Best to leave her be. As if a beauty like her would ever give me the time of day. The sergeant had long black hair (I supposed, as it was always twisted in a bun) and deep brown eyes. Slender. Seeing her in just a T-shirt made my glasses steam up. Michelle's ass looked like an upside heart and the thought of holding her hips made my hands tremble. What if she let her hair down, took off her glasses and boots? Just a touch of makeup maybe, and the scent of coconut shampoo. I could envision my fingers running through her curls. I wanted to count the freckles on her face and give her Eskimo kisses. Butterfly kisses, too! Would she think I was a good kisser? Was the clasp of her bra in the front or back? Could I open it with one hand, with just a flick?

"You still plan on helping?" Donny caught me gawking, a big grin on his face. "Why don't you save that for break?"

"Oh. Yeah, sure. Yeah." I picked up a long pole for the camouflage netting and we continued to place them into the spreaders. We pushed them up together towards the sky with great force, stretching the nets laced with ropes that groaned and shook, tied them down to the desert hard pan with metal stakes, then pounded them in with giant wooden mallets. The earth-tone vinyl strips fastened to the netting fluttered gently in hot breezes. The shade was just enough to cool my skin a tiny bit from the sweat just worked up. When you were underneath the cover of the netting, little shadows moved everywhere like a vivid yet shapeless dream. Michelle worked beside me for a few minutes, just enough for me to sneak good views of the shape of her breasts beneath her tan T-shirt. They were like twin fawns skipping in a new found world. This was going to be a long deployment.

Maybe we'd get a decent meal tomorrow morning, once the cooks arrived and the Mobile Kitchen Trailer (MKT) got set up completely. It was crazy to sweat into your scrambled eggs at breakfast chow.

The pace and the pressure reached fever level in Iraq and never relented. What you did was who you were. The training helped, but ultimately, I saw many people crack and behave badly. I almost cracked up myself a couple of times when I felt like I was coming unglued. Most people did wonderfully well.

The expectation for the duration of an Army deployment was "twelve months boots on the ground." But as time went on, no definitive word came about when we'd transfer our equipment and leave for home. When 2004 began there was still no end in sight. The uncertainty tugged at me constantly. Then units that had made it to Kuwait got turned around and sent back into the fray. Four-month extensions started getting placed on units. The anxiety overcame me and I purposely lost control of myself one afternoon within our massive motor pool. There I experienced the greatest crying jag I've ever had. It lasted a full ten minutes. A poor-me baby episode to be sure. But when it was over, I felt marvelous. I immediately found Master Sergeant Black at his hooch smoking a cigarette and told him all about it. "I feel relieved! You have to try it. When is the last time you had a good cry?" He growled, "You damn fool!" I was just trying to help.

Captain Sanchez, Master Sergeant Black, and Sergeant First Class Anderson raised the Equipment Utilization rate to over 97% for our Combat Heavy Engineer Battalion. It was then and remained the highest percentage within the 1st Armored Division during our deployment. A record never matched. It was unheard of because of the numbers of different pieces of equipment we had on the books. Other equipment requisitioned, repurposed, or procured by other means also got the parts they needed, somehow.

• • •

Water. Your body is 67% water. Have you ever seen a dying cockroach? On its back with its little legs kicking slowly? That's you in the desert in front of your fellow soldiers when you don't drink enough water. Take it from this old soldier—drink water.

It's one of the greatest keys to your health. When Private Snuffy King told First Sergeant Kringle that he was sad because his wife was divorcing him, Kringle said, "Drink water. You'll feel better." Private First Class King was up for promotion to Specialist and Kringle knew it. I hope the young soldier became Sergeant King after the deployment. He was a talented third-year apprentice carpenter, local 264, out of Davenport, Iowa.

When the Chaplain landed at the Battalion Aid Station, he was suffering from heat exhaustion: cramps, nausea, chills, headache, etc. Top (another name for the First Sergeant) visited the medical tent once again and asked his favorite question, "What color is your pee?"

Chaplain Charlie asked, "What?" He'd nearly done the dying cockroach scrounging for building materials from around the LSA for the secret chapel he was trying to build.

"Unless your pee is clear, you're not drinking enough water."

"Oh. OK." CC was in the air-conditioned domain of Doc Baker.

Top slapped him on the back. "I want you to rest for the rest of the day. And tomorrow." First Sergeant Kringle looked him straight in the eyes, "How many sheets of plywood have you got now?" Doc Baker grew annoyed.

Completely surprised he responded, "Oh. About ten." A good First Sergeant knows everything that's going on.

"OK, Sir. Let me see what I can do. Are any carpenters helping you yet? Do you have any drawings?"

"No, not yet."

"Let me see what I can do. But you rest all day tomorrow. You have enough to do." Doc Baker was actually a physician's assistant back home. But his position in theater was as the Battalion Surgeon for the 169th. It might have been Top's company but it sure as shit was the First Lieutenant's Aid Station. He touched both of them, with authority and said, "Are you guys done chatting?" He strained at such niceties; Chaplain Charlie was his patient, after all.

"OK, First Sergeant. Will do," the Man of God said.

We had pallets of bottled water everywhere in the LSA. We placed the plastic bottles in our coolers among the chips off of the blocks of ice we got from vendors just outside the ECPs. The Water Buffaloes were filled every day from the reverse osmosis units. This was an example of an IBU or "Itty Bitty Unit"; the small "Ash and Trash" outfits the Army cannot deploy without or replace with contract work. They took any kind of nasty water and purified it, making it potable, clean to drink. But most soldiers preferred the bottled water.

When Second Lieutenant Shit-for-Brains lumbered through the LSA's stone base, his size 13 boots kicking up rocks, the First Sergeant zeroed in from fifty meters out, walking purposely towards him. Being 24 years old and 6 foot, 3 inches, the young Platoon Leader only shaved every other day and then mostly just his chin. He graduated from a small college in Minnesota majoring in Architectural Design. He wasn't dumb, just greener than grass. He stumbled past the First Sergeant, his eyes blurred, staring at the ground. At 2:00 p.m. in the afternoon (1400 hours), the sun was blazing everyone into a state of "I don't give a shit."

"Hey, Lieutenant." Top was continuing to check on the troops, patrolling the LSA (Life Support Area) and visiting the job sites and the Battalion motor pool. He saw a problem here.

"Huh?"

"Hey. How many times you pee today?"

"Huh? How come?"

"I've pee'd five times today. How 'bout you?"

"Uh, maybe twice."

"I win!" A big grin on Top's face. Kringle was as bald as a cue ball, which made having a regulation haircut easy. "Is your platoon drinking enough water? Have you checked?"

"Oh, right. Yeah, I will."

"We don't need any dying cockroaches."

Second Lieutenant Meredith straightened up, "Yeah, I remember you

saying that before. I'll check. No dying cockroaches. Thanks, Top." The young man could be trained!

When I see First Sergeant Kringle at the next reunion I'm going to give him a big hug, grab his ass, and whisper in his ear, "I love you, Santa."

CHAPTER 3

# Liaison at Al Kashafa Football Stadium

Another trip to the Head Shed/ Battalion Headquarters. What was I being summoned for now? What did I do wrong? What should I have known not to do? Who was pissed off? I kept going until I got to the Battalion Operations Officer, Major Posey. I turned my left ankle again walking through the broken stone. It hurt sometimes. It wasn't sprained; on the pain scale of ten it was a one or a two. I tried not to limp.

"Hi, Kenny, how are you doing today?" he asked, sounding pleasant enough.

"Not bad, Sir. Yourself?"

The Battalion Headquarters was a spacious knit-together group of tents, shaped like the letter "T." They were like medical tents, designed to keep all sand and other contaminants out, eighty feet at the tee with a conference room at its base. The AC was always blasting to protect all the computer systems running 24/7. Being in the cool was always nice, while it lasted. Baghdad slapped you in the face again upon your exit from the air lock.

44

"Good, good. Say, I need you to hook up with the 16th Engineer Battalion as a liaison, for about two weeks."

What's a liaison? I responded with "OK" with a slight lilt in my voice, showing I had no idea what the man was talking about. Tony walked over to listen.

"OK. The 16th is on the north side of Baghdad, and the land owner is 1st Brigade, 1st Armored Division (AD). They need essential services and other stuff, like debris removal, etc., in their Area of Operations (AO). So, you're going to base out of the 16th at Baghdad Island, and then hook up with their higher to see what the Brigade Commander has in mind. But we want projects that have meat on the bone. Know what I mean?"

Major Posey gave me a look like he wished he was going instead. "When you figure out what projects we can do in their AO, come back and let me know. Then we can task organize and hit it hard." He scanned my face to see if I still had the deer-in-the-headlights look. "It actually sounds pretty cool. I need you to leave tomorrow. Captain Berry has the rest of the info you'll need. OK?"

"Yeah, yes Sir. OK. I'll get with her for the rest. Yeah, sounds cool." He slapped my upper arm and walked to another part of the Tactical Operations Center (TOC – pronounced – "talk").

Baghdad Island! It sounded like the place where typhus was invented. The Tigris ran along both sides of this sliver of land in the river. Saddam built an amusement park there. What a nice guy! And now the 16th Combat Engineer Battalion was occupying it. After a mere 20-minute trip north of BIAP, we arrived. There were lots of fun rides. Even a concrete space needle. On day two we climbed the ten stories to gaze over the mega-city nestled with palm trees. Except for the extreme heat (it was the second week of June), flies, lack of air conditioning, and slit trenches for latrines, this was going to be great!

Sergeant Jim Fester, some junior enlisted soldiers, and I got our hooches (a cot and if possible a privacy screen) set up in the park's big clubhouse. It had winding staircases, marble floors, and terrazzo mosaics of quartz on the walls, lots of glass and indoor gardens—neat stuff for the few. The 16th's TOC was established here. The first night we placed our cots in the main ballroom. Thinking of the opulence here reminded me of the massive landfill/garbage dump we had passed on the highway north that morning while moving at a slick 50 MPH. I could smell the burning chemicals from smoldering fires within it at the same moment I made eye contact with a mother shepherding her three small kids as they scoured over the refuse. Our living conditions were vastly better. We tried to use our Army-issued mosquito netting to keep the flies from landing on our skin, tickling before taking a bite, all while spreading their filth upon us. But the netting stifled any breeze, making you sweat on top of your sleeping bag. You had to make your choice.

The clubhouse had a non-functioning pool with a non-functioning bar, both very sad. The amusement park rides hadn't been maintained and didn't run. But with a little work, people could enjoy the place again, one would hope for everybody, not just for the Ba'athists (Saddam's hijacked political party). Still, it was eerie at night to be in an empty amusement park. The carousel's music played in one's head and the shadows morphed into Halloween spirits. Tea Cup rides didn't spin and the Tilt o' Whirl didn't grind away, twisting the little kids up with suspense. Popcorn vendors' carts lay empty, and no smiles emerged from grandmothers watching their families play. When the evenings came and the temperature dropped, after a fine pre-packaged meal and a refreshing bath with baby wipes, as I lay listening to the wind rustle through the palms, it still sucked. If monsters were real they'd be here at night. For our Iraqi neighbors across the Tigris, their monster was hiding someplace in a spider hole. Was Saddam ready to come out after the Americans left? We knew that the minority Muslim Sunnis had violently oppressed the Muslim Shias under the past government. Would it happen again? I bet our new neighbors were equally frightened of us.

Then we heard the auspicious Call to Prayer, or Adhan, from loudspeakers mounted on an unseen minaret across the river. "Listen. Hear. God is great." In Arabic, the song sounded almost mournful. It was strange. Like a church bell magnified a thousand times over, but with a man's voice. Five times a day. It always snapped me back into the reality of where I was, as the trembling voice pleaded, demanding recognition of God's primacy in our lives, a singing call for peace. Amen.

Kenny was now the boy with all the toys. It was my sandbox. Or should I say our military sandbox. The combat engineers from Active Duty could dig in vehicle fighting positions for tanks, clear obstacles, place and recover minefields, and lay concertina/razor wire; but actual, substantial construction was the bailiwick of engineers out of the Army Reserve. Thus entered the stage our crew with a New Jersey attitude and a Midwest "Ah shucks" demeanor.

The landowner (First Brigade, 1AD) was piecing together some sort of Stabilization Operations Plan. The Army had the initiative, but what to build? The officers I spoke with at the Brigade's HQ basically instructed me to drive around their sector of the city and investigate war damaged sites and/or community action type projects they suggested. I spent some time making radio communications with the 169th and entered into the Brigade's radio Network Equipment Technologies (NET). This wasn't easy work. Secure FM communications has always had its limitations. I could pretty much do whatever I wanted, but first I had to do my job.

The Army's Global Positioning System (GPS) was a piece of shit. Overly complicated, it worked sometimes. It took a lot of practice to figure out where you were at any given moment, and it didn't like displaying grid coordinates while you were moving. When you are in downtown Baghdad with your ass in both hands it is far more preferable just to turn a GPS on and be told where the hell you are! But paper maps are always the best for land navigation, anyway. Both means were necessary, though.

Jim and I drove away from the beautiful palace the HQ was in with our two unarmored Humvees and four other soldiers. We were looking for work. We had taken the plastic doors off of our Humvees for ease, the breeze, and of course to look cool. Only a fifteen-year old boy can understand how stupid can equate to cool. And we were very, very cool traversing Baghdad with slight weapons, no route declared, shaded ballistic eye glasses, and balls of brass.

Finding a dirt field between cramped neighborhoods, we pulled over and watched the kids playing football (soccer balls were always an appreciated gift for the kids). The refuse was piling up in every corner. Baghdad administrators were off the job, with no chance of getting paid, at least not yet. No Sanitation Department. In a few months, when the Sunni insurgency began in earnest, hoping that they would get Saddam, or at least their privileges back, garbage became a great place to hide Improvised Explosive Devices (IEDs). Another good place was the carcass of a dog or behind the guardrail beside a highway. The Army quickly got the garbage men to pick up their routes again, and take it to massive lots within the city. Here, people continued to sift through it just as before the war.

We were drawing too much attention at this field, so I told Jim to lead us around the block. A minute later I thought I saw something and asked him to stop. Upon inspection I found it was a 120- millimeter artillery round, just lying alongside the road, and I walked right up to it, turned on my heels, got back in the Humvee and kept moving. I didn't think it was armed, as no wires were trailing from the three-foot long projectile. Later that day I reported the munition with a ten-digit grid coordinate. The proper procedure should have been to back away from the artillery round and call for help while keeping it under surveillance. I guess I caught someone in mid-deployment of an IED. It probably had enough explosive force to kill everything within a 50-meter radius. We'd have to get better before the physical bits of our bodies were blown into spray and a feast for the neighborhood rats.

There are wonderful parks in Baghdad, at least, in favorable Saddam-loving Sunni neighborhoods. We were always well received in places known to have Republican Guard officers living in them. Professional courtesy, I guess. Even in upscale neighborhoods it was common to have mule-driven carts and BMWs traveling the same road. Working off of the list of possible sites, we recon'd a park that needed some cleanup. Not much meat to justify organizing a work mission for the 169th and our host. Bunches of playground equipment, mature trees, and only a few piles of trash were evident.

At another location adjacent to a small college was more refuse in a field. It could have been cleaned up and made into a park or a football field, but when the locals said there were Iraqi soldiers recently buried there from the American invasion, we decided a possible unmarked grave site was a non-starter. I imagined a bulldozer pushing and churning the earth above freshly dug pits with its tracks, and recoiled from the horrible prospect of disinterring bodies with huge steel blades and diesel engines. Tearing and exposing un-embalmed corpses to the sun would probably make the locals upset.

Jim spotted a cluster of bombed-out buildings so we drove towards them. He and I were always the lead vehicle on every convoy we ran on point. I was navigating and doing the "thinking," and Jim was driving, maintaining the vehicle, leading, monitoring the radio, anything. He was also a mechanic, useful when you had your ass in both hands, which we usually did. I never went anywhere without Jim, not once. A few years after we got back to the U.S., he died in a motorcycle wreck.

Baghdad has forever been distinguished for its academic excellence. Students from around the world would come here to study Engineering, Mathematics, the Arts, etc. As we approached this satellite campus of Baghdad University, few folks were around. But soon after we entered the main quad, pointing our vehicles toward a building blown to hell from a missile, the students came out of the adjacent buildings by the dozens. To my shock and horror, they were almost all young women, curious and shocked themselves at the Americans bravado. We were actually "freshmen" ourselves. We wore ballistic sunglasses always, which we later learned was extremely rude not to remove when speaking, because others couldn't see our eyes. We had basic techniques to dismount, protecting ourselves and vehicles with a 360-degree field of fire. Not that it mattered, as my young soldiers melted before the throng of beautiful women. They were typically thin, shapely, healthy girls, with dark straight hair and deep, dark eyes. Their makeup was worn like a model's; and they were tastefully dressed in jeans and blouses. The few male students stayed silent. But several female students began to ask me in English if we were here to fix the school? My guys weren't watching their sectors; they had huge smiles on their faces, understandably so.

"Oh, yeah," I told one of them, a ring of girls surrounding me, "Easy. No problem." I would have promised to build them a new Science Lab if they promised to release me from their gaze. We were being lured in with their enchantments like sailors to shipwreck.

An administrator quickly descended upon us and ushered me into an auditorium, and began to describe in passable English all the war damage that her college had suffered. Being separated from my men, all I could think about was getting the hell out of there and accounting for my guys. It'd be a minor miracle if they were all still situated around the Humvees, not having wandered off in love. Perhaps I made up some B.S. about an initial assessment, because the Dean and I made a quick tour. Getting back, Jim counted heads and we departed. These ladies were the exception to the rule that we should never talk to an Arab woman in country without a male authority figure present. It could be trouble for her. The extraordinarily beautiful Iraqi women were kept at arm's length; US soldiers could only fantasize. We never went back. It would be much too dangerous for us.

The next day, at another suggested stop, we found a police headquarters that was now reoccupied by folks from the neighborhood who were volunteering to replace the local cops. The police were para-military in Saddam's stranglehold on the capital. They worked with the military at times, but served both capacities in addressing some crime and arresting political enemies of the Regime. The station was small, only three stories, with telltale bullet holes pock marking the façade. It was looted of almost all its furniture after the collapse of the government two months earlier. As always, a throng of people roamed in the street. Although it was before 9:00 a.m., it was starting to get hot again. Lots of people were in the building. No one was in charge that I could tell, and of course it wasn't as if I could've called ahead to make an appointment. [One overarching principle of safe travel in Iraq was to never tell anyone outside your chain of command where you were going]. Sure, plenty could be done to renovate this lousy concrete building. Everything was in disrepair. Paint peeling, exposed wiring, plumbing not functioning, trim boards gauged, doors missing, windows broken. It had been ill maintained long before the police abandoned their posts.

The community was certainly overjoyed that their local oppressors were gone. An impromptu interpreter showed me around. Perhaps to demonstrate to me the violence the people had suffered, she took me to the basement where I was told by the group that the police tortured those they arrested. A floor drain in one cell had rust colored stains around it. Rings were mounted into the foundation walls to restrain the victims. The neighbors next door could hear their cries. No one saw prisoners leaving. The space was tight and I thought I could feel the pain reverberating from the walls. My head began to spin and my soul felt sick.

"OK, that's enough of this," I thought. Not going to do it, way too spooky. Too many people around for comfort and the physical security of my troops. Perhaps the next site on the list, the Al Kashafa Stadium, could be the ticket? Built in the 1950's for a visit by Britain's Queen Elizabeth, this small stadium could seat maybe ten thousand, and had recently been used as a barracks for a company of Republican Guards (about 125 soldiers). I suppose it was a psychological boost to quarter Infantry among the imprisoned population in case an alternative to the Ba'ath Party should arise and a demonstration have to be crushed.

It was only a few blocks from the police station. The biggest hazard driving through the residential streets was their maze of overhead electrical wires. Since only favored neighborhoods received juice for twelve hours a day (typically "free"), this unregulated utility was up for grabs. Anyone brave enough to risk serious injury could shimmy up a pole to tap into a live line and string it to their apartment, maybe keep some food cold, or run a fan, listen to radio, watch TV, or use some power tools in their business. Unless we tied our twelve-foot whip antennas down like a bow, they'd snag the electrical lines' weak connections. And more than once, I saw neighbors pissed off as hell running and screaming after our convoys. Sometimes, we'd stop and I'd get out, remove my shades, and receive my ass chewing in Arabic. No way were we ever to touch that tangled mess of wires. The spaghetti was everywhere, looping sometimes less than ten feet off the ground.

As we rolled up to the front door of the stadium, the stench of sanitary sewer backup filled the 105-degree air. It was nauseating. Garbage like pop cans, fruit boxes, and plastic bottles by the thousands were strewn about. But despite this filth, behind the walls that fenced in every little two-story house, the Iraqi family living within would be tidy to a fault. I learned this later through the few times I was invited into a home. But what can you do when the garbage men don't show up for a couple of weeks? The Army knew. Pay them. Finance Officers began carrying around hundreds of thousands of dollars in their rucksacks. But sewage was an engineering problem well beyond my liaison mission, which as I understood it, was to introduce the Iraqi people to American soldiers and us to them, and to do good.

The stink was so bad in front of the Al Kashafa Football Stadium we drove around the complex to get away, discovering a walled-in field adjacent to the stadium where we could safely park and provide security. The practice field, as it would become, was over an acre in size. A twenty-foot opening on an alley side of the practice field held two big rusted swinging doors. The field could be blocked and secured by only one vehicle, riflemen at the ready. The soon-to-be practice field had been used by the Republican Guard as a garbage pit. It was a perfect, small earth-moving project. But first I recon'd the stadium proper. As concrete gets older it gets harder, so the stadium structure was intact with little crumbling or exposed steel reinforcement. The pitch needed some topsoil and grass seed but was level, with burned-out turf. There was even a functioning watering system and I was to meet the long time maintenance man that afternoon as he came to check us out. No worries about the new grass when it sprouted. The lobby was greatly aged, but I knew that an immediate start was required, not a protracted renovation that required the ordering of doors and electrical equipment. Someone else could paint. Reclaiming a neighborhood icon from Saddam's personal guard/hit squads so they could play football again seemed pitch perfect.

The Operations Officer of 1st Brigade, 1st Armored Division agreed. It was a quick project they could have for a song. I was totally jazzed to leave there, return to Baghdad Island, get back to BIAP, and make the pitch to Major Posey. As the Executive Officer (XO) of the Headquarters Company (HHC) within the 169th Battalion, I was second in command of a 150 plus soldier unit. It wasn't hard to convince the other officers that Al Kashafa was a worthwhile, literally "shovel ready" project.

Captain Diana Berry was an African American soldier who worked harder than most out of necessity. I had just recently come from a company command back in Milwaukee, and having a boss in my foxhole was wonderful. The Army needed officers, so where you serve is where there's a need, even if it was supposedly a step back professionally. Diana treated us all like her own kids. Once, months later, about to leave the TOC, I picked up a piece of hard candy from the bowl near the tent flap. I heard her say in earnest, "You don't need that." My hand reflexively sprung open, dropping the apple Jolly Rancher into the bowl, never turning or losing a step. Mom was in charge. I had a big grin on my face.

Before I could begin assembling a crew for the new stadium project, Diana dropped some bad news. "Kenny, I need you to take charge of the Equipment Platoon besides being XO." Wearing another hat wasn't what I wanted, but instantly I was now directly responsible for 63 pieces of equipment and nearly 40 soldiers. All of which upon my discretion could be assigned for a hot mission. I paused a good five seconds, "OK. I guess I should do the property inventory tomorrow." I didn't know Diana well. She had a wry smile and talked in low tones so you had to pay attention.

"Do you know Sergeant Molina well?" He was the Platoon Sergeant and worked full time for the unit back in Davenport, Iowa.

"Oh, sure. Yeah, we talked some. We worked the convoy coming back from the port."

"Just watch your back. That's all I'm saying."

Another pregnant pause, "OK. Fine. Hey, maybe I'll make the trip to the stadium day after next? What about the rest of NCOs?"

Like she was reading the roll, Captain Berry recited the noteworthy sergeants, "Your squad leaders are good. Hendricks is good, Gibson is good. Same way for Thibodeaux." We took a breath at the same time. She was a beautiful young woman, so I missed some of what she said next as her chest rose and fell, but picked back up with "and there's an Inspector General (IG) complaint against Molina from Davenport, just to let you know." Switching gears, she asked, "Where are you getting the topsoil for the soccer field?" I responded, "First Brigade said they got a guy." The Army posted "contractor wanted" advertisements on boards outside our Forward Operating Bases and Headquarters. However, vetting them was impossible or sketchy at best. Muhammed Muhammed usually couldn't be checked for references, as Iraq was in great turmoil. But references could be established by working with the US Army Corps of Engineers in the present. Doing well for us meant these contractors could get more work from the greatest cash cow in the world—the American tax payer.

The Equipment Platoon had three sections: the Dump Truck Section had nine 20-ton behemoths that could move earth extremely fast; the Equipment Section had the vast majority of the heavy junk, including two 5-yard and two 2 ½ yard bucket loaders for the dumps, as well as John Deere excavators, dozers, scrapers, graders, rollers etc.; and the lowly Asphalt and Concrete Section had equipment that no one knew how to operate or maintain. The existing senior Staff Sergeant for this section, Desoto, would have better served the Army as a pastry chef. That would change when Sergeant First Class Gibson was grudgingly reassigned by yours truly. The Asphalt and Concrete Section included asphalt distributors that didn't work and Magical Mobile Mixing Machines far older than the soldiers.

I found Sergeant Hank Molina and gave him the news. He gave me a big smile. "Thank God they finally gave me an officer. You know I'm the last platoon sergeant in the battalion to get an officer. All because of that son-of-a- bitch Sergeant Major Maloney. You know Sergeant Major Maloney? Just watch your back that's all I'm saying."

"Where's your hooch?"

"Oh, I didn't want to bunk with the section sergeants so I got a two-man tent for myself. But then Kris Kringle needed a place to rack out so he set up with me. Where're you going to set up,

Captain Dupar? Did I say that right? That's French right? Well, I won't hold that against you." And he gave a hardy laugh. "I busted Sergeant Major Maloney and some other full-timers two years ago for stealing from the soda fund. 'Waste, fraud, and abuse,' that's what I say. Say, you've been a Commander right?"

"Yeah."

"Well, the most of the sergeants are a bunch of dipsticks, just to let you know. But Hendricks and Gibson are cool. Sergeant T, too."

I called my wife Ellen that evening and gently demanded that she run, not walk, to Radio Shack and buy a Garmin GPS. "Spend a lot of money," I said. "Get the best one they have. Then drive to the post office, today, and mail it to me." The Army equipment was a few years old and not user friendly. The girls were fine. My daughter liked splashing around the little wading pool Ellen got from Kmart. She didn't ask why I wanted the instrument badly. I neglected to tell her about driving around downtown Baghdad with my ass on the line, out of control, too dumb to care.

The first and oldest trick in the construction contractor game is to short the customer with inferior or less material than required. It's all about money, honey. Muhammed Muhammed wore a lot of cologne and spoke with passable English, which was a lot more than I could say for myself in regards to his native tongue, Arabic. We met and recon'd the site to develop a soil estimate. I thought in cubic yards and he thought in cubic meters. I'm pretty sure that 1 meter = 1.09 yards, meaning that whatever I thought I should get via the agreement in yards, that I should receive a visually greater amount on the ground. I knew my dirt. My new friend saw volumes differently. It was a protracted argument for the rest of our time together. But the bottom line was that the stadium field needed decent topsoil (not clay or sand) and the practice field the same. With quality grass seed after that. The contractor to bring us the soil and our grader operators to spread it as flat as a billiard table. I told Tony later about Al Kashafa. He laughed hard when I told him the whole story and about Muhammad Muhammad. As a general contractor himself, the boss had a few tricks of his own. But at least he tried to build to code, usually.

A slice from the Equipment Platoon was busy clearing away the debris to be placed in someone else's neighborhood. The 20 tons made quick work of debris removal. Jim and I stationed ourselves on day two of construction out front, by the lobby, the stench having subsided somewhat. With two vehicles and another soldier, we passed the midday hours trying not to doze in the heat. I walked the job back and forth to stay awake. The dense population of Baghdad stayed indoors, mostly, or so it seemed. A kid and an elder came out of an apartment. I saw the ten-year old running towards us with a rocket-propelled grenade (RPG) cradled in his arms.

"Holy Shit! Goddamn it, Jim, look!" I pointed. His head snapped.

The private yelled, "I got him!" His rifle leveled.

Jim also took aim, "Stop, you bastard! Stop!" he screamed!

"Stop! Goddamn it, stop!" I called.

He started less than a block away. But the boy was not prepared to shoot—he was turning it in. I jogged quickly toward the kid, my hands in the air, weapon slung, and he slowed down, then halted, so close I could have tossed him a baseball underhanded. When I met him, the kid placed the RPG on the ground. It was live. When I placed my hand on his shoulder and thanked him for not killing us he said something I couldn't understand. We both smiled at each other after worrying stares and heavily panting from the accelerated, unexpected drama.

"It's cool. It's cool, kid. Thanks."

I think what he said in Arabic would translate, "Holy shit! I thought you guys were going to kill me! I was turning it in. We don't want this thing in our house."

The Army had passed leaflets to the population that they should surrender all weapons save AK-47s and sidearms to use for their own personal protection. I guess his elder figured there was less chance of us shooting the kid than himself. They did the right thing but in the wrong way. I picked up the RPG, and Jim figured out that it was on "safe." It was time to chain smoke again. I had never seen Sergeant Fester that angry before: "I nearly shot that stupid kid! Goddam it! And that asshole just watching over there!" About ten others were observing from the street now. Dozens of pairs of eyeballs peered from behind curtains.

"Yeah, but you didn't."

"Give me a smoke, Cap."

"You OK, Private Olsen?" I asked.

"What was that dumb ass thinking? Say, can I bum a smoke off you, Sir?"

"Sure. Have as many as you want," and I handed him nearly half a pack. The thought of hurting a neighborhood boy sent a shudder down my spine. "Thanks for not killing the kid."

Adults would have been pouring out of the buildings by the dozens, women screaming, men shouting. We would've had to fight our way out of there, probably abandoning our equipment. Jim asked, "What about next time?" Damn good question. Rules of engagement? Defensive plans? I provided some answers but it wasn't much. Still armed, we turned the RPG in to the 1st Brigade Headquarters before leading the platoon slice back to Baghdad Island late that afternoon. We weren't trained on this Soviet weapon, simple as it was.

The prettiest girl in the Equipment Platoon was a 24-year-old specialist (the rank between private and sergeant) with sandy blond hair always tied in a knot, and big boobs. She never had a boyfriend in Iraq, despite the testosterone-driven constant attention. Outspoken when she needed to be, never pushed around, a face without blemish, she just did her job, soldiering, with never a complaint. She was with us at Al Kashafa. Her butt rode nine feet in the air in the cab of the huge 5-yard loader. Her face was a mix of worry and exultation as she loaded the 20-ton dumps, removing the waste of the Republican Guard, load after load. When she finished, her infectious attitude was, "What now, Sir?" I had a lot of respect for her. She didn't come to Iraq to find a boyfriend. I hope she's a Sergeant Major or a Lieutenant Colonel by now.

It took only a few days for my vision of the stadium to be completed, and it looked pretty good with the grass seed spread and the maintenance man watering. Now it was time for the divorce. My contractor wanted to get paid more than what was stipulated! I was in shock. We met at the Brigade headquarters/ palace and argued again in front of the disburser's office. He waved his hands wildly and I threw my helmet on the ground. "What if the grass doesn't grow?" I demanded.

"It will grow. It will grow. Trust me, my friend." Muhammed Muhammed placed his hand upon my shoulder and I smelled why he wore so much cologne. Both of us were sweating profusely with the drama. His clothes were cleaner than mine. He wore leather shoes well shined and gold jewelry. I looked into his deep dark eyes and knew I was about to get screwed. I brought out an interpreter hired by the Army. She took Muhammed Muhammed's side of the debate.

"I'm going to go and talk to my boss and see if there's anything we can do about the price. We really want you to continue to work for us since you did such a great job. You stay here and I'll be right back." The AC felt wonderful. I've never worked in a car dealership, but I drank a cup of coffee and talked to some fellow soldiers about how well Dusty Baker might do in his first year managing the Chicago Cubs and stalled for more than 20 minutes for dramatic effect. Charging out to meet my Arabic dynamic duo, I said, "That guy is some kind of an asshole! He said either you take the $10,000 or not. He doesn't care." After translation more pandemonium erupted. I touched Muhammad gently on the arm, "Listen to me, my friend. You will get more work from us. Which is a good thing. Please don't argue too much or we won't be able to hire you again. You do good work." It was mediocre at best, but I got enough dirt. I looked in his face and I believe he saw the wisdom in my words, probably hating me as much as I hated him. M&M nodded, and we walked into the disburser's office.

"Pay the man!" $10,000 was probably a 500% profit for this guy.

We shook hands. Never to meet again. Like leaving the courthouse, I felt a huge sense of relief. He did have dreamy eyes though. And that's when I realized it was time to go home. But I hadn't even been in Iraq for a month. I sure did miss my wife Ellen. She's a lot prettier than Muhammed Muhammed. This was going to be a long deployment.

CHAPTER 4

# The White Don King
# of Baghdad

While I was liaising, Sergeant First Class Molina and the Equipment Section of my platoon were helping build secure Entry Control Points at Camp Cropper about a half mile up the road. Photos of the worst of Saddam's Ba'ath party officials were printed on playing cards and if captured, they would probably pass through Cropper. These were the bastards responsible for the greatest atrocities in recent memory in Iraq. The King of Clubs was the notorious "Chemical Ali," or Ali Hassan al Majid, Saddam's first cousin. He was a mass murderer convicted of war crimes and genocide. He had been the Defense Minister and Chief of the Intelligence Service. In 1998, Ali orchestrated the use of mustard gas, sarin, and nerve agent against the Kurds in the northeast of the country. In one attack, more than 5,000 civilians were murdered in the city of Halabja. Ten thousand were injured. Thousands more died of disease; babies were delivered lifeless. The US Army Corps of Engineers endeavored to build a sizeable school there; six years later my office out of Tikrit would help complete it.

Platoon Sergeant Hank Molina and team were also cleaning up bomb damage at an Intelligence Battalion adjacent to the MPs. Always making the deal, Molina sweet-talked permission to use their satellite phones. And, our soldiers got another chance to call home. He was an operator. I liked that. The internet café was still in the planning stage back at the 169th, and the entire Headquarters Company of 145 soldiers had only two satellite phones. You'd sign up a few days in advance for a 30-minute chance to call home, in whatever time slot was available, even in the middle of the night, and you'd set your alarm and get to the TOC on time. Go over your 30-minute slot too many times and your privileges could get suspended. Many times I'd call Ellen in the middle of the night in Iraq, early evening in the States (we were nine hours ahead). Just to ask what was happening, how our daughter Abby was doing, status on the cock-a-poodle, parakeets Lola and Gomez, and how long the grass was. Ellen always cut the lawn like a barber who hated the kid whose hair she had to trim, leaving slender strips of uncut grass between rows. She'd take care of it, she said. It was one of many things that I used to do. She'd tell me she loved me too, that the menagerie was just fine. Ellen read to our daughter incessantly. I loved them all the way to the moon and back, times infinity, plus one.

When I got back to BIAP from driving around northern Baghdad it had just turned the 30th of June, 2003. I was feeling pretty good about things, not having died during my first escapade into the Iraqi capital, and I intended to ask Diana if she had anything planned for the 4th of July. But before I could bull my way through what was required to celebrate the founding of America, a huge surprise waited for me back at my hooch. It was finally the Equipment Platoon's turn to have plywood floors built over the stone underneath the tent/Roman candle we lived under. The floor was sublime. Newly built by carpenters from Delta Company, it still smelled of factory chemicals, not having a speck of grime or dust upon it. My section leaders were still out working. I pulled my dusty duffle bags and cot atop the magnificence and took off my boots and socks. I walked upon a level surface, smooth and clean, for the first time in a month and a half. My back aligned and my toes unscrunched. I felt the joints between the plywood sheets with my big toes left and right. The nails dimpled into the deck with framing hammers felt like potholes. I wish I had someone to dance with right then. No music needed; just grab the girl and twirl her around a time or two. And maybe steal a kiss. Not wanting to appear strange, I sadly put my boots back on and walked out upon the three-inch stone, nearly turning an ankle, again. Combat pay is an extra $250 bucks a month. It was mandated not for the dangers or separation from family, which are incalculable, but perhaps to compensate for the loss of feeling cool long grass between your toes and the soft earth underneath bare feet, and dancing with your love in your arms.

"Because it's going to be the 4th of July and we're in Iraq."

"It's a Thursday. We planned on giving everybody a half day off."

"Why?" Captain Berry asked impatiently.

"Shouldn't we have a cookout or something?"

"Nobody is going to give a shit when it's 120 degrees outside. And we got no grill, no burgers, and no hotdogs. You want to grill an MRE, Kenny?" At least I was amusing her.

Hank was able to hustle the meat and the essentials for Bar-B-Que. I didn't ask how or who he knew at Kellogg Brown and Root. He always had an angle.

"What about playing a baseball game?" I made a slow motion swing of a bat.

"If you can figure it out, Captain Dupar, let me know." She didn't suffer fools lightly. But this was bullshit! Sure, everybody got at least one "day off" a week. Another half day wouldn't mean a thing! So you could stay at your hooch and sweat instead of working and sweating. Great.

I refused to quit. This had to mean something. Why were we in Iraq to begin with? It was a hard question for soldiers to answer. We had to celebrate us. For being on the other side of the planet, building towards something. Everyone was pissed off, tired, stressed, and depressed. Something had to give. Ignoring our birthday wasn't going to happen! We had only a few days to pull it off.

• • •

On one of my jobsite visits to Camp Cropper I had introduced myself to a Company Commander of the 115th Military Police Battalion, Captain Margret Lindskoog. She showed me the 200-foot square compound where the detainees sweltered, and it was a mess, rotting food from MREs baking in the heat, flies whirling around, landing on refuse and crap, then perching on upper lips and noses. The packaging collected on the fencing, the wind blowing the garbage where it would. The fifty plus prisoners waiting for some sort of processing were placed under tents with the sides furled up. They waited until the MPs released them, sent them to the notorious Abu Ghraib prison, or shut them into a cell in another part of the compound. The detention yard was surrounded by high cyclone fencing, with razor wire on the top. Bravo Company, 169th had built four 20-foot high guard towers outside the corners of the compound. Our Equipment Platoon placed the guard towers with our precious all-terrain forklifts. The nastiest part was the rotting food quivering in the hot shade, strewn about the yard, breakfast for maggots. But who doesn't like a Hash Brown Potatoes w/Bacon MRE? Oh, they're probably Muslim and don't eat pork. How insensitive of the MPs. They probably should have thought of that. A couple of Port-a-Potties baked in the sun for the prisoners. Would you want to be the one to service those? The Bravo Company girls and boys kept banging. Big towers sprang up, and darkened holding cells within pre-existing maintenance buildings opened.

Maggie was responsible for more than two hundred detainees and one hundred and twenty soldiers. Wearing thick glasses, she received her Army Reserve commission from the ROTC (Reserve Officer Training Command) at Purdue University. She swore a lot. It was a gimmick, I guess. It got people's attention. But to me it made her look nervous. But then, why wouldn't she be? Chemical Ali had been through her compound recently, as well as other jackoffs from the deck of cards.

Between the 115th's compound and the BIAP crumbling masonry wall was a massive garbage dump. It routinely caught fire as the heat caused spontaneous combustion because of failure to sort the materials—tires mixed with accelerants, mixed with cardboard, mixed with food waste, and all mixed with demolition debris. Every few weeks or so, we'd have an emergency mission, sending our dozers over to push down the piles of burning refuse to put out the smoking waste. I hated going to Camp Cropper at night to have our precious equipment fight fires. If it weren't for my new sisters and brothers there and the risk of an uncontrolled inferno, we should have let the damn thing burn.

We were improving their Entry Control Point daily with serpentines, speed bumps, guard shacks, fighting positions and drop gates. Representatives of the State Department routinely came through their ECP to Camp Cropper. Other technocrats menacingly demanded access to certain prisoners. Intelligence officers from God knows where exercised their influence with malice and took prisoners away without any written documentation. I was glad not to be in this chain of command. How could you protect yourself? Others? Someone made a movie about Camp Cropper. It portrayed the prison as a clearing house for Iraqi government officials, now known by a deck of cards for their crimes against their people. I didn't watch the whole flick. Having helped to build Cropper, I didn't find the film adaptation interesting.

Plywood and 2x4s were pure gold in Iraq. Timber wasn't a normal building material here, and the wood probably came from either Turkey or Pakistan. It was strictly accounted for. Nothing was wasted. We finished our work in daylight at Camp Cropper and sped back for a delicious Kellogg Brown and Root supper at the Engineer Village five blocks south. KBR was/is the mammoth international company that gobbled up federal contracts for serving chow to troops for $25/plate. It was cheap really, when you consider the logistics and the quality of the food, which was actually good. Dick Cheney, once the Vice President of the United States, would be proud of his former employer's effort.

"Hey, Captain Dupar, I hate to ask you this, but we've set up a volleyball court and it sucks just playing off of the dirt. Is there any way you could get us some sand for that?" Captain Lindskoog must have thought she was pushing her luck, especially since the 169th had already done a lot of work for her Company and Battalion.

"Oh, hey. I don't know." An authorized building project where you could justify the use of precious material was one thing, but off the books? Maggie looked somewhat sheepish.

"Give me a couple of days to see what I can come up with." Have I shared with you one of Kenny Dupar's prime credos for success? Always get in good with the cops. It is always worth knowing what the police are planning.

"Thanks, Kenny." What she didn't know was that I had a ginormous stockpile of torpedo sand across the street on the Air Force side. It wasn't fine sand. It had tiny pieces of quartz crushed in it. Perfect for making mortar or concrete, but not so much for playing volleyball barefoot. The Military Police didn't care, though. I found Hank and told him what I was thinking. He got a five-yard loader to the huge stockpile and I got a few 20-ton dump trucks to start rotating between the pile and the MPs' compound. In about an hour I asked an MP NCO a stupid question, "Where do you want it?" She walked me over to the volleyball court. The dumps backed up, the caution alarm beep, beep, beeping. By the end of the day the MPs had enough sand for three volleyball courts. The needs of the many superseded formal consent. Besides, I could get away with it, for now. The five-yard loader came over to push down the piles. It was a thing of beauty only a baseball field away from the detention yard. When Battalion Sergeant Major Maloney found out he tried to chew me out for doing my own thing, making my own deals. I acted like a puppy that had just pee'd on the carpet. My contrition was short-lived though. Hank reminded me, "I told you to watch your back."

The next evening, at our daily construction huddle with the Battalion Operations Officer Major Posey, I floated the notion of building our own volleyball courts. You know, for morale. Tony was in attendance that night. He thought it was a great idea and gave me notice to proceed. A mountain of torpedo sand was available, and by the 3rd of July we had three courts of our own. Poles and cords were made for nets. Success.

Scrounging for baseball mitts, I began searching some of the 40-foot containers we'd brought from Iowa. Lo and behold, I opened a metal box containing recreational gear. The baseball stuff was pretty old, the gloves dry and cracked. There were volleyball nets and horseshoes. I reached in and pulled out a pair of boxing gloves, then another pair, and two sets of head protection. Boxing? A kernel of an idea that would become a legend had sprouted. I immediately began promoting to others the festivities that were but a whisper in my mind. "We're going to have boxing matches for the 4th of July!" I told everyone I saw. "Want to fight?" I asked. Most thought I was crazy, but what better way to pass the time? I prefer crazy. We were going to have fun even if someone would experience a bloody nose. My constant conversations with other soldiers piqued interest. Soon a few expressed interest in fighting. Now I had to develop the fight card. Building the ring was easily accomplished, as I had the ropes, 4x4s and plywood at my fingertips. I delegated the building to Sergeant First Class Thibodeaux. Involving the masses was the art of promotion.

I approached Major Perez, the Battalion's Executive Officer, about the possibility of having boxing matches for the 4th of July, and an opportunity for soldiers to get out their frustrations and the crowd to scream like mad. Could it be authorized? Major Perez was a West Point graduate and an Armor Officer. He played rugby in college and thought my hair-brained idea was a capital one. "Call it 'Combatives Training.' Place it on a training schedule and I'll sign off on it." The next day I went back to solicit the MPs as boxers for the upcoming exposition. The 4th was the day after.

"No way! That is awesome. Yeah, I'll ask around if anyone wants to fight. You can place the flyer on the bulletin board. You said you wanted to borrow a bullhorn? No sweat, Kenny,"

Maggie exclaimed. Now, that's how you get shit done in the Theater of Operations.

"Say, I heard that you've had some escapes? Anything to be concerned about?" That was the wrong thing to ask Maggie and I immediately regretted it.

"We don't talk about shit like that," she snapped. "I'll get a NCO to get you a bullhorn." Maggie walked away. I shouldn't have pee'd in her coffee. But we'd be friends again when the matches started. A few of her soldiers wanted to kick somebody's/anybody's ass, you know, just for fun.

I visited at least seven other units I'd had contact with about blood sport and evening boxing, with varying success. Even after the 4th of July, I'd keep promoting continuously even as the year became 2004. I even advertised on Armed Forces Radio-Baghdad that fall, autumn back in Wisconsin. Iraq doesn't have a change in season where the forest explodes in shades of red and orange. I got chewed out royally for publishing the eight-digit grid coordinate of the boxing ring. That bastard Maloney probably told on me to the teacher. Oh, well.

It was exhilarating to be creating improved morale and being the epicenter of something good, something positive—controlled violence amidst a war. It took my mind off not being able to experience my daughter turning three. It replaced regret with enthusiasm despite the inescapable knowledge that when I got back home I'd be out of work and she'd be a year older, bills mounting in batches, never getting that time back with her. Welcome to reality, you Army Reservist, you Citizen Patriot, you National Guardsman, you Active Duty Soldier. At least I came home with all my fingers and toes. Not everyone did. Thousands not at all.

Diana said, "Kenny, you're nuts!" Yes, but I have more fun this way. I think she started to regard me a bit differently. Not just as her #2/Executive Officer, but as some sort of weird leader with an agenda of his own. Like I said, I served for the welfare of my fellow soldiers, Tony, and the President of the United States, in that order.

A medical unit supplied some mouth guards upon being invited. The Intelligence Battalion had two fighters. I borrowed some flood lights from Charlie Company. Staff Sergeant Thibodeaux completed the construction. I asked Major Perez to be one of the judges and he heartily agreed. Master Sergeant Black was another. Newly promoted Major Sanchez was happy to help.

Little excites the imagination of an American male more than the idea of two women fighting. Recall middle school and the shout, "Chick Fight!" You'd gather a crowd quicker than throwing money on the ground. Note to Don King: I never made a penny. Really. Sergeant Shawna Burgden found me to ask if was true.

"What?"

"Are you really going to have boxing matches, Sir? Can I fight?" Several soldiers had asked the same question in rapid succession. What criteria should I use to pair the combatants?

"Why? Who do you want to fight?"

"There's this stupid bitch in the Maintenance Platoon, says she wants to kick my ass. Almost got into it with her way back in Leonard Wood."

"What's her name?" And thus began a lengthy tale of frustration and hate for which I had no concern. When I found the object of SGT Burgden's animosity, I blushed at finding her but a waif.

"How much do you weigh? 105? You know Burgden is after you." Dramatic pause. "You know I could give you chance to kick her butt. If you'd want to?" She was no lamb. Maybe in stature, but not in courage. Twenty years old, a Non-commissioned Officer herself.

"I hate that cunt!" Don't sugar coat it, tell me how you feel.

"Have you fought before?" (Prior experience placed fighters at the top tier).

"Well, kind-of. Well, a little during combatives training in Basic Training."

"Yeah, but you're going to be giving up at least thirty pounds, maybe fifty. I don't know if this is a good idea."

She got into my personal space. "That doesn't matter, Sir. I'm going to kick her ass. I have to."

"OK. Be ready on the 4th after evening chow." I walked away grinning and thinking about how best to hype my best match.

Tony raced to catch up to me as I scoured our Battalion footprint for fighters, "Say, Cap. How's the card coming along?" He was even heavier than me and was sweating hard, breathing heavily.

"I don't know. OK, I guess. I got five fights locked in. But there'll be more."

"What's the top of the card?" I told him about the females desirous for blood. And some others.

"You're not going to try to make book, are you?"

I gave him a big smile, bounced my head and looked him square in the eyes, and said, "Because that'd be wrong. Right?"

Tony liked a smart ass, "Yeah, right wrong, wrong right." His head tilted the other way. "You got those names?" He hit me up for info three more times before the exposition started.

Chaplain Charlie saw an opportunity during the slap-dash construction of the ring. Sent forth as a sheep in the midst of wolves, he asked me for some plywood and 2x4s for a project he was working on. "Yeah, go ahead take some." My carte blanche permission was a mistake of sorts. He was wise as a serpent and harmless as a dove. His first name was Matthew. Somewhere, it was in the good news. I counted 10 plywood sheets and many 16-foot sticks pilfered the next day. I began to wonder who else was helping him, and kicked myself for giving a man of God access to my precious building material. It wasn't the last time I'd let him "appropriate" from me. A few days later I circled behind him as only a lone wolf could and surprised him outside the TOC. Just to chastise him I warned, "If you're going to steal from me, I want to know how much you want in advance." I gave a hearty laugh. That got his attention. "One piece at a time, brother!" I slapped his shoulder and strode off. I felt bad the next day and examined the conference room/chapel's progress. Others were also helping with material as the raised deck was complete and some exterior walls were getting framed. Some "leftover" concrete that I sort of knew about was placed for footers. He was building our chapel one stick at a time without authorization. He was a gray-haired First Lieutenant, soft spoken, with Jesus in his hip pocket. He built with Christian soldiers volunteering time after evening chow. A true engineer. Another carpenter scoundrel for the Lord.

But I needed to flesh out my fight card. Before my manic 4th of July mission to find enough participants I crossed paths with the BN XO again and asked him, "Sir, who is the Battalion morale officer?"

Major Perez smiled and said, "Well, you are, Kenny." That puzzled me for a couple of days.

Master Sergeant Black introduced me to Specialist Quinn from the Maintenance Platoon. He was a mountain of a man, 6 foot 4, 295 pounds, who had a mixed martial arts background. He wanted to fight. It would take several months before I could find someone to take on "Killer Quinn." I had boxing matches regularly scheduled every two weeks on Saturday nights for the duration of our deployment.

Staff Sergeant Gibson created a baseball diamond with makeshift bases. Hank printed off some flyers and was traveling Baghdad International Airport spreading the news. I needed a referee and didn't have to look far. Staff Sergeant Jones was a brick house of a black man, a body builder with a deep-throated baritone. From the equipment platoon, he had been an amateur boxer. He wasn't too motivated to join the effort, but after repeated pleas reluctantly agreed.

After work hours on the 4th of July the floodlights connected to a nearby generator flashed on. Doc Baker, our Battalion Surgeon, brought the First Aid bag. I organized the fighters by weight and self-reported experience level. Sergeant Denver from Delta Company wanted to beat the shit out of another soldier from his platoon. It was an even match. The other soldier had instantly agreed. The first on the card. Over a hundred personnel gathered at the appointed time, some unfolding the picnic chairs purchased from the big PX on BIAP. Another hundred would gather soon enough. The three-judge panel was seated.

Sergeant First Class Molina and a few other soldiers were running concessions, selling grilled burgers and brats for a buck. It was the only time attempted though, as demand was low. I conned the prettiest mechanic in the Maintenance Platoon to be a ring girl. A Cameron Diaz look-a-like. She paraded around the ring holding up the round number card before the rounds. Her first trip fell flat as she appeared distressed. I told her to smile big, really sell it! When our young soldier did, it sparked the crowd. But she never volunteered again after that first night. And I got the sense it was degrading, so never tried to find a replacement. I think she had been embarrassed. Sergeant First Class Michelle Anderson, her supervisor, shot me an ugly glare the next day in line at the chow hall, and I knew why.

I handed the megaphone to Staff Sergeant Jones, the soldier with the deep commanding voice.

"LADIES AND GENTLEMEN! "A small flurry of excitement ruffled through the 200 plus audience.

"ON THE BIRTHDAY OF THE UNITED STATES OF AMERICA! THE 169TH ENGINEER BATTALION PRESENTS TO YOU A NIGHT OF EXPOSITION," slight pause: "BOXING!" The applause lowly thundered as the crowd was merely warming up.

"IT IS TIME!!" Staff Sergeant Jones crushed the sell, flexing his muscles into an upper body pose, one hand pointing to the sky! He was a lucky choice.

I had the names, weights, and unit affiliation for the first bout. We were still working out the kinks. The crowd was buzzing loudly. He held the bullhorn aloft, his massive arms spread like wings,

"BAGHDAD. ARRRRRRE YOU READYYY TOOOO FIGHT??"

The enthusiasm of the crowd was electric. It wasn't Atlantic City. It wasn't Vegas. It was a neighborhood transported to the other side of the world. He handed the megaphone back to me as I stepped between the ropes to introduce the first bout. The matches were comprised of three, one-minute rounds, which always seemed stretched out as if the timer with the bell was cheating. During the action, I made sure the upcoming fighters were ready to go. A few bloody noses appeared throughout the night. Ten matches in all on the card. It was cathartic for the soldiers. They could scream at the top of their lungs. Grudges were satisfied.

Two Apache attack helicopters buzzed the lit ring twice during the fourth match. The sun was just past the horizon. Aviators were always on patrol around BIAP. Fifteen minutes later I spotted two officers in desert flight suits in the back, so

I approached them during a match and asked them what they thought.

"We flew over and had to see what was going on."

"You guys want to fight?"

"No way, "the Captain answered. "Do you fight?"

"Hell no! I'm the promoter! Tell your unit." And they just smiled in dubious appreciation.

Before the last fight Staff Sergeant Jones theatrically entered the ring and announced, "LADIES AND GENTLEMAN. IT IS TIME... FOR THE MAIN EVENT!!!"

Sergeant First Class Michelle Anderson brought her young fighting waif into the ring. Barely five-foot-tall, the mechanic kept flinching, moving her hands and arms, with an expressionless, glassy look. I imagined the back of her robe advertising a Philadelphia meat-packing plant.

When Sergeant Shawna Bergden entered the ring, you'd have thought she was Apollo Creed. Working it, she threatened to beat the shit out of her opponent and the entire crowd. Holding her arms up already, Shawna kept screaming, "One and done! One and done!" I wondered if there was a book maker out there and if so what the odds could be. Soldiers were going berserk with rants and screams! The lamb gave up a half a foot in height, and I had a sick feeling about leading her to slaughter. Just as I began announcing the bout I saw the Chaplain staring at me, his arms across his chest. This was some bad, bad juju. Perhaps the waif was a congregant?

The young un' landed a left upper cut to Bergden's chin, about thirty seconds in the first round, sending her mouth guard flying! Sergeant Shawna had stormed across the ring and chased our hero around until the lamb stood firm and then, POW! Sergeant Jones stopped the fight to retrieve and place the mouth guard back in. Oh, they flailed away at each other for a few more minutes, but the contest was already over. The first good shot usually determined these super amateur fights. Apollo Creed sat panting like a whipped dog between the rounds. She had two rolls of belly fat and looked dazed. Rocky refused to sit. Before the third round, Bergden threw in the towel by refusing to answer the bell. Muttering, "No mas, no mas!" I guess their grudge was settled. The young'n danced, holding up her arms!

The boxing matches continued twice a month until I left. Sometimes the crowd was around 200 soldiers or more, but the novelty was diminishing. Major Sanchez crossed paths with me and informed me that one of his soldiers, Staff Sergeant Duran, wanted to fight my heavyweight, Killer Quinn. I was elated and found the young man that afternoon. I hadn't presented a head-liner in a while and my program surely needed a big bounce. When I found him, he was working a speed bag he'd gotten from his home in New Mexico. He had at most 8% body fat, and I had just found my new prospect. The rhythm of the bag was hypnotic. When he paused he said, "Hey, Sir."

"Your boss says you want to fight my big man. You're no amateur, I can tell. But you'd be giving up too much weight."

"Don't care. I just need to fight." SSG Duran weighed a trim 175.

"How many fights have you had? What level? Quinn's back-ground is mixed martial arts. He weighs at least 285." My Iowa boy was starting to sink in my estimation.

"I won most of my fights at the club I was in."

"Where was that?"

"The El Paso amateur boxing club." Another soldier crossed-leveled to the Iowa unit was about to make his mark in 169th fame.

"OK. I'll ask Quinn. But I'm not sure. Why haven't you fought in my ring yet?"

"Couldn't find no one to fight."

"I'll let you know. Cool. Buen dia, Senor."

Staff Sergeant Duran chuckled, "OK, Sir."

Quinn was in. I couldn't tell if he was prepared or not. I guess I forgot to ask. In the meantime, I crisscrossed BIAP telling everyone that the heavyweight fight was finally on. It sparked some increased interest. At the next exposition they fought at the end of the card.

"BAGHDAD. ARE YOU READY TO FIGHT?" It never got old.

I hardly had a chance to put the bull horn down when Duran charged his opponent and landed a combination directly on his chin. Then again, and again, and again. Killer Quinn's knees buckled and he was immediately on all fours in the middle of the ring. Now, I was always neutral in the fights. It didn't matter to me who won. But I heard myself screaming at my greatest volume, "Get the hell up, you goddamn bastard!" I wasn't alone in the shouts. SSG Jones got him back to his feet but it was effectively over. Another combination and he stopped the fight. I didn't know my headliner had a glass jaw. Oh well, there's always another prospect, another top dog. And of course I made a big deal of Staff Sergeant Duran's victory, holding his hand high, big smiles. Now I had to find him opponents.

I talked to Specialist Quinn the next day about his retiring from the ring. He'd had several dozen fights back in Iowa. Was he susceptible to being concussed? I wish him well. He never fought for me again.

I guess being a bastard is part of being a promoter, but at the end of the day, it's all about the gate.

On 11 July, 2003 Lieutenant Colonel "Dynamite Dan" signed my appointment order as the Morale, Welfare, and Recreation Officer for the Battalion. I had a third hat now, besides being the HHC Executive Officer and the Heavy Equipment Platoon Leader. Now I figured we should build/supply workout tents with weights, benches, and kettle bells. But I had to figure out how to buy the equipment. The Asphalt Section should build a running track. Muscle men in the Maintenance shop built squat racks. Why not build basketball courts? My mind bubbled. A library of books and movies donated by soldiers and folks back home was established at a new MWR (Morale, Welfare, and Recreation) tent. I bought big screen TVs and furniture on America's dime. I hoped this would help my soldiers, besides giving me a hobby. As the Battalion Morale Officer I continued scheming. When would Bob Hope visit? In his service to our nation the man had visited and entertained the military overseas always, through every American conflict. Could I meet Bob Hope?

On July 27th 2003, Bob Hope died, so too my scheme to meet him. This war was becoming a big disappointment. Drew Cary and entourage showed up instead. He swore profusely. Kathy Kinney (Mimi – from the headliner's show) had a good set on the giant aircraft hangar stage. Blake Clark, who was a decorated infantry platoon leader in Vietnam, was the most memorable. He told jokes about the living conditions then and now, how the senior officers were dummies then and now, and honored our sacrifice, telling the crowd that whatever happened, you can always tell people that, "I was there, man. I was there." That meant a lot.

The biggest dining facility (DFAC) on BIAP was named after Bob Hope soon after that. President George W. Bush showed up at Thanksgiving, 2003 to dish out food there. Because of security concerns the number of soldiers allowed to push through the Bob Hope DFAC was limited, so most soldiers on post came to the DFAC at Engineer Village. I waited in line for two hours to get in. We had all the fixings and sat elbow to elbow, thanking the American people and Kellogg, Brown and Root for the spread. If you're talking, you're not eating, and if you're not eating then someone else is waiting, so you ate quickly and got out. But George W showed he cared by giving us his own Thanksgiving and that meant a lot, too.

# CHAPTER 5

# Abu Ghraib

If you remember the photographs from 2003-2004 of Iraqi prisoners from Abu Ghraib being forced into naked human pyramids, or blindfolded before snarling German shepherds, then you know how it gave the Army a huge black eye. The junior soldiers who did those things weren't properly supervised. Where was their First Sergeant? Where was their Company Commander? What were they doing to take care of their greatly overworked troops? The Military Police were tasked to control Iraq's entire road network, plus administer all the prisons. They received only a third of the soldiers requested by the Army to do the job. "Do more with less" was the mantra from the Neo-cons like Rumsfeld and Wolfowitz. It took Big Daddy and the troop surge years later to prove thinking like that is extremely dangerous. You can't grow soldiers from seeds.

What were the Battalion Commanders and Sergeant Majors doing when Intelligence officials were giving back door direction to their MPs to "soften up" the detainees? I read the 15-6 investigation findings a few years later online. It was disgraceful. Except for the punishments meted out to the individuals directly involved, little justice was served. The juniors spent a few years at the Fort Leavenworth Detention Center to think about it. The MP Brigadier General was demoted and sent home. It was a failure of leadership up and down the line. And a gut blow to the Army Reserve soldiers who'd finally gained some respect from our Active Duty sisters and brothers for all our hard work.

Everybody shit in the pool on that one.

• • •

Dynamite Dan loved everyone. So in the spirit of brotherly love he had Charlie Company construct a billboard outside the small Baghdad suburb of Abu Ghraib. During the weeks I worked as a liaison, the Equipment Platoon also did some small projects at the prison there, and the carpenters gave Dynamite a ginormous good will sign. His driver looked a lot like "Napoleon Dynamite"—very tall, pimply, skinny, and young. They would disappear into Baghdad, exercising Dynamite's own agenda. It was extremely reckless. Lieutenant Colonel Dynamite dreamed of having two hands coming together grasping in a handshake, with some motto like, "America and Iraq in partnership together building for the future." Or some such bullshit. But since we Americans can't read Arabic, we had to trust what his interpreter had written. As soon as the paint was dry on the billboard, the neighborhood kids started shooting at it with their dads' AK-47s after school. Once, an unexploded round from an RPG stuck into it, the back fins easily seen.

During the invasion the Marines mauled the city of Abu Ghraib pretty badly. Lots of civilian deaths were incurred while US forces gained control of one of Saddam's biggest prisons, to which the town lent its name. It's directly north of Baghdad International Airport (BIAP). So ingrained was the fear of the place that when I let the name Abu Ghraib drop during a particularly frank discussion with a contractor of mine, it brought an instantaneous consent to my demands. Perhaps it evoked memories of relatives or neighbors never seen after internment there. I didn't repeat that remark. I guess it was bad form during negotiations to hint of possible imprisonment and torture, like unto the days of ol' Saddam Hussein himself.

Here's how contracting works in theater, at least at the micro level. After some short readings and filling out of forms, senior soldiers could become a contracting agent "light." At the most basic level, they could buy goods and services for a total of $2,000 a month. Which I did, to buy weight lifting equipment, basketball backboards, volleyballs, etc.—for the troops. The reconciliation was completed for approval every month. Another soldier provided oversight to make sure my paperwork was in order and the vendors got paid. That wasn't good enough for Dynamite. He started buying land from local Iraqis whose plots were on the other side of BIAP perimeter wall, next to our huge battalion motor pool, for no specified reason. Maybe Dynamite Dan was planning to build himself a house? He bought a one-megawatt generator sight unseen for $60,000. It was a great idea as we had to build our own electrical grid in our Life Support Area. We could finally get rid of the generators that dotted the camp and their requisite spaghetti of electrical cords running to the tents.

When a particular convoy arrived at the rendezvous point to pick up the huge machine, there wasn't anybody there. In the south side of Baghdad, the link-up point had been determined by the contractor. Not good. When the small contingent of our soldiers arrived, it was too quiet. This packed-in neighborhood was behind doors. Where were the kids? If something is messed up, look around for kids. If they're there, cool. But

if there's nary a one in an urban environment, you have a seriously dangerous situation on your hands. It meant the parents
were tipped off about trouble ahead. Our soldiers waited for a
few minutes while Dan worked his satellite phone. A motorcycle
carrying two teenage boys approached the tiny convoy, stopped
in the middle of street, and then turned around and sped off
from the direction they had come. This was not good. Another
twenty minutes ticked by before the NCOs could implore the
Battalion Commander to abort the mission. The convoy also
turned around, and after traveling a few blocks, a maintenance
Humvee was ripped apart by an IED.

The front suspension was obliterated by the exploding
artillery shell hastily placed inside a guardrail beside a cul-
vert. Spinning, standing vertically, the vehicle smashed back
down, twisting and cracking the frame as it absorbed the shock
wave. It was a wonder anyone survived the blast, detonated
by a simple garage door opener. A female soldier riding "shot-
gun," in charge of the Humvee and the occupants, broke her
teeth against her rifle butt. Her leg was torn, exposed, out of
its socket, blood spurting from a bloody stump of tendons and
arteries, sticking to clothing, accelerating to match her beat-
ing heart. Smoke exploded with dust, releasing monster echoes
between the buildings, shocking the Americans, as did the vehicle fire. One soldier from the back right seat released his safety
belt and crawled from the hulk and into the street. The driver
had a bloody nose and a death grip on the steering wheel. Their
ears rang, some for days, others for years. A medic placed a
tourniquet to staunch Alecia's bleeding. It was like a quart of
crimson paint spilled upon the floorboard. Three injuries were
relatively minor except for concussions, cuts, and night terrors.
Alecia, from the Maintenance Platoon, was soon evacuated to
Landstuhl Army Regional Medical Center in Germany, then

Walter Reed National Military Medical Center in Washington. Her mother and father were flown at government expense to see her in a hospital bed.

BANG, and your daughter goes into shock, too far from the soccer fields in Iowa from where she had played left wing. Shattered glass cuts flesh readily. No up-armor anything existed in 2003, and ballistic windshields were not built as yet or placed into new vehicles. The equipment now destroyed was a hand-me-down from Regular Army to the Reserve. The fourth soldier grabbed the fire extinguisher, but upon his exit a NCO took him away from the wreck, grabbed the red cylinder, and began spraying the engine and everything underneath. The fire melted uniforms into flesh. Without proper planning and preparation, "leaving the wire" was risky. Good luck. Roll the dice. You don't have a choice when your leader says "Go."

We'd later learn that no trip ticket had been placed with the Engineer Brigade for the movement, which basically meant it wasn't an authorized convoy. So First Armored Division didn't know the convoy was there. But Dynamite didn't care about that kind of stuff. We officers heard stories of how he would disappear with his young driver and venture into Baghdad alone, just to have dinner with prominent Iraqis. At times his staff didn't know where he was. Major General Martin Dempsey, who would later become the Chairman of the Joint Chiefs of Staff, must have hit the roof when he was informed that he had wounded soldiers in his Area of Operations (all of Baghdad and its environs), but that his 1st Armored Division staff didn't know in advance such a mission was being conducted.

The soldiers had removed the wounded and abandoned the Humvee, but forgot to take the encrypted radios padlocked within. The radios cost $15,000 apiece, but the codes inside were as invaluable as the lives of fellow soldiers. The insurgency could now possibly intercept military communications. Careers are cut short for less than this. Another mission was immediately scrambled to go back and recover the radios and flamed-out hulk. So hasty was the organization for the return trip that the freaked-out NCOs actually scrubbed soldiers who were married from going on the mission. A trip ticket was quickly filled out and submitted, covering the names of personnel departing, where to, the what, the why, times, weapon systems, and bumper numbers of the vehicles going. Sergeant First Class Michelle Anderson, who had pledged her life for her troops, was hell bent to go on the recovery mission, as it was her mechanic who was now in emergency surgery.

She pulled up with a wrecker, jumped out, and got into the Convoy Commander's grille, "Put me down, I'm going."

"We already got a wrecker."

"FUCK YOU! Those are my soldiers who got hurt. I'm the one who's going to have to help fix that blown- up piece of shit!" Pause. "I'm bringing the contact truck, too." It was then that she realized she'd just told a commissioned officer to fuck himself. Michele straightened up a bit. "Sorry about that, Sir."

The Lieutenant considered briefly and said," I need the bumper numbers off the vehicles and the names of the maintenance folks going with us. Quickly! Like in two minutes." He smiled at her, "Oh, and Sergeant, hurry the fuck up!" All was forgiven. He had to amend the trip ticket, no big deal.

"Yes, Sir," she said with a relieved grin, as she turned and jogged back to her truck and gave direction to her troops. Soldiers buzzed about making last minute preparations before the rescue mission left out. Michelle was good at her job. She and her crew could easily swap out a Deuce's transmission in a day. Michele had been in the Service for 17 years, and I noticed she tried to hide her hands, unconsciously embarrassed about the grease beneath her nails, drawing them beneath her desk when I came to ask dumb questions. She managed an oil change shop in Davenport and probably would get her job back upon her return. Active duty was a pay increase for her fragmented family. When she got back to the shop she feared being laid off, but thanked for her service to the country. She was going to get her Humvee. She had allowed Alecia to go on the convoy instead of herself.

The better organized and authorized convoy had seven vehicles, 18 personnel, one 240B machine gun, 14 rifles, three 9MM Berettas, a route with times to start movement, and frequencies practiced. They left BIAP with their backs to the setting sun, into Baghdad, traveling Route Senators to the east. It was twenty minutes from leaving the wire to the objective. Would more soldiers get hurt and permanently lose their hearing? Lose a limb like Alecia?

I guessed that SFC Anderson was exhilarated by the danger. Right behind the point vehicle, her driver down shifted the wrecker and Michelle asked her, "Deb, what was the name of your best boyfriend in high school?" Just to ease the tension.

"Eric was a total asshole!" The highway swung to the south. The natural light was diminishing rapidly.

"What was wrong with him?" Michelle asked.

"Besides a needle dick and a mother who hated my guts? I don't know. He never held a job more than three months. No ambition. Just fishing, hunting, and playing with himself." Both Deb and Michelle grinned from ear to ear as the element slowed and exited the highway toward an unknown grid coordinate, a street intersection. "All he wanted to do was play computer games. I'm lucky I didn't get knocked up before I dumped him."

The convoy pulled up to the blown up Humvee. If the soldiers had had time to rehearse they would have secured the site first, and then moved the recovery vehicles to the broken machine, but in their haste, fear, and inexperience they merely occupied the street by force. It was now nearly 1900 hours and it'd soon become pitch dark. Now the residents came out in force, too. Everyone was screaming chants in Arabic, threats in English. Few lights shone from the houses. The streets were lit by the soldiers' vehicles. The soldiers pointed their weapons at the crowd, screaming at the top of their lungs, "GET BACK! GET BACK! I'LL SHOOT YOU, YOU PIECE OF SHIT!" Again and again. A circle of people widened around the object of the mission, but the chant reverberated among the houses loudly, "Almawt li'amrika!" "Death to America!"

The question was how to recover the vehicle from the previous ambush. The IED had detonated from the front right side. It wasn't a direct hit, thank God. The soldiers' injuries were mostly due to flying glass from the smashed windshield and smoke inhalation. Alecia had been severely concussed, was unconscious, and bleeding from her mouth and ears when shoved into another Humvee.

Sergeant First Class Anderson was the first into the vehicle, bolt cutters in hand. Her rifle was getting in the way, strapped across her back. The two radios were still there. "Thank God," Michelle thought. Bolted and padlocked within their mount. She snapped both shanks and spun the locks loose, handing the cutters to her young sergeant outside the Humvee. Like a nurse to the surgeon, Deb handed back the screwdriver and pliers needed next. From the time the pair started until Michelle pulled out the first $15,000 radio with the invaluable encryption code stored inside was less than thirty seconds.

"Deb, put this in the Lieutenant's Humvee!" With the other secured as well, the maintenance NCO placed it with the other and found the Convoy Commander.

"Sir, got 'em both. They're in your vehicle. Your driver has eyes on them."

He was trying to keep a lid on the situation in the street. "Great job, Sergeant Anderson!" he bellowed. There wasn't any reason to raise his voice, since the crowd had started to thin and had quieted. But Michelle wasn't done yet. Could the vehicle roll? Other soldiers were trying to figure it out, too. An NCO from the equipment platoon backed a lowboy trailer toward the hood of the Humvee. Young men milled between the houses and alleys, some with AK-47s and some with pistols. They all saw the woman soldier. The ambush of Jessica Lynch was well known throughout Iraq. The men knew what had happened to her in the street. Some wished to repeat the offenses.

Michelle raced back to her wrecker and swung it wide in the street, nearly clipping a building, and bringing its bumper to the ass end of the disabled vehicle. The ramp was down on the lowboy and the winch attached to the huge shackles in the front bumper of the hulk. The cable pulled and the wrecker pushed. The front right tire was bent inwards, but the others scraped the lowboy's deck, the shredded tires ripping against the frame. The Humvee lunged along the deck and was quickly chained down. Michelle was exposed in the street, along with the Lieutenant directing the vehicle marching orders for the convoy back to BIAP. The sky was black now, except for the neighbor's lights. She wore a Vietnam vintage flak jacket like us all. The Americans were ready to roll out.

A young man from a second-story house with a direct view of the scene peeked out the window. His AK was loaded, safety off, and a round chambered. He would shoot her in a moment. The would-be assassin fought the weakness to kill when his mother barged in to the second-story bedroom screaming, ranting, crying, and slapping her son. "The Americans will kill us all!" Every member of the house piled into it, older sister, father holding baby sister, younger brother, all crying not to do this thing. "From where will we get bread tomorrow? Your father will be sent to Abu Ghraib; we will lose you both forever!" And they took the rifle out of his hands.

• • •

The obvious solution to the problem of the billboard getting shot at every night was to bring a generator on site, along with a light set to blaze up the painted handshake between new friends. The 169th Engineer Battalion didn't have any to spare, but this was extremely important stuff. Dynamite Dan paid two local Iraqis to guard the Army's equipment and the sign. Everything would be all right. Right? On the other hand, the boys from Abu Ghraib thought it would be fun to smoke some hashish and go shoot at the sign again. And now that it was lit up, who could resist? The new condition existed for a few days. Each little gang leader worried that another would beat them to the punch again. The sign was less than a half mile from the prison.

One evening, as soon as the sun went down, a little gang fired their rifles on full automatic towards the billboard, from about 300 meters away. This was great fun. AK-47s aren't accurate past 100 meters and their precious ammo was soon spent. Shooting from the hip betrayed the boys' complete lack of marksmanship training. But it was more than enough of a spray of bullets to scare the shit out of the two guards who started running towards the prison. Rounds whizzed past their ears, bouncing off the ground, muzzles flashing fast rhythmic bursts from across the field. The 169th Battalion Commander hadn't armed them. That would have been reckless. The commotion was quickly detected by the infantry boys inside Abu Ghraib prison and in less than a minute the Quick Reaction Force launched their vehicles outside the gate. The first target the gunners picked up were the two dumb bastards running towards them; it was pretty obvious. The contractors better put their arms up and stop, or their machine guns would split them in half.

"We work for Dynamite! We work for Dynamite!" they screamed at the infantry boys, in broken English. It was time for the little gang to go home and see what Mom had for supper. Hopefully, their fathers wouldn't catch them with the family AK-47. Replacing the rounds was like filling Dad's liquor bottles back up. Who knew, their parents might not even get mad.

When it all got sorted out, Dynamite Dan got fired. One morning he was gone. Criminal Investigation Division (CID) came in the middle of the night and simply said, "Pack your shit." I guess that the First Armored Division Commander had had enough. But that was OK. Dynamite Dan was given a new job with more responsibility as a contracting officer, and lots of money to play with. A classic case of "screw up, move up."

• • •

The Engineer Brigade Commander, Colonel Jimmy Davies, was getting it from both directions. This was his last rodeo. No Brigadier's star for him. He had all the battalions in Engineer Village under his command. The preliminary reports of the generator fiasco were spotty at best. They left out what the Senior NCOs really did on the mission. Several general officers were crawling up his ass. He got up from his desk. He liked going to the boxing matches that I put on at the 169th, smoking a big cigar, cheering with the other Soldiers.

"Sergeant Major?" Col Davies found his battle buddy in his office.

"Let's roll over to the 169th. The After Action Reports about the stupid generator are weak. I can't tell who did what."

"We can ask that dipstick Maloney, but I'm not sure what good it would do."

"You can ask him. Keep him busy while I find the Maintenance NCO Anderson." He wiped the lenses of his glasses. "When are you going to let me fire that Sergeant Major? Jesus."

"Sir, we can't just get rid of the entire leadership team in the middle of the night." Dynamite was out, another Battalion Commander had to be appointed. Jim liked to laugh. "Why not?" He wiped his eyes, then his glasses with a handkerchief. "Anyway, I need to go over some stuff with Major Perez, too."

"Can you keep him in command there?"

"Don't know yet. Probably not, since he's not promotable from Major. But as XO he can pitch hit for a while." And the Engineer Brigade Command team rolled the half mile to the 169th footprint to rescue, once again, their problem child.

Colonel Davies wiped his bald head and glasses as he entered the maintenance building. His battle buddy was giving Sergeant Major Maloney an "anal exam" while the Brigade Commander went unannounced to find Michelle. He approached a soldier half his age while tugging up his pants towards his belly. "Excuse me," he said in a soft tone, "do you know where I could find Sergeant Anderson?" The kid stared at the eagle rank centered on his chest. It wasn't every day a Full Bird came walking around, especially without an entourage. By all rights the 169th Battalion Commander should be there with him. But that was still an open issue.

"Uh, Sir." The young'un was still a little spooked.

Jimmy thought to himself, "Jesus, kid. I'm not Mick Jagger." Still smiling, with the subsequent thought that he may not even know who that is.

"I think she's over here." COL Davies waved his hand low as if to say, "Lead on, good man, lead on."

Michelle got spooked too, and withdrew her hands under her desk as they walked up. "Uh, Sergeant, I saw the Colonel here wandering around so I brought him to you."

The Colonel squeezed the bridge of his nose hard, trying not to exclaim, "You little shit!" When the private was dismissed he did say while shaking her hand, "I wasn't wandering around your motor pool, Sergeant. I came to talk to you about the generator mission." They sat down. "After that, you're going to have to tell me about how you have your operational readiness rate so high. No smoke and mirrors, I hope?"

"No, Sir, no smoke and mirrors," she smiled. "At least not much." Jimmy chuckled. He liked to laugh. Michelle was freaked that he was in her space. The Brigade Commander didn't just wander around. What did this officer want? It could spell big trouble for her.

"Let me get right to the point, Sergeant Anderson. The reports of the aborted generator mission are basically crap. And I've got only one about the recovery mission. The Convoy Commander wrote your name down like ten times in his report on the recovery mission. I need your perspective." He paused briefly, "Your help?" The Colonel continued, "Were there shots fired, for example? I don't know." Colonel Davies looked at his hands. "You do. If you write me the truth," he paused again, picking at his fingernails, "it'll help take the heat off of this outfit. You know, somebody doing good. Maybe, probably you. I could really use a good news story, so to speak."

"I did write a sworn statement, Sir. I gave it to Sergeant Major Maloney."

"I never got it." That dipstick Maloney again, pissing in his coffee. "Do you have a copy?" It took her about thirty seconds to print it off and hand it to the Colonel. He read the four short paragraphs and said, "Cool. Now I want the no bullshit version in any format you want to provide. You can give me an actual After Action Report or whatever, but I need hard copy from you by close of business tomorrow." Colonel Davies leaned forward. "Put whatever you got on my desk. Don't know if I'll be there. And of course, I don't want to have to come looking for you. I might get in trouble with the private again," the Colonel said with a grin.

"He's a good kid. No problem, Sir." It was a problem; this officer might just be looking for someone to blame besides the former commander of the 169th, Dynamite Dan.

Annoyed, she responded his previous request, "What I wrote was the truth, Sir."

"Hey," He put both of his hands up, "I wouldn't imply that you didn't, but this statement is pretty short." Glancing at it again. "I'd appreciate if you'd give me more details. A lot more details. Quickly changing gears, he asked, "How's your soldier doing?"

Five seconds later she replied, "Her parents are with her. I talked to her once, but she was so doped up I doubt she'll remember. That was a few days ago."

Jimmy just nodded. "God, that's sad." They talked shop about the 97% Equipment Operational Readiness rate for a while, but the Brigade Commander felt the need to leave as inconspicuously as he had arrived, without more soldiers seeing him there. Michelle walked him to the door. "Dynamite has left me a huge mess to clean up." He shook her hand. "I need to know who the good people are. That's really why I'm here. Believe me, you're not going to be any trouble."

She overstepped her bounds by asking, "What's going to happen to him?"

"Don't worry about him!" The question sort of pissed him off, sort of not. "And by the way, how are my Massy Fergusons working for you guys these days? It took me a thick rug to soothe those wounds." Of course he knew about that theft. Michelle had a guilty look on her face. "Email me your report on the Humvee recovery mission, too."

"I want to make sure Alecia's parents have you as a point contact." The Colonel was switching gears confusingly, "OK? I won't give them your email if you don't think it's the right thing to do."

That snapped her back. "You've talked to them?"

"Yeah, couple times." I wasn't sure anybody else would do it." Jimmy walked towards the door, and waved with his back turned, "See you at the fights."

"How she's doing?" Michelle asked.

The Colonel turned and met his weary eyes to hers, "Not too good. They had to amputate her leg below the knee. Same leg is going to need a hip replacement. Her jaw was broken and she's going to need a lot of dental work done." As he walked out of the room, he said, "Not good at all." Alecia was young. She wouldn't die, just be disfigured. The medical care would be top notch. Physical rehabilitation and pain management would be the tricky part. Pushing away multiple tears rolling from the edge of his nose and upper lip, the Colonel found his way out of the motor pool without escort. Jimmy dreaded having to write another, "Your loved one died/got hurt in service to her country" letter. He had more important people to explain to about what had happened than just generals.

A few months later he'd pin Michele with the Bronze Star for valor. He wrote the nomination taking most of the verbiage from her own amended After Action Report.

• • •

The 169th Engineer Battalion eventually got a new boss. Major Perez wasn't up for Lieutenant Colonel so had to step back again as the number two soldier in the outfit. In came Lieutenant Colonel Barnacle. The Engineer Group Headquarters, once knowing that Barnacle was leaving, popped corks from non-alcoholic champagne bottles upon his transfer to their subordinate unit. The Brigade Commander, Colonel Davies, chose from a pool of one. LTC Barnacle's infesting grip on the 169th was felt immediately. He and Dipstick worked well together for the rest of the deployment. Barnacle was like the Grinch who stole Christmas, not in Whoville, but in Iraq.

A few months later, as the Morale, Welfare, and Recreation Officer, I had written an appeal to the Des Moines Resister for readers to send the battalion holiday decorations. Boxes showed up forthwith and we had our Life Support Area lit up like Bourbon Street at Mardi Gras. I was pretty proud of that, until the new boss outlawed happiness. Let's just say he didn't like me much. I guess he wanted to make his command a flaming boil on everyone's butt, and had crosshairs was on my back from his day one. The argument was that the enemy would now know where we were, being lit up like a Christmas tree, so we were ordered to take down all decorative lights. Noise and light discipline, boo hiss. We had built Engineer Village, had been there for six months and were mortared pretty regularly, so I guessed, like a dummy, that the insurgency knew where we were. Besides, the Engineer Battalion across the street had a fifteen-foot-high inflatable Santa emblazoned with lights on the roof of their TOC. But I was only a captain and couldn't easily stem the tide of stupidity by myself.

I countered by finding a restaurant at the Baghdad International Airport that would seat uniformed American Soldiers. Instead of the usual Denny's in the Desert, this place had tablecloths, metal utensils, place settings, cloth napkins and waiters. I brought a small group of favorites on the inaugural mission there. I was even able to tuck Diana's chair beneath her as any true gentleman should. What a rush. The only glitch was that we had to leave our weapons with our drivers, so the juniors had to wait outside. We brought to-go boxes out for them. The food I remember was just OK. But the next morning Sergeant Major Maloney shut my effort down.

"It isn't fair," he told me while rendering his decision.

"What's not fair?" I asked stunned.

"The drivers can't go in to the restaurant."

"Sergeant Major, this was only our first time through. You should come with us next time. They have tablecloths and everything. I'll work out the bugs. This was only our first go through."

"Sir," he choked on saying that. "The fact is that you led personnel to an unauthorized location and told soldiers to disarm just so that YOU could have a nice dinner!" The man had a slight point and I couldn't recover quickly enough.

"This will not happen again!"

Damn, I hate getting dressed down when I am trying so hard to blur the lines. He turned on his heel and walked away from me in disgust.

# CHAPTER 6

# Why I Stole a Bulldozer

If you're going to steal something, it's always best to do it in the middle of day. When the sun is cooking central Baghdad at 120 degrees, people don't care what's going on. Just act like you know what you're doing, and go forth boldly. I have based a few careers and relationships on that. I remember Bob Uecker, Mr. Baseball, the voice of the Milwaukee Brewers once saying, "If you're going to go for it, you might as well go all in." This guy was spooky smart! I've always tried to follow his advice, especially when it didn't make any sense.

Ellen was a dear and got me a Garmin Global Positioning Device ricky tick (fast). The ten-digit grid coordinate was tiny in the little screen but it was always accurate; with a push of a button I had my position within ten meters anywhere on the globe. Along with a military map, I was now golden to navigate anywhere, in real time and with total confidence, anywhere on or off the road, a dangerous man on the loose. The Army hand-held GPS devices had breadstick-sized non-rechargeable batteries. Mine ran on AAA's.

The Head Shed called me again. Major Posey was jovial, "Hey, Kenny. I got a big one for you!" Did he think I was willing to do anything upon request? I hadn't brought my knee pads so the answer was no. It was a cool, pleasant 75 degrees in the Tactical Operation Center (TOC). "OK, Sir. What can I do?"

"There's a D-9 high track in the central railroad yard in Baghdad. You know, up-armored with the massive blade, ballistic glass all around the cab. I need you to go get it. It's not far." His eyes danced awaiting my response.

"Whose is it?' I responded with a residual, honest curiosity. That was the wrong question to ask.

He paused, taking a serious tone, "Well, it says Caterpillar on the side, so it's America's. Go get it!"

I contemplated the ethical, moral, and legal repercussions of what he was asking me to do and with a goofy smile responded, "Well, okay." And I immediately started planning in my head. Moments later I wished I'd said, "Yeah, Tony. No problem." I love a hot mission. Could someone take it before I got there? Not likely. It was time to put the pedal down. Gotta go, gotta go. Roger that, Sir. Funny, I never felt any anxiety during the mission I conducted the next day.

The D9 is a beast, known as the "Teddy Bear" to the Israeli Defense Force. They probably built the up-armored bulldozer that I was about to "appropriate." The ballistic glass was placed turret style around the cab in six-inch-wide slats. The driver could therefore maneuver with impunity against machine gun fire or an RPG launch. At 474 horsepower and weighing over 50 tons, the D9 high track could really push. It had a front blade as wide as a two-car garage door and was taller than Shaquille O'Neal. The overall height of the Teddy Bear is 13 feet to the top of its armored cab. Its multi-shank back rippers could loosen boulders from frozen tundra.

If some Iraqi government agency or a contractor like Kellogg Brown and Root can prove that they had a Teddy Bear come up missing in a railroad yard in Baghdad around July of 2003, tell them we gave the one I stole to the United States Marine Corps. Go get it from them. It saved American lives in the assault of enemy positions. THAT'S THE WHY!

If ever charged for the offense, I will demand a court martial. After a few days of bloviating for the record, I would surely create enough confusion to lead to my acquittal. I hope. What's the worst case scenario? Making big rocks into little rocks during the day and writing my next book at night. All rent free at the disciplinary barracks at Fort Leavenworth. Where's the downside? No beer, no girls, no Saturday nights?

• • •

Kellogg, Brown and Root had built a dining facility adjacent to Engineer Village. Pakistanis did the cooking with American civilians, who were the lead men and women, directing the work. All to serve a $25 meal to a soldier. It was a blessing. AC blasted triple-wide trailers had multiple soda dispensers for numerous soldiers at a time. Like a Denny's in the desert. The Army determined that the nastier the living conditions were the better the food should be for the soldiers. Less for us to grouse about, as we soldiers had traveled on our stomachs for millennia. I learned to drink mango juice and peel kiwis. Life was good for Captain Dupar's belly.

One lunchtime meal we heard, "THUMP!" A few moments later another "THUMP!" Telltale sounds of a mortar outside BIAP. "WWZZZZZZIIZZ BANGG!" The windows of the dining facility shook violently. Soldiers yelled, "Incoming!" and dived beneath the tables. Many, disappointed with the interference between themselves and a decent burger, reluctantly took a knee.

"WWZZZZZZIIZZ BANGG!" Please, Lord, let no one be hurt. Please Lord.

We rushed outside to look for wounded. A 75mm mortar had a blast/kill radius of 100 feet. Many took cover in five-foot by five-foot concrete reinforced rectangular tube-shaped bunkers, as we were trained to do. I did, then waited for the "All Clear" to step out. Lack of discipline and impatience infected standard operating procedures. Dummies wandered everywhere, disregarding their own safety. In the Army you have the right to be stupid, but not the right to get yourself hurt needlessly, making other soldiers have to take care of you because you are stupid.

Resistance to American involvement in their country was forming. Enemy mortar teams with lousy ammo, lousy marksmanship, and no professional training cooked off rounds from folks' backyards, then ran. As what they fired were mostly duds after being buried in the sand, there typically were no soldiers injured or equipment damaged from the attack. Typically.

"THUMP. THUMP. THUMP."

First Armored Division's radar technology could detect any ballistic fire 50 caliber or greater. [A caliber is an English measurement, 0.50 of an inch, or in other words, a half-inch wide bullet]. Division TOC had a 10-digit grid coordinate on the location of the bastards in moments, pinpointing the exact site to within 10 meters. But you couldn't respond with counter battery fire with 105mm (four inches at the base and almost four feet tall) high explosive artillery rounds into a neighborhood. That'd kill dozens of human beings, maybe more.

"WWZZZZZZIIZZ BANGG!" Pause. "WWZZZZZZIIZZ BANGG!" Pause. "WWZZZZZZIIZZ BANGG!"

Being mortared always made you wide awake, wondering if it would be your flesh ripped apart, your family traveling to the military cemetery at Arlington, Virginia or a hospital back home. The status report from the 169th Engineer Battalion to the Engineer Brigade and then to First Armored Division fifteen minutes later was that there was no injury to personnel and no damage to equipment. This time. The Quick Reaction Force (QRF) launched immediately north of Baghdad International Airport with the grids. The door kickers were pissed, hesitant, hyped on energy drinks, and scared. Hurt my folks? It was time to see what the infantry boys could do to influence the situation, but how?

"Who was just in your backyard?" The soldiers threatened to take men to Abu Ghraib prison— those who resisted the demands for information. The heads of households remained silent in English and their native tongue. Before the occupier's language, most fell dumb due to neighborhood gangsters. They would risk the familiar prison now administered by Army Reserve soldiers instead. Men followed US troops quietly, hands bound behind their backs with plastic quick ties, glances shot to their girls, hoping that they might come back soon.

• • •

It's a miracle that society has progressed as far has it has in Iraq. Not because of the recent homicidal dictator who was shaking in a spider hole somewhere, or the British Empire that invaded the place in both World Wars, imposing straight line national borders, but because Iraq is damn hot in the summertime. Work is much harder therefore, and intensifies in heat

I saw only three or four civilians in the abandoned train yard that was only a five-minute drive from BIAP. It wasn't hard to find the bulldozer. But if the mechanics couldn't get it started, the mission was toast. Just like my ass felt resting against the 120-degree hood of the Humvee. Navigating to the railroad yard was a snap with my new GPS and military maps. No one was there. Saddam hadn't resourced rail infrastructure much. The equipment was crumbling and oddly rusting in the torrid waves of heat. No maintenance was provided to the boxcars on sidings. Decay between steel and timetables began long before Americans invaded. But like a big toe, my objective stuck out plainly. Well, shit! If I didn't take this prize someone else would. What do American children say, "Finders keepers; losers weepers?" You'd do the same thing. Bet you would.

A gentleman rode his bicycle past us. I gave him a wave and smiled. He waved back and kept going. We spaced out the Humvees to provide some security, but there wasn't anyone around at 1300 (that's 1:00 p.m. for you non-military folks), just like I wanted it. All metal was burning hot. We had big igloo coolers filled with ice and cool bottles of water, but when it melted, so did we. Perspiration ran down our backs, down sleeves of flak-jacketed arms. I sure hoped the Mic-A-Nics (mechanics) could pull their magic once again.

For the soldiers of the 169th Engineer Battalion, picking locks was like something we had learned in grade school, like drawing a picture for Mom with Crayons. One intrepid soldier was in the cab within minutes of arrival. Bolt cutters were on the pre-execution checklist for every mission. Getting the engine to crank was another matter. Hell if I knew how. I'm a carpenter by trade, a wood butcher. The Teddy Bear seemed to want to come with us. To be fired up. To be useful. The Mic-A Nics did a quick inspection for any missing scavenged parts. There weren't any. I wanted to ask every five minutes, "How is it going?" But I remained stalwart in confidence and said nothing.

The battery had a charge and there was pressure in the hydraulic lines, therefore no massive leaks. Some ether sprayed in the carburetor and, "VAAVOOM!" The engine shook, not serenely constant in its growl, not quite yet. It was really, really loud. It belched, sputtering to life. How long had it been since it'd been lubed? Pissed off, this Teddy Bear was awakened. The same young soldier who got into the cab continued to take charge, and raised and lowered the blade. The diesel exhaust shot dense fumes through the stacks, enough to make one proud. He climbed down the behemoth and had a drink of cool water. I had to ask the question. His short response was, "let the fluids warm up." The oils circulated, arousing the beast. Me, too. The danger of being caught by somebody thumped in my ears with each cyclic cough of the engine trying to find its massive rhythm.

Back in the driver's seat, the soldier hit that bitch hard. You have to manhandle the Teddy Bear. Gunning it, the mechanic made the tracks squeal, forward and reverse. "CLACK CLACK CLACK CLACK CLACK CLACK." The metal roared, decibels spiked! Another sergeant from my Equipment Platoon took over the beast and drove toward the trailer. Like a bull mounting a cow, there was nothing gentle about it. They both hollered and screamed! The tracks of the Teddy Bear twisted and broke the running boards out of the lowboy. Tons weighed upon hardpan, and now tires bulged. Idling loud and seemingly panting, the Teddy Bear required the operators to chain it down. The shimmering heat was broken by the sound of the United States Army Reserve on the make. When we got back from the railroad yard I told Tony that we'd "done the job." This was getting easy.

Back in BIAP, Sergeant First Class Anderson and her Maintenance section would drain all fluids and do a complete technical inspection, which would take a full two days. Then she would order $30K worth of parts, which would take over three weeks to get from Illinois, another ten to build back up. She was nothing short of beautiful; the system was working. The 169th eventually brought the D9 up to operational standards after SFC Anderson hung the parts with her own greasy wrench, with dirt beneath her split fingernails forgiven overseas, a badge of honor.

• • •

The reason the armored bulldozers were so prized was offensive in nature. Walls are obstacles that must be either gone around, under, over or through. Engineers would say breeched. The assault of an enemy fortification means to reduce it, tear it down enough to destroy their covered and concealed positions. The Teddy Bear does that with it's massive blade.

Consider that every hamlet in Iraq produces its own concrete block. There is a wide differentiation from the standards we have in the States. It is their basic building material, and the reason few structures were over two stories high. Proper steel reinforced concrete was rare. The mortar and block the locals produced hadn't a high enough cement content, and included contaminated sand or dirty water which in total produced walls more like tissue paper to bullets and armored vehicles. When the Marines had two D9's abreast during an attack, buildings and walls collapsed readily with a slight push. The drivers, behind ballistic glass on the dozers were impervious to small arms fire, and would just climb over the debris they created.

Suppose you are an insurgent/patriot (depending who wins the war) in a compound made of such a block wall. Then at 0300 (3:00 a.m.), the silence is disturbed by "CLACK CLACK CLACK CLACK CLACK," without pause, from behind a palm grove, approaching at 7 mph with Marines coming forward from a thousand meters out, night vision goggles on.

Never shoot a firearm at American Marines. You'll just make them mad. No better friend. No worse enemy.

When the world calls 911 the answer on the line responds," United States Marine Corp, how can I help you, Sir or Ma'am?"

A youngster, his butt nine feet in the air pushing through an Iraqi wall like paper mache, calling, "Get some!" I imagine his sister Marine drove the other Teddy Bear in tandem, through and over all obstacles, imagine buildings crushed, riding up and over.

But you would have run away before then, if you are a smart insurgent, that is.

CHAPTER 7

# Magical Mobile
# Mixing Machines

In early July we received the mission to build from scratch a Life Support Area for a Battalion of the 82nd Airborne Division just north of Engineer Village. They were not going to be good neighbors. The 82nd was known by the Army since World War Two as the biggest thieves in the service. We were amateurs compared to them. We had a three-strand concertina fence between us and them. The razor wire barely reached three feet in height and wasn't much of an obstacle to the paratroopers. Within hours of their arrival, our trucks were missing headlights and batteries. The fact that we, the 169th, were from the Army Reserve made it justifiable to steal from us. And such fun!

In anticipation of their arrival, we began pouring concrete pads for hard-stand buildings using the Magical Mobile Mixing Machines. No one knew how to use the Vietnam War era concrete mixing machines. The maintenance platoon was still figuring out how to order routine parts to maintain the familiar rolling stock like Humvees and bulldozers. We had three

MMMMs all shipped from the Reserve Center in Davenport, Iowa. One was built in 1967 and the other two in 1971. They had large compartments on a truck chassis which contained, in order of volume, stone aggregate, sand, and water and cement, the components of concrete. Steel wheels, cranked by hand, controlled the admixture, depending on the concrete properties desired. Once the soldiers got the hang of it, and the mechanics figured out how to replace ancient parts when needed, and I coordinated the purchase and delivery of the material, it was magical. Concrete on demand, 30 yards a day, every day, quality. More than enough to place two 20-foot by 30-foot pads every day. These three machines paid for themselves in spades.

We contracted Iraqi vendors to bring in the majority of the concrete required to build the huge Life Support Area in preparation for 1st Cavalry Division (which replaced 1st Armored Division). The vendors used what we called "jingle trucks," named for the tassels and bells the local drivers used to gaudily adorn their vehicles. If they showed up, it was always a huge pain in the ass to escort them to where we needed to place the concrete. Our guys and gals worked six days a week, as sure as the sun came up in the morning. In the construction world concrete is God. There's no mistake in placing concrete that doesn't cause an extreme amount of ass pain. Is the pad at the proper elevation? Is it square? Is it level? Is there a slight twist in the column? Are the edge forms plumb? Running a jackhammer to demolish isn't fun. But what we did in Iraq was the simplest variety of concrete placement, slab on grade. Think pads, like your driveway squares. Incidentally, you don't pour concrete, it's placed. Concrete in the mixer is a solid in liquid form, but I'm probably geeking out now and shouldn't describe compression strength or how hard it is. Because it is very, very hard, you don't want to screw it up or you'll be pounding it out. Sorry, the psychosexual aspects of construction never stop. Screws, nails, male and female ends of an electrical cord, don't forget vibrators (also known as donkey dicks) for the 'crete. You have to strip the formwork as soon as possible and you'd better have oiled them up prior to use. Engineers hammer and drill and on and on. The presence of female soldiers on the jobsite provides some check in the lewdness, until they become just as bad. Swearing conveys importance, and you rely on your teammates continually. Idiots and the lazy need not apply. It becomes a matter of production. And the crew running the Magical Mobile Mixing Machines was a source of great pride.

The Concrete and Asphalt Section also had asphalt distributors. With these pieces of equipment, compacted stone would be sprayed with a black tar-like liquid and rolled to form a road. This was another mystery within the section, as no one had done this before. Coming from a dead stop, this smallest of the Equipment Platoon's three sections needed the most love, which is why I pledged to them that they would build every day, and that we would do chip and seal operations and asphalt BIAP. Bituminous pavement makes me excited. The gasoline smell when it is being placed is like none other. When it gets hard, it is so fresh and hot you just want to touch it. The coolest thing about construction is that at the end of the day the product of your labor is physical, tangible. It's there and no one can say otherwise. You write your name on it whether it's sound or not. The solders needed goals so they could come home proud, and we pushed each other mightily. It took three months, but eventually we built an acceptable running track around the inside of our Life Support Area. Yeah, the rabbits among us needed to blow off steam every day too, safely, and the runners were on it the afternoon it was finished getting rolled flat, their sneakers slightly sticking. One of my proudest moments was coming to the daily construction meeting Major Posey hosted, my boots and trousers splattered with tar. Very soon we had more requests for asphalt placement than we could handle. Everybody wants you when you're good.

The Concrete Section made a mistake. While loading sand into the hopper at the tail end of a Magic Mobile Mixing Machine, the operator of the five-yard loader accidently mashed it by not having the bucket high enough when he tipped it down. It was a $3,000 mistake. A routine report of survey was initiated to investigate the incident, and my statement provided the view that "shit happens in construction." It's inevitable that equipment will get broken, no big deal, a cost of doing business. Sergeant Major Maloney didn't see it that way and shaped the result so that three of my guys would have to pay out of pocket! It was absurd and I confronted the Battalion Command Sergeant Major about it. The dipstick's attitude was that soldiers weren't being careful enough and he wanted to send a message. By the end of the month Finance had already taken a grand from each soldier's paycheck without prior notification. Try to explain that to the young wife and kids of the private operating the five-yard loader. I developed an abounding hate for that man that lasts until this day. I wasn't alone.

Revenge came later in the form of a fish named Freddie. I'm embarrassed to recall such juvenile hijinks but let's just say a carp from the Tigris doesn't smell too sweet after a couple days. Don't tell Tony. It wasn't a dignified moment for a member of his crew. More about Freddie later.

• • •

Section Sergeants Gibson, Hensen, Thibodaux and I were playing a riveting game of Risk one evening after chow when the second-ranking soldier of the Asphalt and Concrete Section entered our tent and whispered into Gibson's ear. His eyes popped wide open and he sprang out of his chair, taking the poor NCO with him. We who remained around the map of the world exchanged quick worried glances at each other. Another roll of the dice. Thibodaux had control of Australia and was invading Asia.

Moments later Sergeant First Class Gibson reentered the tent, "Desoto lost his weapon. Can't find it anywhere."

We all shot to our feet. "How long?" I asked.

"Two hours."

"Oh, my God!" gasped Hensen. The shared fear at that moment was chilling, the blood running out of our faces.

Desoto would have better served the Army as a pastry chef rather than an Engineer without a weapon. The search began at once. As word spread, a panic was lit among the higher ranks. I hurried to the TOC to tell our Company Commander, Captain Berry. Platoon Sergeant Molina reacted like his hair had caught on fire. I roused Captain Berry from her tent and told her the God-awful news that we had a missing weapon. Diana was angry, "What if the 82nd found it?" My blood ran cold again. She went to report the lost weapon to Battalion. Quickly our front gate was closed, as if that would do any good.

The thought of having to personally grovel at the feet of an Active Army Lieutenant Colonel for the return of my soldier's rifle filled me with tremendous dread. I imagined a faceless officer asking me, "What's wrong, Captain, don't your soldiers want to be in the Army?" I grabbed Staff Sergeant Desoto and he showed me the row of Port-a-Potties that he'd left the weapon in, now two and half hours ago. He'd taken a leak and had a brain fart and walked away. A few minutes later he ran back, but it was gone. He was of no use to me after that. Going into every tent nearby, I asked everybody I came across and widened my search. The shitters were just along the concertina fence with the 82nd. Coming to the tents occupied by our cooks, I found Sergeant Grant sitting on his cot and asked the question, "Have you seen a rifle? We're missing one." Sure enough, he reached underneath his cot and pulled out the weapon.

I snatched it out of his hands kind of pissed off. "Why didn't you report it? That you found a weapon?" He looked at me through his Army unflattering birth control glasses and said, "Well, I just figured I should hang on to it just in case someone came looking for it." Somehow his answer made sense in the moment.

"Well, hey, thanks. Thanks a lot Sergeant Grant!"

Skipping to the TOC, I felt sublime relief. In the meantime, my battle buddy had formed up the platoon and threatened to personally beat the shit out of everyone if the weapon wasn't found. I was later told that the strings of vulgarity Molina uttered in two languages were masterful. Command Sergeant Major Maloney saw it differently and fired him from his leadership position. He ended up working in the Battalion Operations cell for Major Posey. Sergeant Molina was pretty down in the mouth when I checked on him the next day. He had to move to another tent within the LSA. His cot was now next to the Battalion Commander's driver, "Napoleon Dynamite." The kid liked to listen to techno music and badly draw fantasy creatures. The young soldier acted like everybody else was an idiot.

Cheerfully, I pointed out that all the pressure of having to babysit nearly forty soldiers was now gone. "And just think, Hank" I said with a grin, "No one is going to bug you when you're working for Major Posey. You're free. Now we can really go into business." Molina's eyes started to twinkle. He always had an angle playing, usually several. It was in actuality another classic case of "screw up; move up." I never got a replacement for my fired Platoon Sergeant. I tried to get Staff Sergeant Henson to step up, but he wasn't interested, so I just left things alone. Besides, we had a lot of concrete to place and the work was going smoothly. Staff Sergeant Desoto was given a written counseling statement for losing his weapon, but hey, scary stuff like this could happen to anybody.

CHAPTER 8

# Battle Rhythm

Organizations purposely get into what we call a "battle rhythm" to create efficiencies. Example: At 1700 (5:00 p.m.) every day Major Posey had his construction meeting. You didn't have to think about where you needed to be or do. Think of Ground Hog Day, the movie. The routine tested your ability to cope over time. Days of the week became immaterial, a weekend an absurdity. A lot of folks crumbled. Personal growth was a mirage. You persevered. Even the wailing sirens echoing from loudspeakers became routine, the warning that mortars were in the air.

"POP POP POP!" Sirens blared. "BANG BANG BANG!" By the time you got to the nearest bunker it'd usually be over. You'd wait in the concrete square tube until the all clear was given. If it was given. Or more likely, Soldiers were lazy and simply stayed where they were. The Army developed battle drills to react to the aftermath of indirect fire, which was basically to find out where the round detonated, then search in concentric circles for hurt personnel or damage to equipment. How often it happened depended on where you were in Iraq. Even then, those procedures vanished as almost no one got hurt. Considered not to be serious unless it landed in your hip pocket.

By the winter of 2003, the insurgency was stepping up fast. Shoot and scoot. IEDs along the road. American casualties were rising. We'd change our tactics and they'd change theirs. This lethal cat-and-mouse game lasted until US Forces retrograded out of theater. The Iranian mullahs shipped bomb parts by the truckload into Iraq for years. NCIS-Baghdad (Naval Criminal Investigation Service) was able to trace the components of IEDs after detonation and link them to Iranian factories. Hundreds and then thousands of Americans were killed and maimed for life due to the orders of the Ayatollah. A grim bargain with fate enveloped Soldiers. If your convoy got hit by an IED it was just the luck of the draw.

One morning I woke up and walked over to the bank of Port-a- Potties that was about 100 feet from my hooch. I saw yellow construction tape around them like a half ass cordon around the area. Another soldier asked me if I hadn't heard the mortar attack the night before. I hadn't. I always slept like a baby in Iraq. But sure as shit, I spied a tail fin of a small mortar sticking up ten feet from the pissers. The explosion would have sent blue crap everywhere. I witnessed two big-balled bastards holding a conversation above the unexploded munition, smoking cigars. That kind of bravado/stupidity eventually gets other people killed/hurt. Military traffic passed just meters from the UXO (Unexploded Ordinance). It was reckless, a failure of leadership, betting that vibrations wouldn't set the munition off. I walked to a different set of Port-a-Potties. Complacency had replaced battle drills. People stopped caring and started making mistakes, like losing your weapon or failing to call home.

• • •

Sergeant First Class Molina was working with Major Posey now, developing Life Support Areas all over BIAP for incoming Army outfits. Hank had contacts with lots of folks, including vendors from outside the base. One afternoon, after a wonderful meal of baked chicken, mashed potatoes, and chocolate ice cream, Hank disclosed a dastardly plan. I was going to be the lookout, supposedly. Every day we ate the same food at the same place at the same time. Living in Iraq had become almost normal by now and our unoccupied minds turned towards evil.

Command Sergeant Major Maloney was vigorously enforcing a new rule that the rugs sold at the Haji Marts inside BIAP couldn't be placed on the floor, wall decoration only. Political correctness stated they were actually prayer rugs, and as infidels, we must not use them as rugs beneath our feet while changing our socks or clipping our toenails. It was disrespectful to Islam. Tony was seething, "Even in our own hooches? Who's going to know?" The vendors certainly didn't care what we used the rugs for. A blow for justice had to be struck. The Sergeant Major also banned the use of the word Haji to refer to Iraqis.

The Hajj refers to the pilgrimage to Mecca. A Haji is someone who has successfully completed this once-in-a lifetime obligation. As compared to Zipperheads, Chinks, Commies, Japs, Krauts, Hun, Johnny Reb, and Yankees, it was a mild dehumanization of the "other." Haji became part of the American lexicon despite official attempts to suppress it. To our minds it was kind of like calling someone "dude" or "sport".

The plan was simple, the potential effects horrid. Around the outside of our tents were stacked sandbags about three or four feet high, just in case a mortar landed close and the shrapnel,

or twisted bits of metal flying above the speed of sound, punctured canvas, sheets, skin, and sinew.

"Why don't we throw a fish outside dipstick's tent, between
the canvas and the sandbags?" Molina suggested. I looked up
from my pudding pop. "Right by his cot."

"And where's that?" I asked. I was intrigued by the juvenile
audacity and cruelty of a rotting fish somewhere near a man's
pillow.

"Oh, I know," said Molina. "The only other person in his tent
is Sergeant Major Clinton." I liked Sergeant Major Clinton. Soft-
spoken, tried hard, good people. It seemed unfortunate that
those two had to bunk together.

"Where you gonna' get a fish, smart ass?" I was trying to gain
weight so I went to the desert carousel and got a piece of red
velvet cake.

"That's easy. What are you doing around 2:00 a.m?"

"When? Why?"

"I'll get the fish and then..."

"Wait, wait, wait." I said in a hushed tone. "Stop talking like
that. It's not a fish. Call it something else."

"What?"

"Listen, Molina, from now on in the operation we talk about
the thing, like a code."

It didn't take long for him to spout off, "Freddie! It's Freddie
the Fish!"

"OK, don't get excited." I saw cookies stacked on the way
outside the dining facility.

"Aren't you afraid you're going to get fat?" He asked me.

"What do you mean, going to?" I asked. The bastard. I've
always been very sensitive about my weight.

The fateful evening came. Freddie was procured, wrapped in
rags. It stunk awful, getting ripe under Molina's Humvee most

of the day. The unmistakable smell of death was just beginning to come from Freddie. I shuddered to think about the flies this would produce. Few soldiers would be walking around at 0200. At this point my memory comes and goes as far as who did what. Chagrined, I learned later that Freddie landed beside SGM Clinton's cot, with only canvas between it and his dreams. Collateral damage.

• • •

After six months of existence in Iraq it seemed everyone's personal relationships were unraveling. The need to have somebody care for you banged like a bass drum. A sad rhythm of loneliness permeated the LSA. Soldiers got one day off a week, which was indistinguishable from any other.

Oh, you could go to the work out tents and lift weights (I bought those using MWR money). Maybe go to the Haji Mart on your time off and buy your wife pearls. Soldiers had nothing to spend money on except rugs, metal wares, crap perfumes, knock off leather Versace purses and colorful bronze bowls. I set up a big Morale tent with donated movies and books. We built basketball courts and of course the running track. The internet was used to pick at old worries.

One beautiful soldier served in the Survey Section and had the reputation for liking the fellas. She was very "affectionate" supposedly and her supervisor tried out his crude come-ons. She threw the bullshit flag and complained to the Inspector General. A talented and married electrician, he lost his position and worked alone on the LSA's electrical infrastructure for the second half of the deployment. His prosecution was deferred until his homecoming. The Soldier got sent back early, pregnant. His career was over after seventeen years, no pension. In the LSA fishbowl the gossip spread quickly.

The internet café was both a blessing and a curse. Hank's girlfriend had "heard" that he was screwing around. The rumor mill churned now electronically. It was absurd. I spent more time with Hank than anyone. He was madly in love with her. I witnessed on his behalf, but my Email didn't matter. She dumped my battle buddy during the deployment.

Ellen was distant during correspondence. It took a few weeks for me to figure out that something was definitely wrong. When I finally was able to get her to spill, the reality was that my neighbor was making moves on her. He was a runner and wasn't opposed to wearing short shorts. It had been an open joke that you could see the head of Bill's penis through his speedos. Hank and I devised a plan to be executed upon our return. Bill didn't know him, so a visit to his front door with a baseball bat intended for his kneecap was definitely a course of action. But my favorite course of action was that I'd draw him to the side of my house with the ruse that I needed an opinion about the shape of the siding, (I helped him on the fascia and soffit of his garage before I deployed). I'd turn and grab his balls, twist hard, get him on the ground and start stomping. I planned to tell the cops that the piece of goo that had been Bill had tried to kiss me. What would a month in the county lock up be to me other than a vacation?

Ellen, as always, handled her business and confronted his wife. They moved before I came home. It was a pity. Getting back to Wisconsin, I had a few anger issues. The violation of respect for our family at a vulnerable time, our lowest ebb, is still hard to understand.

Everyone had a sob story and seemed ready to fall to pieces. There may have been truly resilient Soldiers whose personal problems diminished in Iraq but I never met one.

• • •

Chaplain Charlie unexpectedly attended a daily construction meeting hosted by the Battalion Operations Officer, Major Posey. The agenda usually just went in order: Me (Headquarters and Headquarters Company), Alpha's XO, Bravo, Charlie, then Delta Company. We'd been doing it seven days a week at 1700 hours for so long that my feet just naturally took me over the crushed rocks to the spot outside of the TOC. Month after month, it was the same basic song, until the man of God walked up.

"Whatcha' need, Chaplain?" Major Posey asked.

He looked a little sheepish, "Well, Sir, now that the chapel, I mean conference room, is almost done, I've run out of materials to finish. And now we need to do the roof. Do you think we could get some troops to help finish it up?" I thought the guy was going to cry. CC was smooth.

"You're kidding me, right?" I never saw Major Posey angry before. He just realized he'd been hustled. A conference room/chapel wasn't on the approved project list for the battalion. But he took a breath and said, "OK, let's go take a look." And the entire meeting adjourned to the mostly built chapel, about three hundred feet from the TOC. Right under his nose a building had taken shape. In those early months all building materials could only be used for mission critical projects like showers, doors for tents, an internet café to connect Soldiers to family, and at least one boxing ring. Someone had denied the project to build a hardstand building for a chapel, instead of just a tent (probably that atheist prick Maloney). Some people disagreed with the Command's priorities.

"We really need some windows, too. Do you think the carpenters know how to build...?" He paused looking confused, "You know—rafters?"

"Just stop, Lieutenant! We'll see." He was pissed. Or was he faking it? He had to know what had been going on. Tony wasn't above play-acting either. Maybe he just wanted to see how far we'd get before they had to step in with dedicated resources, like parents watching their kids build a "secret" tree house. We had done pretty good up to then.

"And chairs. We really need chairs, too."

We company XOs looked at each other, some with big grins, some with looks of boredom. It was framed, just needed the roof, AC, doors, and windows. It was pretty big, forty feet by thirty feet. And we did end up using it for meetings. The Chaplain had even partitioned some offices and had an empty bookshelf on display. It was very sad in its uncompleted state.

Major Posey looked at us Executive Officers and asked, "OK, who has a squad of carpenters that isn't overly tasked right now?"

Alpha's XO, Captain Rodriguez chimed in, "Well sir, our 2nd Platoon isn't too engaged, and besides, Private King has already been the lead man in the construction so far."

"The third-year carpenter apprentice you got?"

"Yes, Sir." Switching gears, Al Rodriguez continued, "Looks like we'll have to build some columns for inside support." Al loved to build, you could tell. "Lieutenant Meredith could figure the load-bearing requirements and design the roof." So, it was a conspiracy after all.

"He hasn't already?" Now Major Posey was in on the game.

"Uh." Long pause. "No, Sir."

It was my turn: "If we do that, we'll have to pull up the deck and build some concrete piers for the columns. No big deal."

"Just like the concrete footings that you already placed, Major Dupar?" the Battalion Construction Officer shot at me, just for the fun of watching me twist. I had grown complacent in my unprincipled behavior and forgot that sometimes, it is far better just to stay silent and not answer the boss.

Major Posey looked around at the group an exclaimed, "You know, I've just been hustled." The wry smile crooked through his reddish mustache. CC looked like his sin was unpardonable. This was some funny shit. The Engineer Officers continued, now that the conspiracy was out in the open. We couldn't leave a half-finished building halfway through the deployment halfway around the world. We had enough problems. Why make Jesus mad now?

Looking at Rodriguez, Major Posey said, "All right. Get me a bill of materials for what you need to complete the conference room. And get the thing finished pronto." Turning to CC with a wicked smile, "Is there anything else you need, Chaplain?"

"Oh, no, Sir. No, Sir. At least not right now. But maybe later."

And that's the way it was with the 169th Engineer Battalion. All the real movers and shakers were constantly playing the angles. The cool kids had gravitated to the same table at lunch, always in some sort of trouble.

# CHAPTER 9

# The Russian Embassy and the Diaper Rash Miracle

On August 7, 2003, a car bomb attack, pinned to the developing insurgency, occurred in front of the Jordanian Embassy in Baghdad. Witnesses reported the driver walked away before the bomb detonated. No blast walls protected the building. Seventeen innocents were killed in the street, another forty wounded, all Iraqis. The soft target was immediately looted.

This attack made the Russians extremely nervous. Force protection measures around their nearby embassy were non-existent, and it wasn't protected from Vehicle Borne Improvised Explosive Devices (VBIEDs) at all. Only a few blocks away from the Jordanian embassy, it was a five-floor concrete box built in the 1970's as a hotel. Like most things in Iraq, the grime never got washed away from the façade.

The deck of cards of wanted Iraqi members of the Ba'athist government didn't include Abu Musab al-Zarqawi. However, he was trying to make a name for himself with Al-Qaida in Iraq (which would later morph into ISIS -Islamic State of Iraq and Syria]) by masterminding mass casualty events. The playing card idea had been used since the Civil War to help soldiers identify enemy commanders, ships, or airplanes. Without ideology except to kill, al-Zarqawi became the "Joker" in the deck. The idea terrorists wish to impose is the helplessness of the governed to be protected. Three months after the Jordanian Embassy bombing, al-Zarqawi murdered dozens of his own people with nearly simultaneous explosions at hotels in Ahman, Jordan. The butcher's bill was the greatest against celebrants at a wedding. The local boy was popular at home for killings against the "Other." Jews and Americans were targets that could be understood. Eventually, Abu Musab al-Zarqawi's blood lust brought his own folk against him. It took NCIS-Baghdad three years to hunt him down.

The day after the bombing at the Jordanian embassy I was having a nice KBR (Kellogg Brown and Root) veggie burger for lunch. KBR charged the American tax payer over $25 per plate for fresh veggies, soft serve ice cream, and acceptable burgers. I got another "hurry up and get to the Head Shed" through my Motorola. Who was mad at me now? What had I done that I probably should have known not to do, but did anyway? I walked fast.

MAJ Posey was in a hell of a hurry. "Kenny, get over to the Engineer Brigade Headquarters. We're organizing a mission to protect the Russian Embassy from car bombs. We have to get Texas barriers over there this afternoon. We're assembling the tractor trailers now. The other Company XOs are supposed to get the HQ, too. How soon can you be there?"

"Five minutes." I was already caught up in the excitement.

"Go!"

Texas barriers are fourteen-feet long and nine-feet high, with a square base at the bottom making an inverted "T." Everything's big in Texas, and each barrier weighed nearly seventeen tons. There's no going around that with your white Toyota pickup laden with rusted artillery shells, diesel fuel, 16-penny nails, and fertilizer. Jersey barriers are much smaller. You've seen them around for traffic control. In the civilian world they're made of plastic and maybe filled with water. In Iraq, Jersey barriers are seven feet long, three and a half feet high, made of concrete and rebar and weigh almost a ton. We were to use them by the dozen around the Russian Embassy, blocking sidewalks, in between the Texas barriers; basically anywhere the white Toyota pickup could wedge itself through. The goal was to protect the staffers inside, and perhaps keep the building from collapsing. A formidable insurgent network was at work.

I called Sergeant First Class Molina on the radio and we met briefly in the motor pool. I jumped out of the Humvee and asked, "Hank, what the hell is going on?"

"We're getting all the lowboys (equipment trailers) hooked up and we're supposed to get over to the Brigade Headquarters and load up Texas barriers."

"You getting a crane over there?"

"No, our cranes are to offload. We're going to save the Russian Embassy!" He had this huge smile on his face.

"You're such an asshole."

"Thanks. Where you going, Captain Dupar?"

"To the Brigade Headquarters. See you there."

This was not good. A slapdash unplanned emergency mission was extremely dangerous. I'd been inside the BDE HQ once. It was air-conditioned. Nice. When I entered, the Engineer Brigade Operations Officer, Major Rigsby, was briefing and planning over a Baghdad map in the conference room with another officer. I hadn't met them before and quickly introduced myself. The Major showed the location of the embassy. It was on a major thoroughfare. The back of the building faced an upscale neighborhood. Several roads and alleys led towards the embassy. Another officer came in, red-faced and sweating. He had recon'd the site and wasn't enthusiastic about our prospects.

"Sir, there's electrical lines everywhere around the embassy. Some as low as only ten feet off the ground. There's no way a crane can operate in these tight conditions. And it's going to be rush hour soon."

Major Rigsby looked at me. "What do you think, Captain Dupar?"

In the Army there's an old credo—"never volunteer." It was entirely ignored by the post-Vietnam all-volunteer force. But then, that was our first mistake, volunteering for military service. Strange how hard it is to leave it, though, something you love. I could shoe horn a stack of sixteen foot 2x4's into the boss's igloo cooler with a crane, so I felt somewhat confident. Like a moron I said, "We can do it." I had confidence in the guys and gals of the Heavy Equipment Platoon.

"Go!" said Major Rigsby.

He gave me some other directions but my head was beginning to spin. It felt like my ball sack was trying to crawl back into my body. I started shaking like a dog pooping razor blades, again. I had the feeling that I was now in charge of the mission leaving the gate, although not specifically appointed as such. There was so much activity. I was swimming in confusion. How was I to get on top of this thing?

It took another two hours before the T barriers were loaded. I used an old convoy organization trick, pulling the element forward about a half mile to scare the shit out of everyone, and then stopping to re-organize. The purpose of this was to uncoil the staged vehicles and ensure they were in the proper order. Convoys don't wait for stragglers. I wasn't gentle when I ordered all

officers, NCOs, and drivers to get to the hood of my Humvee
for a half-assed convoy brief. Barely fifteen soldiers ran up. You
can usually tell who doesn't know what they're talking about
by the volume and frustration in their voice. I had no idea how
many soldiers we had and I knew only a fraction of the faces, as
the other units from Engineer Village had soldiers and equipment mixed in with the 169th. We reviewed the route. The Russian embassy was only fifteen minutes away in the city. We had
radio communications, for now. I started to holler at folks. Bad
sign. Not good.

Jim and I were on point, the first vehicle in the convoy, as
always. Lighting a smoke, I jumped into our unarmored Humvee with the vinyl doors removed, looked at Jim and said, "Hit
it." God, was that cool = stupid. But he started driving too fast
and I had to slow him down. A highway around the commercial
runways was called "the race track" because it was wide and
banked. We crawled at 15 mph, and then picked up speed. We
were the only traffic heading outside BIAP. NCOs waved us forward leaving the Entry Control Point, with nothing but green
lights for us this afternoon, God willing. Steering quickly onto
the Joseph Stalin Memorial Tollway, Jim picked up the pace
to 40 mph. Within three exits the convoy was heading north
through a cloverleaf exit. The civilian traffic was heavy. The EZ
passes atop each vehicle's dashboard saved a lot of time, avoiding the cash-only booths, otherwise we'd have had to return to
the base to get a shit ton of shekels. We found the boulevard,
swung to the east, and pulled right up like we owned the joint,
snarling up traffic mightily. Thousands of good people moved
through us and around us, trying to get home, like a river pulsing
past newly placed stones. It's funny how people won't look at
you when you're heavily armed, or pretending to be. They take
directions for their tired bodies like fish in a stream, struggling

for a restful space to reside momentarily before avoiding a new danger.

We started setting up a crane by the main entrance of the Russian Embassy, at the south end of the 1970 era concrete box/former hotel. Our big rigs backed up the low boy trailers, each with one Texas barrier. Hank and I argued about how to swing between the spaghetti-like electrical lines above. He was right this time. The boulevard traffic dodged around us, the pedestrian traffic heavy. Hank's and my instructions created a logjam in each direction. The crane had to be repositioned after I had set it down. Hank didn't like where it was so overrode his officer's direction. Outriggers up, mud pads moved, another ten minutes before the first pick. In the meantime, six tractor trailers were lined up with Texas barriers south of the embassy. The drivers and shotguns would wait for hours, isolated in their cabs, before being summoned for their cargo, as the tumult eased into curfew.

An intestinal parasite from the crowd approached me with haste. I watched as if through slow motion. An American journalist walked right to me and with a slight quiver in his voice, announced: "I'm Robbie the reporter from CNN." He flipped out his notepad. "Can you tell me what is going on here? Who's in charge?" Sergeant First Class Molina appeared at my side like a magician's assistant, but an ugly, really ugly one. He cleaved to me. He had some sort of Navajo pheromone that discounted fear and attracted women. Or maybe that was his Black Irish half. I told Robbie, "I have no idea" and stopped talking. The press maggot directed his attention to Hank, "What about you? Do you know what's going on here?"

"Hi. I'm Sergeant Molina." The same wide grin on his face, "We're from Iowa. And we're here to save the Russian embassy!" I looked at my battle buddy with shock, my mouth wide open, and walked away before I could say anything stupid for the record. Hank was in an opposite, helpful, vainglorious mood.

Hank would work the building from the six o'clock position clockwise around the west side of the building. I took the east side, circling counter clockwise towards the twelve o'clock (north), where we'd meet up. At least that was the tentative plan. An American Infantry Major came out from the embassy to find me. He knew who I was! We walked the perimeter together. He was agitated and proceeded to direct the force protection requirements with a quick stern patter. He used phrases that began with, "You will," and "without fail." He acted like a West Point officer having to direct a silly Army Reservist. This was getting curious. An American Military Officer posted at the Russian embassy in Baghdad, reporting the effort to protect the Russians from a possibly imminent VBIED attack? I still had a half pack of Marlboros on me so I guessed things would be OK. This effort might just be getting reported all the way to Chief of Dental Affairs at the Pentagon, as if I gave a shit about the Major's problems, except for the immediate mission to place Texas barriers, which was a problem for both of us. I answered with, "Yes, Sir" repeatedly. The Major went back inside. Better him than me. At least outside I could smoke and do what I wanted. I never saw him again.

An alley two blocks long approached the embassy's east side. I directed the nervous drivers back down it, a crane at the ready. With no way to turn around, the vehicle beep beep beeped loudly backwards, then gratefully forward upon unloading. We repeated this process hours on end. Often I found myself alone, save for the crane operator in the cab. My Motorola wasn't working well and I wouldn't talk to Hank for the next eight hours. The T barriers arrived about every thirty minutes at best.

I wondered how Ellen was getting along with cutting the grass back in Milwaukee. She hated doing it, making it look like a haircut given to a squirming boy. Once I mowed after she did, just to do it right. That was a mistake. Important things like this entered my mind, when a middle- aged local neighbor surprised me with the offer of cool water. He invited me a few steps into his home and demonstrated the gift by pouring water into a glass from a plastic jug. He even drank some himself to demonstrate its safety. I chugged several glasses, not realizing how thirsty I was. A woman with a head scarf stole a quick glance at me. I thanked him profusely in English, and he responded in Arabic. A cynic might say he didn't want a VBIED going off in his alley, but probably he was just a good person.

The curfew was imposed, the streets grew quiet, the temperature dropped, the stars came out, my Vietnam era flak jacket chafed my shoulders, and the day's sweat began to chafe my inner thighs. Walking back to the Embassy entrance, back to the placement of barriers, directing the crane, walking, walking back and forth, slowly making progress, again and again, walking, walking.

Several hours later I walked back to the Embassy front only to discover an American soldier asleep on the boulevard's curb like a bum. He had been Dynamite Dan's driver, the Napoleon Dynamite look-a-like completely exposed to possible danger. It was disgraceful, so I kicked him in the butt, literally, and found an NCO to look after him as we fulfilled our mission. All eyelids weighed with anchors. The vat of adrenaline was drained except for occasional drips in the empty streets. I got to the 2:00 o'clock position in front of some spiffy houses, with front doors made of teak, very expensive. BMWs were parked in little driveways. Sometime after midnight the residents emerged from their homes and set up lawn chairs, I guess to see the show. Set up the crane, back in the tractor trailer, swing the Texas barrier. Unhook, repeat. Walking,

walking, I began to stride like John Wayne having ridden a horse for two straight days

"You can't put that there," said a kid about seventeen years old, speaking perfect American English and wearing a Hard Rock Cafe T-shirt. This little shit came right up to me. "I said, you can't put that there," he said, pointing to the mammoth Texas barrier and taking a swig from a can of Pepsi. My diaper rash felt like a forest fire. I just looked at him. "You're going to block my driveway." Sure enough, he'd have to drive on his "lawn" to get out to the cul-de-sac that abutted a road to the Russian Embassy. I was stunned at his speech and bravado. I felt privileged as an American Army officer, and blew him off. I can't remember what I said to the young man. It was probably filthy. I had a mission to accomplish, and had just made a huge mistake. I waved him off. Just watch me. Yep, I set the T-barrier right behind his BMW. It was in the ring of obstacles I was setting to prevent a mass casualty event. And that's how we get things done down on the farm.

Another hour passed. Progress still being made. It was 3:00 a.m. when a First Lieutenant approached. "The Major says you can't block that guy's driveway." A long pause, "OK." That son-of-a-bitch had some kind of pull. Did I mention that former Iraqi Republican Guard officers resided in that neighborhood? And that's how they get things done.

It would have been humiliating if it wasn't for the fire down below. Each step was an effort. I tried not to accentuate the gimp of a man in an unrelenting walking creep. The crane operator and I went back the two blocks, set the crane back up, outriggers spread, mud pads down, hooked the Texas barrier, swung it twenty feet, unhooked, picked the crane back up and drove back to where we were. What was another 45 minutes of my night? I was as contrite as I could be.

The sky began to glow. I saw Hank about 50 meters away and slowly strode to him.

Where you been?" He looked at me like I'd been malingering all night long.

"Oh, I don't know? Just hanging out."

"Everybody's gone except for us. I guess we're done." OK.

I got into the back of the Humvee behind my battle buddy. Then the miracle happened.

Something was under my feet. I looked down and read, "Desitin" on a white tube. The vehicle moved west towards BIAP, the morning light behind us. Immediately I dropped trousers and spread the cream.

"We placed over thirty T-barriers last night."

"Thank you, Jesus," I praised. We weren't talking about the same thing.

Upon getting back to my hooch, I changed my clothes to Army Physical Fitness (PT) shorts and T-shirt, used some more Desitin, opened an MRE, and contemplated sleep in the awful morning heat.

An NCO found me sitting on my cot. "Captain Dupar, the Head Shed needs you right away." Too tired to swear, I put my boots and uniform back on. Swung my flak jacket back over my shoulders, grabbed my rifle and hobbled to report to MAJ Perez.

"Sounds like you had quite a night, Kenny." He rolled an unlit cigar between his lips.

"Yes, Sir."

"Tell me about it."

I debriefed the Battalion Executive Officer as best I could and asked if I should stay for the morning Commander's meeting.

He said, "No. Get some rest. I'll talk to you tomorrow."

All personnel were accounted for, no injuries or damage to equipment. Mission complete. Team effort.

I finished the MRE; my brain was on fire as well as my thighs. I slept through the rising temperature.

The next day I received, through the telling of Alpha Company's XO, Captain Rodriguez, to me, the greatest compliment I have ever or could ever receive in my lifetime. MAJ Perez told the officers of the 169th at the morning meeting that, "Captain Dupar knows how to take chicken shit and turn it into chicken soup."

I had a lot of help.

And it is a great relief when the Creator Being is saving your butt in wartime. Don't tell me God doesn't have a sense of humor. You can bet your ass She does.

CHAPTER 10

# Special Operators –
# Men in Black

W here was the Ace of Spades, Saddam Hussein Al-Tikriti, president of Iraq? Nearly seven months into our deployment, that question hadn't been answered. In July 2003, when Uday (Ace of Clubs) and Qusay (Ace of Hearts), Saddam's sons, were killed by Task Force 121 in conjunction with elements of the 101st Airborne, we heard Iraqi celebratory gunfire for days. The eldest was infamous for torturing athletes when they lost football matches, and raping brides during their wedding receptions. Qusay was the heir apparent, due to his older brother's disfavor with Dad for murdering men Saddam still needed. Perhaps the biggest affront was big bro's open disapproval of his father's new wife.

The suppression of the Marsh Arabs after the 1991 uprising was directed by the younger son Qusay. Shias had lived in the delta created by the emptying of the Euphrates and Tigris rivers into the Persian Gulf at Basra. The Marsh Arabs had dwelt there for centuries. They had believed the US reassurances of support after the abrupt suspension of offensive operations during Operation Desert Storm. When that didn't come, Qusay struck, draining the marshes, destroying habitat, and pumping the water into the desert to deform and waste. He forcibly displaced the Marsh Arabs throughout the country into the worst lands. They attempted bare subsistence farming and the raising of a few sheep. Those that survived have slowly reclaimed their lives in the Marsh, twenty years later. The rivers went back to their courses, and water species slowly rebounded. Understandably, the Iraqi people abhorred these men. The jubilation over their deaths was real.

But in the fall of 2003, the counter-insurgency had begun in earnest, and IEDs were becoming routine, their use spreading rapidly, and techniques to thwart them evolved. American commanders developed templates for letters addressed to loved ones of the maimed and killed. The Ayatollah in Iran sent bomb parts. Body parts mounted by the bushel. The explosives of choice were artillery or mortar rounds, which were both plentiful and resistant to poor storage, as in buried. They could be initiated with a radio control like a key fob, garage door opener, or cell phone; command wire with a physical wire led back to a plunger that sent the signal. VBIEDs were the variety most feared, as the vehicle that bore the bomb was mobile and could strike an Entry Control Point, or a crowd of women shopping, with few tell-tale signs about the carnage soon to occur. It took only a small amount of electrical current to detonate munitions.

Most remember pictures of the spider hole from which mangy Saddam was yanked. He indignantly told the young soldiers who captured him that he was the President of Iraq. Too bad the president didn't have a toothbrush, or a barber, or a clean pair of underwear.

I clearly remember Staff Sergeant Gibson telling me the news, outside the Command Post tent. "No way!" I said.

"No shit, we got 'im."

"No way."

"It's the truth." Yeah, everybody was ecstatic for the rest of the day. Somewhere, champagne corks were popping, but not at BIAP. His capture was strategically mega-important. It was a gut blow to the Sunni militias that dreamed of placing Saddam's Ba'athist political party back in power, if not the dictator himself. Now he was a prisoner of the Coalition. NCIS-Baghdad and Task Force 121 had hunted him down to a farmhouse near his hometown of Tikrit. The Men in Black had gotten their man.

The next day I was able to call home at 1:00 a.m. local, dinnertime in Wisconsin. My daughter (three-and-a-half at the time) asked me on the phone if it was true: "Daddy, did you get the bad guy?" Her voice was innocent and wondering. This would explain my absence, to a little girl and to a country. I paused briefly, considering. Doesn't a little girl deserve to see her Dad as a hero? I told the truth. "Yes. Yes, I did. Me and my friends." In baseball that's called grand slam.

I think just being there serving gives everybody some bragging rights, albeit microscopic compared to the Special Operators (the REAL Men in Black) and Infantry Boys taking most of the risks. I know that Will Smith and Tommy Lee Jones made a movie about aliens having invaded our planet, some nice, some not. The name for it sounded tough. But nothing could erase from my memory my chance encounter with the actual Men in Black. It was a shock when I was suddenly among them. There weren't two or twenty, but more like fifty. Everyone was nonchalant; it was just another work day, no reason to get excited about anything. We were like ghosts to them, and they to us. We had no reason to speak to each other. Their eyes never made contact with my astonished gaze. The Men in Black live in an altered state of being. The experience was similar to when I first realized humans aren't alone in the universe.

. . .

Two days after that dirty, mangy, lying dog Saddam was cornered I got the call from the Head Shed. Our primary means of communication within BIAP were encrypted Motorola radios. Major Posey, the Battalion Operations Officer, S3, had never before called me on the radio. He knew his construction people, and whom to call within his crew.

"Four-five, this is three." My heart skipped a beat. He never called me. Not like this, over the Motorola.

"Three, this is four-five, over."

"Four-five, do you have a stockpile of dirt somewhere close? Over." His patter was quick, worried.

"Roger, I have a mountain of sand by the runway, right across from our LSA, over."

"Four-five, need you to get that fill by the Air Force, time now. Break." He paused to shorten the length of each transmission. "Get the names of the soldiers with social security numbers to the TOC. We have to fill Hesco bastions now! Break." Pause. "Get me those names and numbers to the TOC in the next fifteen minutes. Come see me. Acknowledge, over."

"Roger, over." That was a lot of direct information to put out over the radio NOT face to face. Something was extremely hot.

"Three out." And the Motorola went cold.

Oh, great. Not that I was just sitting on my ass doing a whole lot of jack shit. Please let me jump through a bunch of bullshit hoops just because someone decided to panic, by all means, yes, Sir! Social Security Numbers? Oh, shit. I didn't know I was about to meet the real Men in Black.

I quickly organized the effort. All we needed was to get the 5-yard loader by the stockpile, and the twenty-ton dumps moving between it and the Hesco bastions, to some still undisclosed close compound on the Air Force side of the road. One of our 2&1/2-yard loaders was in convoy, with Jim and me at the lead.

Hesco bastions are steel and fabric collapsible baskets that can be filled with dirt. They come in cube sizes of typically 2ft x 2ft or 4ft x 4ft, with the purpose of blast protection. They are stacked to provide three-tiered walls that become security from very, very large explosions.

At BIAP, the Iraqi Air Force stored their munitions in concrete pyramidal structures twenty feet high. A good place to store things. I had three copies of the list of my guys and their SSNs. We had to drive all of four blocks. Jim and I drove slowly to a gate, the dumps full, the front-end loader right behind my Humvee. I presented the paper to an NCO, not leaving the vehicle with no doors. Soon, we were waved in.

This is the part where the hairs on your neck should stand up on end. Scary men were everywhere. Totally in shape. Special Operators. I never saw them again. They wore only black, but uniformity was in color only. Black stocking caps over the skull, hat size eight. Long sleeves. Black tank tops. Shorts. Flip flops. All manner of weaponry and vehicles. Beards, Mohawks, long hair half way down the back. The real Men in Black write their own rules, and brush alongside the ordinary only by mistake, or necessity. Fulfilling the American President's direct intent, and their own.

Those guys got all the equipment they needed, and anything they decided to steal. All with full authorization and no recriminations. And a stack of flat Hescoes were waiting for dirt. The Special Forces Officer, who was super nice, greeted me and explained that he needed a serpentine built, followed by walls, all leading to a specific ammo pyramid/bunker. I didn't ask why; we knew. Saddam Hussein was being guarded at this compound and the extra blast protection was required in the very remote possibility a truck bomb came to disrupt justice. We Army Reservists were agitated. The Men in Black were not. Saddam was properly subdued with MREs and zip ties.

A few months after Saddam's capture I got reliable third hand information that a dentist we knew had indeed examined Saddam at BIAP. Poor bastard had to stick his fingers into his nasty maw. I'm glad I never became a dentist.

Jim and I split soon after our gals and guys started filling the Hescoes. It wasn't complicated work. And in a few hours the mission was complete. It was only 500 meters, as the crow flies, from my bunk to where Saddam Hussein was nestled.

The Arab judgment process was quite chaotic. It took a few years to convict him of genocide against his own people. When the end came it was unorganized, with a lot of yelling going on when his neck was finally stretched. I would have rented out Texas Stadium. The White Don King of Baghdad would have had the Ace of Spades execution on pay per view, then spread the proceeds thin.

# CHAPTER 11

# Ba'ath Party Bingo

S addam Hussein al Tikriti fashioned himself from Joseph Stalin. Both were tyrants from distinguished nations of learning and culture. At the 1940 Tehran conference with Prime Minister Churchill and President Roosevelt, the leader of the Supreme Soviet infamously remarked, "I know the Devil. And He is a good Communist." Joseph was an Eastern Orthodox altar boy from Crimea's Georgia, before he followed the voices of violence and hate. Both were wicked rudiments, Stalin and Saddam; they murdered with zeal, just like the Devil they followed.

After the invasion an attempt was made by Iraqi police, and politicians to stabilize Ambar Province. It failed completely. There, all roads literally meet in Fallujah. In December 2003, the Infantry boys flushed the last Ba'athists out of Fallujah. The insurgent Sunni fighters fled east forty miles to the paper mache walls of BIAP. When I heard the unmistakable sound of the Ma Deuce firing 200 meters from my cot, my Saturday morning respite with a book came down in a snap. CHUGGA CHUGGA CHUGGA CHUGGA! Again and again. CHUGGA CHUGGA CHUGGA CHUGGA. It was outgoing! A tightness you never want to feel gripped my chest. There could be only one reason this would be happening—Engineer Village was under attack by enemy infantry!

Someone's M2, 50-caliber Browning (Ma Duece) was unloading. Another fighting position opened up. Then another to our north toward the 82nd Airborne Battalion and the M2s north of them. Hundreds, then thousands of rounds were being fired from platform positions along the wall by soldiers placed in only a 25% security posture. Only every fourth position was manned. Soldiers rushed to the wall.

I quickly changed from my shorts and T-shirt to my desert combat uniform, threw on my newly issued 21ST Century SAPI (Small Arms Protective Insert) ceramic plated vest, and ran to the HHC Command Post looking like RoboCop, but armed only with my 5.56 millimeter, M16 rifle and a half pack of smokes.

Some rectangular ceramic inserts were the size of dinner plates covering your chest and back; others were like saucers protecting your sides; and still others kept your arm from maybe getting shattered from your shoulder to your elbow. A flap called a codpiece (like medieval suits of armor) would supposedly help protect the family jewels.

The AR 15 gets people excited because supposedly it's an "assault" rifle, which actually doesn't exist. It has the components of the venerated M16, and it can be modified illegally to cook on full auto, but it still throws a small round. In the hands of trained soldiers, it is the rifle's accuracy that impresses. Hitting a target 300 meters out is the standard for an expert. It sounds like a small "POP" compared to the growl of the 50-caliber Ma Duece. People can hunt tasty animals with an AR 15. The forward handle and short barrel make it designed for room clearing, not massacring unarmed people. Any firearm can do that, as long as the evil behind the trigger has the will.

The Army gave us Engineers mostly "light" machine guns that threw small bullets, as they were a lot easier to move around than the Ma Duece. They were called SAWs (squad automatic weapons). The rounds were the same as the M16—the ammunition was interchangeable. Size matters. A caliber is an American measure based upon an inch. A 50 caliber at the bullet's base is one half of an inch or 0.5. Millimeters are metric. Velocity also matters in punching holes through flesh and homes, and the Browning 50-caliber air-cooled machine gun has it all. The will and expertise to use it is a soldier skill. Nothing sounds like the Ma Deuce in rhythm, laying waste to all before it with a range of over a mile. According to the Laws of War, an automatic weapon of 50-caliber or greater cannot be fired at troops, just equipment; like armored personnel carriers, trucks, aircraft or belt buckles.

"POP!" Twelve seconds later, "BANG!" The mortars whistled over our heads. Again and Again. They were close. WIZZZH BANG! WIZZHBANG! Outgoing POP POP POP POP, CHUGA CHUGA CHUGA POP POP POP. No time to search for casualties. Everything was ear splittingly loud. Each explosion sent sub-sonic jagged bits of metal flying to tear at you. Fifty meters close would change your life, if not take it. Within fifteen meters the blast concussion would liquefy your brain, making bodies into rag dolls and bloody bits to get sent home in bags and boxes.

Captain Smith was directing soldiers to get to the wall, but most had taken cover in shelters. I made my way alone, screaming a few times to those personnel moving away to reverse course, to no avail. By the time I got to the motor pool just two hundred yards from the Head Shed the enemy mortars had ceased. The wall was only another hundred yards away. It was just like in the movies; I felt the whiz of bullets passing cleanly through the wall and heard their ricochet about me from the cabs of tractor trailers and the blades of bulldozers. I paused against a dump truck's front tire, my back to the wall. WHIZZZ CLUNK. WHIZZ CLUNK. I guessed it wasn't a good time to blaze up a cigarette. But I did anyway. Is that you, John Wayne?

This is when the training takes over. You see yourself in a surreal pageant. Go to the point of attack. Who's hurt? Is anybody hurt? Go forward; go forward. I ran to the wall after a few drags from my smoke, remembering high school and hot boxing/sharing nicotine with fellow students between classes, hearing Motley Crue's "smoking in the boy's room," and scrambled up the wooden ladder to the firing position atop. Soldiers returned fire. Sergeant Bergden was throwing lead down range. I guess she still had fight in her after her boxing match disgrace. We had only the SAW, which fired a mere 5.56MM NATO round matched with our M16, but a well-aimed shot in succession is lethal. But bigger is always better—that's how the American Army rolls. But right now it was a fair fight at Engineer Village. The nearest Ma Deuce was 500 meters north of my position. Not good. When I peeked over the wall I saw muzzle flashes only seventy-five yards out, between the palm trees and the buildings that Dynamite Dan once tried to buy the land beneath. Now it made sense. The former Commander wanted to build defenses further out, away from our precious machines and people.

"HOW'S YOUR AMMO? SHOOT THERE!" I pointed between the palm trees. I guess the other soldiers appreciated an officer being present. Sergeant Bergden was ready to listen, and immediately resumed fire. It was so loud at times I pressed against my ears. You don't have hearing protection like you would at the firing range. We were rapidly running low on ammunition. I called the Tactical Operational Center with my

Motorola to report and request support. My transmission was received, but no acknowledgement of our needing ammo was pushed back. We had to have more ammo. I called again but with no response. Commo was down. As the Executive Officer, I'd inventoried our ammunition each month. It was within a small container adjacent to the TOC. I called again with my Motorola without success. It was now up to me to go back to get ammunition. I knew where the keys were, if it came down to that. WHIZZ, POP POP POP WHIZZ, fire being returned by attacking Ba'athists thudded as it passed through the wall. I saw no American casualties. Not yet.

Scurrying down the ladder amidst the ricochets, I ran to the maintenance building, which was just beside the wall, only fifty yards from my firing position to the south. I couldn't find anyone, but did hear the firing from its roof as I climbed up and through the open scuttle hatch. I wanted to check to see if anyone was hurt. I was sure they would need ammo, too. I'd only been on the roof of the maintenance building once before to inspect the so-called fighting position. Just a few sandbags built up five high to form a shallow "U." Bounding toward a shaft of light leading upwards, I climbed through towards the soldiers. Slightly hunched over, I ran to Michelle. Everything a surprise, she looked through me. "HOW'S YOUR AMMO?" I screamed. She gasped as if to say, "Where'd you come from?" But nothing came out. "HOW'S YOUR AMMO?" Only she and one other soldier returned fire. Her brunette hair smashed between her Kevlar helmet and scalp, she screamed, "We're almost out!" Pretty Michelle and her buddy continued to place rounds with their rifles towards people and muzzle flashes. The intent with each aim and trigger pull was to stop another human being from trying to kill you or your buddy.

"OK. I'LL GET MORE!" Going down the scuttle, relieved at not facing death in that instant, I looked back up and missed the last two rungs of the ladder, landing on my back and twisting my left knee. I got up, my breath knocked out of me. Thirty seconds later I stepped slowly toward the ammunition container by the TOC three football fields away. Precious minutes ticked by as I was handed three ammo cans by Captain Smith and reversed course. I screamed what I was doing, still hearing "POP pause POP pause POP," the sound of sparing rounds. If I knew we were almost out of ammunition, the enemy did as well. Limping, I returned to the maintenance building adjacent to the wall.

Quickly grabbing two bottles of cold water in Sergeant First Class Anderson's fridge, I went back up the ladder, one rung at a time—right leg, pull, right leg towards the scuttle door. Now it was shut. I had water bottles in my pants cargo pockets, pants drooping low to my hips, but I couldn't open the scuttle latch with my rifle across my back and the ammo box in hand. The latch wouldn't turn! I banged on the scuttle door with my left fist. It was open before! I screamed, "Michelle!" I pounded on the hatch 'til I felt my right hand about to break. "Michelle, Michelle! GOD DAMN THE DEVIL TO HELL, I LOVE THAT GIRL!" Thirty seconds, a minute, it didn't matter; someone was alive up there on the roof!

The young Mic-a-Nic opened the door, and I pushed though, handing him the ammo box. The rhythm of the fire fight ebbed like fighters between rounds, subsided for the moment, before the bell clanged again. In the morning heat everything was momentarily silent. Both sides took stock of the clash, birds stayed silent, the wind abated. It became still. Nothing seemed to move. It was 100 degrees already and folks were drenched with sweat. Soldier's voices between tenor and alto shouted between fighting positions, "I'M HERE. YOU THERE?" taking advantage of the momentary silence to reload. I handed the two fighters on the roof their bottles of cold water. Michelle looked at me with dismay as we loaded rounds into our magazines.

After resupplying them I spied a most disturbing sight. SFC Anderson had a full up pimple on her chin. It was revolting. That ten-month superficial fantasy was gone. Not just a red mark, but a whitehead had appeared, probably from the stress of the enemy trying to kill her and her returning the favor in full.

"NICE ZIT."

She gulped some water. All three of us lay prone close together on the roof, pausing before resuming the fight. "What?" she asked. Our knees pointed towards each other, very close. Mine and Michelle's almost touching.

I pointed to my chin. "Nice zit."

"You're weird!"

I wish I had a nickel every time a girl has said that to me. I think she wanted to smile, but didn't. And I sure was glad she still had the choice. I left her again and regained my original post on the wall with more ammo. Did I embarrass her? Well, my fantasy love was alive for a few minutes more, at the fighting position to my left. Returning to the wall with more rounds we began to become elated; we were holding our own! That's when I first felt the deep vibration and then heard the CLACK CLACK CLACK of two Abrams tanks maneuvering on our side of the wall. Tanks are extremely dangerous to be around. That was when I was the most scared. All of a sudden everybody, friend and foe, started firing their weapons again. The combat was as loud as the front row of a Rock n' Roll show.

Being a former enlisted Tanker myself, I knew there are only two kinds of Tankers—those who get killed, and those who do a lot of killing before they get killed. There on our fighting position, my blood ran cold. The chance that the driver, loader, gunner, and tank commander would bust through the wall at any moment to explode their main gun on the enemy was more than I would risk. I ordered the four soldiers with me to abandon our position and retreat back to the motor pool as the tanks crawled by slowly.

SFC Anderson unloaded on the fighters in her field of fire. The enemy sprang back up, returning fire. The tanks kept moving up the wall past us, north towards Camp Cropper. Realizing my error, I led the small crew back to the fighting position on the wall and we shot back toward the muzzle flashes pointed against us until we saw no more. Sergeant Bergden screamed once while firing the light machine gun, "GET SOME!" Is that you, Jane Wayne? It had been nearly an hour since I'd been serenely reading a book on my cot, covered with an air mattress from the PX, the Army's expensive fart sack, followed by sheets and pillows sent by Ellen.

When it was over, I searched out soldiers to our left and right for casualties. There were none. I can't explain it. The adrenaline rush was like none other. I felt like the most courageous man in the world! I realized from talking to other soldiers within that moment that everyone felt the same way— astounded, and eager to tell their brave tales. But I was full of myself; I couldn't listen. I lit the best smoke of my life. There's nothing like a Marlboro to send hundreds of addictive chemicals streaming into your brain as fast as possible to stimulate the pleasure centers of your mind. Yeah!

Soldiers were now streaming toward the fighting positions, now that the threat was extinguished. Michelle, I, and everyone on the wall had just passed through the fire. There can never be anything like it. The Infantry boys might just nod their heads at this account, for to them, the sacrifice is continual; they give everything they have, every day.

Because I'm a goofball by leadership style, I found CPT Smith and suggested, "I guess the boxing matches are cancelled for tonight?"

She agreed. "Not tonight, Kenny." That got a laugh from a couple of folks.

# CHAPTER 12

# Cut Me A Bottle

A fter we'd been deployed five months, the holidays were right around the corner. No deer hunting after Thanksgiving this year. The grind was wearing on us all. The same grimy, dusty, walking-on-gravel, ankle-turning Life Support Area, the same chow day after day, the same BIAP, the same don't know when we're coming home. Kids getting older, missing their moms and dads and acting in hateful ways, marriages breaking, and marriages getting stronger. A lot of people, especially the younger soldiers, saw mental health counselors who doled out anti-depressants and sleep aids like they were Halloween candy corn or Skittles. The chaplain was busy. The workout tents helped some people. The internet café helped and hurt. SSG Jones and I created a morale tent with books and a big TV that played movies on tapes, all donated from the folks back home or unit soldiers. We even built two basketball courts, where an unknown NCO painted the stripes and marks. The running track offered some solace, I suppose.

The more I tried to make Iraq like home the further away home got. Calling home regularly became unnecessary. Just the same frustrations. Families with big problems getting worse.

Money going out the window. Getting mortared now and again. Getting shot at now and then. Once, I saw SFC Anderson walking out of the internet café. I was about to say hi until I saw the near to tears look on her face. I should have asked what was wrong. I didn't know her well, but should have. It was easier for soldiers to just shut down. To stop caring about anything at all. Sometimes people cracked up, lost their bearings, and started to imagine things.

But it was GO time for Captain Kenny. I was going to do some real damage on this one. The 115th MP Company was going home. They had arrived in theater during the buildup prior to the big push north. With the maneuver brigades in February, 2003, they fought their way into Iraq. And since we'd been partners, engineers building and cops providing security on our more hairy missions into the city, it was agreed between commands that I could help our buddies get their storage containers back to the world's biggest ashtray.

To the fabled port of Arifjan we were ordered. Too bad we'd have to bypass Kuwait City, as I wanted to see this city of glass. But Arifjan supposedly had a food court, a pool, and clean sheets on actual beds. You could place your weapon in racks and walk around unfettered by the responsibility. It wasn't that big a deal driving south, especially since the MPs were running the convoy. We used our cranes to place their containers on our trailers and moved out. I wanted to go just for the opportunity to get out of godforsaken Baghdad and go see something else.

Hank informed me of a place in Arifjan called the "Frustration Yard." In other words, it held badly needed replacement parts that were "frustrated" in transit north due to administrative glitches. It was an ideal situation to go "shopping." How did Hank know that? "Get with SFC Anderson; she'll tell you what she needs." My battle buddy's eyes glinted, "Maybe what she wants, too."

Before I could make my way to the motor pool, Major Sanchez found me: "Hey, Kenny, I heard about your mission to Arifjan and it's a golden opportunity to get some parts that are held up in transit. We've had a hard time getting spare parts for the Massey Fergusons and the Marines need more parts for the Teddy Bear. Since that stuff isn't on our Property Book, it's been hard to get it shipped from Kuwait. I have SFC Anderson making you a list now of what we want. They're waiting to get picked up."

"Where would I go to get them, Sir?"

"All you got to do is find the Frustration Yard." I had a way in now. This was falling into place way too easy. I had the uneasy feeling that Tony was setting up a big heist, with me in the middle. When I broached the subject with my mechanic friend, Sergeant First Class Anderson, the dispatch counter was between us.

"Major Sanchez said you have a printout or something for stuff lost down in Kuwait?" She put her elbows down and leaned forward and talked in a hushed tone, "I'm putting together a list of parts we still haven't received." She looked straight through me and smiled. I noticed for the first time SFC Anderson had beautiful, straight white teeth. "And another list of parts that we really need to have extras of." She moved her face close to mine. She had a few pretty freckles, one near the tip of her little ski slope nose. "It's better to have than not to have, you know?" My imagination betrayed my ability to speak.

"Yeah, sure."

"Come back early tomorrow and I'll have what you need."

"Yeah, sure."

Real smooth Kenny, real smooth. But I was hypnotized by Antonia (her new nickname—it means "priceless." I looked it up). She was in on the heist, too. I was getting confused, the blood rushing from my head. I wondered if at my court martial anybody would bring up the point that I had actually brought cops to the job just for cover. Pretty slick if it worked. I think my tutelage with Tony was about to pay off big.

When I came up to Jim with the news, he was reading a filthy magazine on his cot. "Hey, Sergeant Fester! You up for a road trip?"

He answered, "Where to, CAP?"

"Arifjan."

"Hell, yeah!" He got right up in my grill. "When we going?" I loved that man.

"How fast can you get the crane over to the MPs?"

"Like now, like tonight."

The word got out fast. Probably like, "You hear Dupar is going to Arifjan?" Everybody had heard of it, but only a few in the Battalion had experienced the opulence of an enclosed shopping mall with an arcade, swimming pools, spas within casinos that offered Swedish massages, and an actual Dunkin Donuts. It was like preparing to go to the Emerald City in the movie Wizard of Oz. The stories spun out of control. The chaplain's assistant mentioned a basilica. Mechanics had heard of a drag strip. There was something for everyone at the fabled port of Arifjan. I had volunteers up to my eyeballs. We would leave early in the morning, day after next.

They made a movie a few years back called The Hurt Locker. It portrayed the "bomb squads" that contended with IEDs. The first time I saw the flick I loved it. The second time, not so much, as I had too critical an eye for the fictional tactical environments the actors were placed in. But I guess that's Hollywood for you. Boring doesn't sell. And when you're gridlocked on Route Tampa going south to paradise waiting for hours in the heat for the Unexploded Ordinance team to show up, it's boring. They didn't have robots to handle these crises in November of 2003. And the boys took their time. I didn't blame them, because blowing the bomb in place was the preferred method of disposal, unless it could damage the major artery connecting Iraq with Kuwait.

Just an hour south of Baghdad an IED exploded, tearing apart a semi-trailer. Probably command detonated by some asshole in the nearby palm groves, either by wire or remote control. The truck jack-knifed and got smashed from behind by another semi. There were three serials (segments) in the MP convoy, spread apart by about five minutes each. The bomb went off just in front of the third serial—the serial Jim and I were in. I don't know if anyone got hurt. The IED was daisy chained to several other bombs along Tampa, but only one went off. At least that was the scuttlebutt up and down the stuck line of vehicles. This could have been a lot, lot worse.

With no movement in sight, some trucks stuck in the backup started to bypass. Or just turned around to go back to BIAP. The MP serial commander decided that getting back to the USA was more important than waiting, so like "monkey see, monkey do," he led us off road. Thank goodness the tractor trailers were with the first two serials. Driving through the palm groves, losing sight of Tampa, in the same terrain that hid the initiator of the IED, was unnerving. Trying to get back onto the highway, we got snarled again as dozens of military vehicles from scores of units converged in the one place that made sense to get back onto Route Tampa. Eventually, we were back rolling again and by late afternoon, the third serial was fueling in the moon dust of Scania. With gray talcum to the tops of my boots, I found the lieutenant who was leading us out and tried to review the route to Arifjan. He acted like he didn't need my help. Could it be that someone didn't like me? Impossible. We rolled towards Kuwait, passed the lousy hamlet of Safwan, and approached the bypasses that ringed the City of Glass, Kuwait City.

We buzzed past Nine-Mile Road, then Seven-Mile Road, the bypass on our route. The serial blew by it. I called the MP Lieutenant on the radio and said in effect, "No problem. You just missed our turn; just take Five-Mile Ring Road and we'll bypass the downtown. No problem." Except that Lieutenant Ding Dong decided that I was a brain dead idiot and instead gave me a bunch of "yeah, yeah, yeah, shut the hell up." Right about then Jim said that he'd hope we'd be stopping soon 'cause he had to pee.

Well, gee, Son, why didn't you go at Scania? Ding Dong kept driving and was leading us to where no American convoys were ever allowed to go, into the heart of opulence unbounded. The neighborhoods got ritzy fast at 55 mph heading east, all the way to the Persian Gulf. Three and four-story single family homes, painted art deco. Jim really had to pee, but I was too astonished by the wealth to care. Besides, there are no unscheduled halts in a convoy, unless the convoy commander decides so. Because he was probably pissing his pants himself and because he was in the process of getting us inextricably lost in the richest city on earth, at night, he probably wouldn't much care if Captain Idiot called him again to tell him his good friend and driver had to use the bathroom. Water and electrical towers loomed everywhere. The sun was setting fast to our backs. Jaguars and Porsches wove between our Humvees, and we slowed as the highway became a boulevard. Kuwait City was as clean as a whistle. Pakistani sanitation workers with orange vests worked among the smartly dressed business men in silk suits. The women wore dresses from Prada or silk burkas without seam or wrinkle.

There it was! The Al Hamra twisting steel tower. It looked like an enormous 40-story drill bit sliced on one side, lighting towards the sky in the dusk, shimmering blue glass reflected the fading light from the Persian Gulf. Architectural marvels were everywhere—a space needle, vast spans arching over plazas, mosques in rich mosaics, skyscrapers out of square, geometry uncertain. We were down to 20 mph and Jim was driving erratically.

"Keep the damn thing on the road!" I shouted at him. I wanted to gawk. He almost sideswiped another parked car. Some general gibberish on the radio squawked about us being completely lost.

"I'm pulling over."

"There's no place to pull over. How come our lights aren't on?"

"The lights aren't on!" Jim yelled. "I have no electrical to the dashboard!" It was true, none of the dials were registering.

"And when were you going to tell me this, Jim?"

"I got to pee! I just noticed we have no electrical."

Sounding as patronizing as possible, I gently told my driver, "If we were to pull over so you could pee against the tire of a Bentley in the business district of the financial capital of the Middle East with several other vehicles behind us, it would break the convoy; and oh, by the way, if you shut off the motor then it may not start again. Wonderful. Thanks, Sergeant Fester."

By this time Private Olsen in the back had the giggles, listening to the two of us going back and forth, with a pinch of nervousness and also awe at the sights and sounds. He stood in the bed of the two-seat Humvee, with a light machine gun on the vinyl roof. I wondered if the sheiks and their wives and children would freak out by an American soldier exposing himself in public.

"I got to pee, asshole! I can't hold it!" Asshole? Is this what our relationship had degenerated to? What inappropriate language to use in addressing a commissioned officer. I was a bit put off, though I was enjoying the ride, however scary and hysterical.

"I'm sorry, Sir, cut me a bottle. Cut me a bottle, CAP. Please cut me a bottle. I gotta' pee!"

We had empty plastic bottles strewn about the cab from the all-day drive. And I had a knife. The contagion of giggles got hold of me, too. Trying to relieve oneself into the mouth of a plastic water bottle while moving was a scenario for pissing all over the cab, the dash, yourself, others. "Oh, sure. I'll cut you a bottle." I punctured the side with the blade, tears of laughter falling one after another. "Gonna' cut you a son-of-a-bitch jagged-ass saber tooth cut-your-balls off bottle!" I had to jab back due to his calling his superior a bad name.

"Cut two! Cut two!"

In fairness, I tried to make the edge fairly smooth. With our weaving and almost smashing into things, plus ours being the only vehicle obscured in darkness, the soldiers behind us must have thought someone was having a heart attack.

"I ain't holding the bottle, Sergeant!"

"Take the wheel! Take the wheel!" I was crying from laughing so hard, we were still going slow, and the traffic seemed to be clearing up ahead. I could see the Persian Gulf! We had to turn right!

"AHHHHHH!" Have you ever timed your pee to measure its length in seconds? Probably a guy thing. "One Mississippi, two chimpanzees." Jim peed for almost 120 Missipanzees. It was a modern record to be proud of.

"Keep up our speed!" We lurched and paused, accelerating and braking, as Sergeant Fester tried to keep steady pressures on the pedals while his bladder emptied. I cried through the giggles, tears running down my face, my birth control glasses steaming up. After a solid forty seconds, Jim needed the second bottle and threw the full one out the window. So much for avoiding being the ugly American. But it was insightful of my friend to ask for two bottles to be cut. But the last one he tossed over the back, spraying Private Olsen. "Goddamn it, Fester!" Now Jim was laughing, too.

"Turn. Turn!" I shouted.

Jim grabbed the wheel. He was back in the saddle, end of problem. We passed the only three-story glass McDonald's I've ever seen. We saw a Rolls Royce dealership beside a gleaming British petroleum station. I wanted to scream out the window at the service attendants, "Hey, any of you fags know how to replace an electrical fuse?" But the convoy didn't stop. We were now going south, out of the financial district, which was an improvement as we were slowly and inexorably driving back into the Kuwaiti desert. Then the local cops showed up. The Toyota flipped its yellow rotating lights on, U-turned, and led us gently at 40 mph to the gates of Arifjan. Forty miles away. What a nice guy.

The food court was about to close up. The first two serials were pissed we got there late. Jim and I checked it out real fast after claiming a bunk and putting our rifles into a weapons rack. The pizza from Pizza Hut was okay, I guess. It was a food court, though, with camouflage netting throughout for shade. Kuwait in November would probably only reach a temperature of 110 degrees. As they always say, "but it's a dry heat." They'd have USO concerts there, Kid Rock playing several times. There really were bowling alleys and a pool. No beer for solders, though. Maybe in the next war they'll have us clothed in bubble wrap. Arifjan didn't live up to the hype, but it was the best facility in theater. Best I've ever seen.

It was time to part with my MP buddies the next morning. Their containers were swung off of our trailers. We'd worked a lot together in the last six months. The ubiquitous, "shoot me an email sometime when you get back to the States," was often heard. We were no longer going to be "peas and carrots" in Iraq any more, besties. It was sad, saying good bye to your friends, probably forever. Captain Maggie Lindskoog had survived the deck of cards and the CIA.

But I didn't need any cops around for what I was about to do the next. After a night between clean sheets and crescendos of snores within a warehouse with two hundred bunk beds, today was the day to score, load up, and the following day to head out. I found the Movement Control Center and gave them my head count, weapon serial numbers by type, and vehicle bumper numbers. They assigned us to a larger element that was moving out the next day. The Signal Company that was pushing to BIAP wasn't thrilled we were piggy-backing with them, but that's the way it goes.

The mechanics could smell the boneyard a half mile away, panting and crying like ole hound dogs. I unhooked their tethers and watched them run. It was beautiful. They spent the rest of the day scavenging a needed transmission from the hulk of a Deuce. That was a freebee. It gave me time to find the Frustration Yard. This time, the hype lived up to its reputation. The compound was a good fifty acres of warehouses and sun shades—open lots of God knows what. One/third mile by a third/mile, twelve-foot-high fencing with razor wire surrounded it. Both the entrance and exit had small Entry Control Points with guard shacks and drop gates. I was in awe. It was the mother lode of unaccounted-for Army equipment. The biggest part of the facility was where we would pick up legitimate parts ordered through the system. The other part was the Frustration Yard proper, a place where millions of dollars of stuff waited for someone to take it. If you could prove it was yours, supposedly, I guess.

Not getting caught is always extremely important. No cameras that I could see. I asked Jim to get the tractor trailers lined up. We only had one shot at this—in, then out. As I rolled through the front gate, a sergeant directed me to the admin trailers where I could get started. We stopped in the big staging area and I put on my happy face. With my printout I started the process. These were the parts the 169th needed, according to the system. The soldiers behind the counter started to verify the shortages with their computers. This was going to take a while. "No rush," I said with a smile, and went outside for a smoke. Nobody knew except for me what was on the "have to have" and "good to have" lists.

"How on earth are we supposed to find the stuff we want to steal in this mess, CAP?" asked Jim.

"Beats me. Hey Jim, take a look at this," and I showed him what Antonia had written down by hand. As a carpenter, this shit wasn't near and dear to my heart. I didn't recognize the nomenclatures. What's a "Hose Assembly, nonmetal 4720-00-356-8571 Acetylene hose for HEMTT Wrecker Torch, 25' with fittings HEMTT Wrecker"? It was as if the maître de had invited us to do some shopping while we waited for our table of authorized parts.

Would the soldier at the rear gate actually confirm what we were taking? I didn't know. We spent the next three hours waiting for the parts from the authorized list to be loaded and tied down under the blazing Kuwaiti sun. You had to wear gloves to handle anything made of metal. Jim and I attempted to scrounge for the items from Antonia's wish list, but it quickly became impossible, and I didn't care after an afternoon of roasting. My thieving apprenticeship had taught me that sometimes you have to walk away. The Frustration Yard had boggled me. We loaded up and headed for the exit gate. The soldier there took all of thirty seconds to "verify" what we were taking. He didn't know or care either in the heat. I could have taken whatever, if I knew what "whatever" was. But I didn't. I didn't steal anything. Nothing at all.

I couldn't bear looking at her dark brown eyes when I got back. I felt like a chicken shit. However, I do believe that proper appropriation of Army equipment should be based upon an actual need for the greater good. We did get all of what we quasi-legitimately came for. The Teddy Bear would get it's parts. Still, I felt like I'd left everybody down.

Tony never said a word about it until years later. "Hey, you didn't get pinched. You never got pinched." I came damn close a few times though.

Hank and Kenny

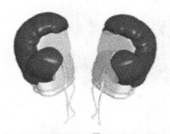

# BIAP BOXING

169th Engineer Battalion Presents

## SATURDAY NIGHT FIGHTS

**DATES:** 31 JAN. / 14 & 28 FEB. 2004
**TIME:** 1800-2100
**WHERE:** ENGINEER VILLAGE, WEST BIAP
       **Grid:** MB282774

**NOTE:** All entries and weight classes are welcome. Individuals interested
may sign in up to 1 day prior to event so that fighting card can be
generated for Saturday's matches.

**Sign up forms at 169th MWR tent, or call DMVT # 551-9504
(Name, weight, experience, unit & phone # required)**

### 'LET'S GET IT ON!'

## PROPER UNIFORM IS REQUIRED
### (PTs, DCUs or BDUs)

Please contact CPT Dupar or SSG James
(MWR STAFF)

169th Boxing Promo

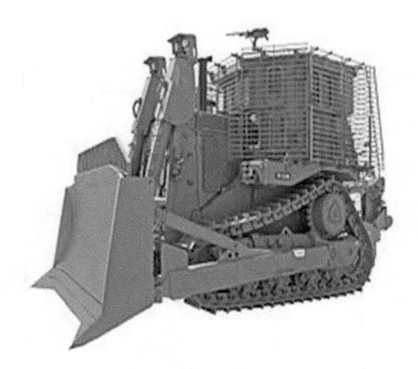

The Teddy Bear

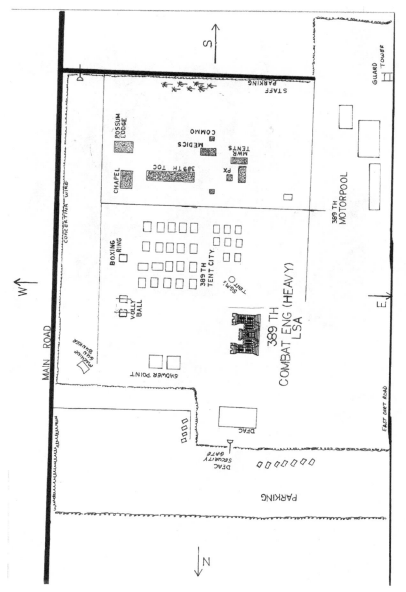

LSA Map

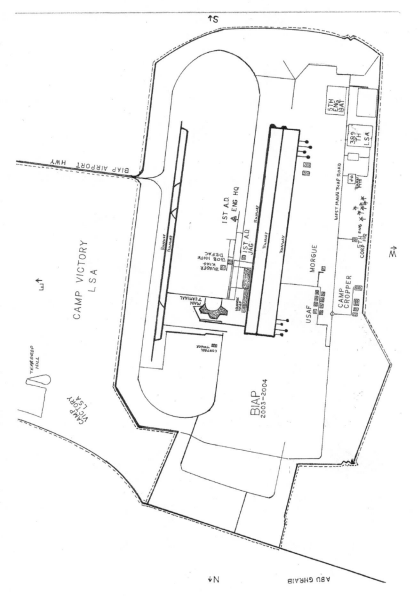

BIAP

# PART 2

# McCoy

# CHAPTER 13

# Medical Hold

In 1999, during a span of three months, I had gotten married, been promoted to Captain, unintentionally partnered in Chicago in the conception of our honeymoon baby, was entrusted with a company command of 110 soldiers, and went into heart failure. I was only thirty-one years old.

Fluid had accumulated in my lungs and liver. My temperature spiked to 102 degrees. I could barely breathe. But with modern pharmaceuticals, I was soon able to continue making a living bending nails. Furosemide, Lisinopril, Toprol, potassium, Hydrochlorothiazide, and Digoxin kept me alive. I lost ten pounds in two days when the extra fluid was pissed out.

In May, 2003, prior to deployment, on the last afternoon of our only battalion field exercise, out of the blue I was called to report immediately to the Fort Leonard Wood Hospital. A choke chain called cardiomyopathy became taut. I had dreaded this moment and knew why my tether was being reeled in. Within an hour a buttwipe in a lab coat asked me why I thought I could be in the Army. It felt like all the blood rushed out of my head. He was in charge of my entire future, but never once made eye contact with me. I was soon dismissed, subject to administrative review of my medical status. The pages of my military career fell to the floor to be stepped over, then discarded. I was about to be benched from the biggest challenge of my life, never able to prove myself. I imagined being asked, "What did you do during the war? After 9/11?" "Well, I got sent back home because of my heart condition." This humiliation would dog me for the rest of my life, however long that might be. Going to war seemed my gamble to take, not some administrator following regulations who had no stake.

I had already received a four-day pass before shipping off to war. Ellen picked me up and then later dropped me off at the airport in Milwaukee. Abby was hilarious, in everything she did. Both Ellen and I would make voices for the puppy dog, the cat, the birds, the hamster, our daughter, always funny.

CAUTION! Pre-deployment sex is complicated, don't do it. It's hard to concentrate when your girl is crying. Then you feel like you should be crying. In the moment I was thinking about baseball, to keep from crying, which isn't conducive to, well— you know. But could this be the last time? It is probably mandated by law to "do it" prior to going to war. On the fun scale up to ten, it was probably only an 8.7 or 8.8. Like I said, it isn't recommended, but hey, the law is the law.

I begged my cardiologist at the time to write me a letter promising that I wasn't going to die (as long as I took my readily available meds). It was an absurd request and his statement was as helpful as tits on a bull. The physician wasn't keen on predicting the future. I had a six-month supply of my prescriptions before I left Milwaukee. By deployment end I had nine months' worth in my travel case. Getting pills in theater wasn't a problem—any sort, any flavor.

When I returned to the Fort, it was a Sunday. The administrative offices at the hospital were closed, with hardly anyone there. Without any control of my future, would I ultimately just get sent back home? My cardiologist had sent the letter to the staff via fax the Friday before. When I found the right office I told a young soldier I wanted to see if a letter had arrived over the weekend. It was really important! What would I tell my wife? My family? Why was I discharged out of the Service? Would my Army family leave without me? Seventeen years down the crapper? No retirement benefits. My identity was dressed in a uniform. The young soldier at the counter said that I couldn't go and check for any fax as only authorized personnel were allowed in this restricted area. It was just the two of us there. The policy certainly made sense.

**1st General Order**

"I will guard everything within the limits of my post and quit my post only when properly relieved."

**2nd General Order**

"I will obey my special orders and perform all of my duties in a military manner."

**3rd General Order**

"I will report violations of my special orders, emergencies, and anything not covered in my instructions, to the commander of the relief."

I noticed boxes of soldiers' medical files organized by unit, just beyond the counter on tables. Some boxes were labeled "non-deployable." The files for the 169th soldiers about to deploy were there before me and I suspected that my file may be in the wrong box. I told him my abridged pity party story and pleaded with him to look for the fax. It worked. He left me alone by walking around a corner and looking for a minute or two, but unfortunately, he found no fax from my cardiologist. Oh well, better luck next time. I thanked the young soldier for his effort. I resigned myself to my fate and skipped back to the barracks, whistling the melody from the Seven Dwarfs, a hopeful hop in my step, "Hi ho, hi ho, it's off to work we go..."

This is why I was thrown out of Iraq a month before the rest of the outfit.

● ● ●

Eleven months later in Iraq, Doc Baker, our Battalion Surgeon, informed me one pleasant 100-degree April afternoon, 2004, that the Fort Leonard Wood Hospital had misfiled my medical records and I shouldn't be in Iraq. I was shocked! Whatever could have happened? My military career still hung in the balance, though. A Physical Evaluation Review Board in Washington DC would decide whether I could still serve in our blessed Army. But I was determined to hang in there like a hair in a biscuit.

It seems that when the Army finally found their paper medical file on me (with everybody else's), someone figured out that I shouldn't have deployed because of my cardiomyopathy (enlarged heart). I was ordered back to the Fort Leonard Wood Hospital. It was only a few weeks before the rest of the outfit would arrive back in America. Anyway, I was emotionally finished with being a stowaway. Oh sure, Dynamite Dan had done me a favor by putting me on the manifest to fly to Iraq, but I did have to promise him that I wasn't going to die. My argument to him was that I had done concrete formwork the previous summer. Hot conditions, physical work, day after day; hell, Iraq would be a piece of cake compared to that. As an officer, it wasn't like I was going to be doing any actual work.

Soon after being informed that the "jig was up," I received a letter signed by the First Armored Division Commander, Major General Martin Dempsey. It contained strict instructions to report back to the Fort Leonard Wood hospital. Tony and I took a walk before he drove me over to the Air Force side of street, where the Freedom Bird took off. I told him I'd see him in a month when the rest of the outfit arrived. He kidded and said he might just stick around Iraq.

"I couldn't have gotten through it without you, Tone."

He cupped the back of my neck and pulled me to him, planting a kiss below my right ear, "Me neither, kid." He straightened me out so I could only see his face. "Now be careful with those medical folks. Be patient. Be nice." I smelled his breath; it was like coffee and fatigue. "This is going to take a couple of months. Don't bullshit them at all. Make friends all over. And don't make me come to Fort Lost in the Woods to bail you out."

"OK, Tone." I met his eyes only for a moment, trying not to tear up.

"You know I would," he said.

"Yeah, Tone. I know you would." He was a part of me now. Tony was in my hip pocket for life.

• • •

When I had the magical letter from Major General Dempsey ordering me out of Iraq, I got onto a plane to Kuwait, and then waited for a plane to the Czech Republic, then to New Jersey, then to St. Louis, finally a bus to the Fort. I was going home. "I broke the law, and the law won."

In Prague, the Signal Battalion I was traveling with looked nervously to their commander as he went up to the terminal bar and bought a beer for himself and his Sergeant Major. Prohibition had been repealed! I got two warm Coronas in the rush.

At Fort Dix I went to have a smoke and a man wearing too many clothes bummed a cigarette from me and asked if I knew where I was. He was lost. So was I. Two lost souls having a smoke together.

That morning, the Air Force flyers let me peek inside the cockpit of the transport plane they flew, as I hitched a ride to Missouri. Just as we gained altitude over Philadelphia, the ship banked. The view was awesome. The crew even gave me a box lunch, an apple, bologna and cheddar cheese on white bread and two oatmeal bars. Down at the Air Force Base, the post Commander came to shake my hand. I was confused. No Military Police, no charges against me.

I had been back in the States for less than a day when a Post cop at the Fort Leonard Wood gate cut my military ID in half right in front of me. I nearly freaked. New identification cards were required since the latest installment of the war had begun. I'd been awake for 48 hours and only wanted to lie down. After the cutting I waited for the duty NCO to pick me up. It was well after midnight. He got me a bunk, a pillow, clean sheets, and a good old-fashioned, warm, scratchy, Army olive drab wool blanket, which is in the top ten of the greatest objects that God ever created. Only the best will do.

There's never a parade when you want one. A Stop N' Go gasoline station paired with a Church's Fried Chicken was where I found my family again. Outside the gate of Fort Leonard Wood, I rode a bike I bought for $50 from Community Services. It was all uphill to the service station. I didn't even have a flip phone yet. Within the cloud of that wonderful gasoline smell, Ellen pulled in, right on time. She saw me, but released Abby from her car seat first. Almost four years old now, she ran toward me. She knew who I was! I wasn't sure if she would. Twenty feet, five feet, her little body gasping in embrace. My daughter's lungs spasmed, her tears running down my neck. I couldn't break away but we were at a gas station. I kissed

Ellen hard, and then threw the bike in the back. My loves were strangers and I to them. The little one buckled into the car seat, I rode in the back with her, nothing but smiles, holding hands. We got through the gate, registering the car and the rest of our tiny family and checked into the soldier/family hotel built for just these occasions. Ellen was nervous, but I didn't know why. Forty bucks a night for three nights was just great for us. We settled in quickly, then hit the PX to look around, then the adjacent Class Six for a bottle of wine, and finally, the commissary for foodstuffs. It was a homecoming Army style. I came back with all my fingers and toes, stirred but not shaken.

CAUTION! When you finally have the opportunity you've fantasized about for a year, and you have little ones that must not ever be left alone, don't be disappointed if it happens quickly in the bathroom. I think the earth moved. Smiles. Everyone smiles. I'd gotten us a condo off post within days. Ellen left and then returned again from Milwaukee with clothes and a cat. I was desperate for them. A moment alone was another moment wasted. I'm not too sure about the cat.

I had a "job" in those months within the Medical Hold Company assisting in administrivia while my disposition wrangled through channels. One afternoon I called the St. Louis Cardinals asking if I could get about twenty tickets for wounded warriors. Always the morale officer, I knew what their response to me would be: "Kenny, what do you want?" They sent a bus and placed the soldiers on the Jumbo-Tron during the Star Spangled Banner. Once a morale officer always a morale officer. Ellen not being a big fan of baseball, the family and I went fishing instead that weekend. It was fortuitous, since someone else could bait my hook for me.

The outfit arrived and began their out-processing from overseas service. Soldiers want to get home no matter what. I helped in the medical processing, slightly. At least they saw a familiar face. But in the crush of lines, it was questionable whether soldiers would truthfully report any and all ailments, physical or mental. They knew the Army would keep them from going home if they needed medical care. It was a "catch 22." Damned if you do and damned if you don't. Report you needed help and you didn't go home, or fib and you'd hope for the best.

When I actively advised full disclosure and patience to my folks going through the hours-long lines to see health care providers, it quickly became known to a physician, a retired Brigadier General, Medical Corps, who was working a station. He confronted me before everyone. We went nose to nose. He made sure I knew that I had no authority to counsel anyone. But these were my people. The stalemate ended with my holding my ground. The hospital folks later asked me if I knew who he was, as if I should be impressed. I continued to encourage people to seek help while still at the Fort.

Michelle came by my table and I tried not to tremble. I hadn't thought about her much since I'd been away. She was pretty. I was infatuated. I didn't really know anything about her. She said, "I appreciate what you're doing, Kenny." She grasped my upper left arm and with a loving look in her amazing brown eyes went to the next station within the packed room. "Be good," was the last thing she said to me. I wish I could have held her hand across the parking lot going somewhere, someplace else. But she, I hoped, had someone else waiting expectantly, somewhere, someplace else.

• • •

You of good hearts and minds,
Care managers to the broken,
We came home with wounds to bind,
Brains traumatic, at times shaken.

Would our jobs still be there?
In employment lines we waited.
The debts piled on kept us bare,
As marriages dissipated.

Volunteers gave their all,
Once only in the realm of men.
Women answered country's call,
A faded flag, she bled with them.

CHAPTER 14

# Hero to Zero

Spring had sprung. Flowering trees budded amongst small orchards, empty of peaches. It suggested renewal but I was broken. At least the Army suspected so. The smoke screen had lifted and it was time for the reckoning. A Medical Review Board would determine if a Physical Evaluation Board would be necessary. The latter, somewhere in Washington DC, would determine my fate. However, I had a good chance of being retained, since I wanted to be. And I experienced marked improvement in my heart health. Iraq was like a year-long spa for me (without the hot bubble baths, massages, clean warm fluffy towels, facials, and cucumber slices on my eyelids).

The rolling hills and red clay of central Missouri sent the almost daily rain into innumerable streams. Farming was hard scrabble here. The mega Walmart under construction in the little town of St. Roberts was a mixed blessing. Outside Fort Leonard Wood, orange barrels and construction dumpsters told of investment following in the wake of war. Little stores got pushed out.

As in most of the South, strip clubs and adult book stores were neighbored by tiny churches with pithy messages like, "Sinners Welcome!" The townhouse I rented for four months had carpeting, AC, indoor plumbing, cable TV—I could go on. A true marvel when you've been without. You get used to the prosperity fast, but I became dually sensitive to the unpainted houses and caving barns when we traveled the small state highways. Litter in the fields and roadways is always a sign of communities run amiss. Abandoned automotive projects would be parked by gravel driveways, usually for years. Refrigerators, tires, and playground equipment rested and rusted amidst tall grass, bidding mosquitoes to come and lay their eggs in stagnant pools of water.

The Fort Leonard Wood Hospital, like all hospitals, was a maze with many floors. The broken gathered in formation each morning for the newly organized Medical Hold Company. Summertime was most pleasant at 0730 when the roll was called. Personal accountability in the Army is as necessary as pulling your socks on before your boots. However, spit shine toe now bowed to desert camouflage. No longer would a soldier drink beer and polish garrison boots into mirrors (as opposed to boots only worn in the field) during the cool of the evening, just to "outsoldier" the comrade to the left and right in formation.

As an officer, my attendance was a professional courtesy of sorts. The non-commissioned officers went bonkers when a young'n wasn't present. It didn't matter if les misérables had appointments with providers or not. Our routine was to traverse the labyrinth of medical regulations, physical pain and familial anguish, all at the friendly slow pace of a southern drawl. If the enlisted soldiers weren't otherwise occupied with physical therapy, they'd be farmed out to cut grass and any other free labor projects that Sergeant Majors across the post requested. Often times, we hid somewhere, pretending to be busy. I had a job but it wasn't a real one. I did some minimal record keeping, nothing for an officer to sink his teeth into.

At 1630, Ellen would pick me up and the girls would tell me about their day's adventures. Their voices were a loving kindness. My daughter and I would spy upon the other drivers, making up songs about who was the biggest loser among the multitude of minivan drivers. Abby and I enjoyed "fly" safaris inside the townhouse. We hunted our prey, each with a loaded Walmart swatter. The tension ran high as the screaming and bashing began. The flies reset soon after our misses, and although indoors, usually one or two found their way into our temporary home. The true mission was still to find my way back to Wisconsin. And I hadn't a clue when that might happen. But any time with my daughter drove all concerns from my mind. We always had a filthy fly to kill—the enemy. Shouts, hoots, and silliness reverberated between slabs of brand new drywall, and we made many squished marks for future painters to cover—confirmed kills. We went fishing on and off post. One of the girls would bait my hook for me and we'd while away the time watching the red and white bobber, hoping to see it make little rings in the pond from nibbles below.

Once, while we were playing cars in the living room, my daughter banged the top of her head directly on the outside corner of a wall. Both Ellen and I witnessed it simultaneously. It was one of those kinds of kid hurts that is so off the charts that the little one looks at you briefly before the true magnitude of the pain registers and the monster scream ensues. As a parent, even an ineffectual one like me, I can't stand seeing my kid get hurt. That's universal.

My case manager was also a captain. We met my second day back in the "Land of Beer and Pizza." As you may have guessed, I'm not a normal soldier. Normal is boring. Normal is a setting on a washing machine. All soldiers in the Medical Hold Company (which had about twenty soldiers assigned but was growing rapidly) were waiting an official disposition of their military duty from Uncle Sugar. In the military, just like the NFL, everything is great until you get hurt. Now, the team wants you back. But rehab takes months, with surgeries. Who knew when a young soldier might get home or back to active duty status? Most folks were in pain from back injuries, orthopedic concerns being primary. It ran the gamut of human bodies being burnt, torn, and shattered. Me? I was in the best shape of my life! My heart condition had improved mightily in Iraq as my heart's injection fraction had reached 46 (low normal) from 27 (heart failure). My circumstances were unusual. No beer at the point of a gun had been the obvious remedy.

Because I was an officer and had practiced communicating effectively in Army style, I had a monstrous advantage over the rest of les misérables. They wanted to get out. I wanted to stay in. It was a strategy that paved my path through the Department of the Army paperwork noodle with grand effect. In record time, a Physical Evaluation Board found me to be worldwide deployable. Victory! This maze was only the entrance to my next, much tougher, civilian one. When I took off the uniform, the fear gripped me and called me its own for the next year and a half. I called the Carpenter's Hall in Milwaukee to find out 250 guys were on the bench in August, '04. Not good.

If 2004 was tolerable, 2005 was grievous. I never felt like a hero. I'd never had to pick myself off of the canvas as often as when I returned from war the first time. I was at my best in theater. In the States I was just OK, average, nothing to look at, and fighting for a job like every other Jane and Joe. Like a vapor trail, our little convoy of a U-Haul filled with new furniture and a Nissan sedan given to Ellen by her parents sped from Missouri back to Wisconsin. The only wrong turn came ten miles from our little three-bedroom ranch. I was leading in the truck and

Ellen was flummoxed on the phone. The city next to ours is old, not laid out in grids; it is easy to be turned around on streets that were once deer trails. I was frustrated at myself and angrily told her into my new flip phone, "This isn't Iraq!" Calm the hell down! There won't be any ambushes, no chance of being hauled out from a flaming hulk to be beaten and sexually assaulted in the street. I quickly learned to apologize and shift down from fifth gear to a steady emotional third.

Perhaps my memory of myself is inaccurate. I had changed, but couldn't discern it. I felt as hard as a concrete block thrown unused into a dumpster. It wasn't Ellen's fault. All my relationships had to start over again. And I didn't have a job to come back to. Coming back from war was more pressure than leaving for it. I'm sure I wasn't a treasure on my return, or an agreeable husband, with my penchant for beer, computer games, and solitude. A sea of dandelions waved at me as I approached my two-thirds of an acre paradise. I had the worst lawn in the neighborhood. My man card was in severe jeopardy of being revoked.

The NCO in charge of me called the next morning, asking where I was, and I apologized for not telling him I was leaving. Personnel accountability, you know. But I had been as excited as a newborn puppy to go home. Like a calf finding her legs upon birth, shaky and unsteady. I was home. With lots of money in the bank, many credit cards demanding minimum payments, and no prospects at all. I attacked the weeds with relish for years to come, admonished repeatedly for harming the pretty yellow flowers. Yard work was a safe escape where I was alone with my thoughts and fears. I could repeat my adventures in my head like a movie, until an unrelenting voice ordered me to write them down.

The last good hand the carpenters' union could deal me was fixture work at a new Target store. Coming home from active duty was a card I placed immediately, but the job played out after only three weeks. One morning a violent wind storm knocked the two Port-a-Potties upon their sides. Blue water, waste, and toilet paper covered the asphalt. The shitters were upended and used again without service—a metaphor perhaps. I identified with the Port-a-Potties. I wrenched my back in week two building a display column and I had to call in sick, unable to stand up straight. Just before the snow began to fly, I was laid off.

Every contractor had established guys they'd call back if or when work picked up. I placed applications by the dozens. Many employers thanked me for my service, and I suspected threw my submission into the circular filing cabinet, afraid of an employee subject to another deployment absence. The out-of-work list was long and I didn't get another carpenter gig for about six months. The state of Wisconsin was grateful for my service and had on the books a reciprocity agreement with my union's pension fund, under which it would fund my donations for the time I was overseas. So, I got 2,000 hours credited towards my pension for nothing. Hey, I don't make the rules. Thanks, Wisconsin. Love you, Honey.

The Army Reserve was built to support Big Army; however, in practice the United States Army Reserve broke itself in the endeavor. The Engineer Battalion I had "grown up" within was fragmented and reorganized into two small engineer detachments. With a third of its strength brought onto active duty during Operation Iraqi Freedom, the flag was folded, the unit decommissioned, and another home was lost to me. I needed another place to soldier.

Without a clue, I turned to the Yellow Pages. To those readers too young to understand the reference, the Yellow Pages was a book published by the only existing phone company that listed businesses and government references. It was a means of advertisement as thick as a brick. Before the invention of computers, we old people used it frequently to contact folks via the landline. Then we scratched directions onto slate boards and drove the buggy to where we needed to go. I found a unit that needed me and had at least one part-time paycheck.

Resurrecting my military career, I found a Reserve unit that made me their Battalion Supply Officer and Headquarters Commander. Like I said, my previous unit, the 169th Engineer Battalion out of Milwaukee, had been picked apart by mobilizations of personnel and reorganized until it was a shadow of the proud outfit it once was. The wars in Iraq and Afghanistan took from the Army Reserve without hesitation to meet the needs of combatant commanders. I straightened out my new unit's property book, making sense of unaccounted for or missing stuff while filing several "Reports of Survey." These reports initiate an official investigation to determine who's responsible for the unaccounted-for equipment. And no, a bulldozer wasn't among the items. It was ironic. I wondered if anyone initiated an investigation on the Teddy Bear that was appropriated. I doubt it.

We hosted Ellen's family that Thanksgiving, and when it was my turn to say what I was grateful for, this unemployed, buzzed carpenter could only respond with, "the Green Bay Packers." Brett Favre was still playing for us back then. I encountered a lot to clean up the next day to occupy my time. My turkey was OK, and the giblet gravy awesome. My apple pie was gobbled down.

I started going to religious services again. I tried to sell Jesus on having a pity part for Kenny but he wasn't buying. "God is the last refuge of a scoundrel," they say. But I stayed with it even after favorable times returned. I haven't forgotten about putting down 28K on my tax return in 2005, or losing our health insurance, or the panic attacks at 2:00 a.m. My earthly father staunched the financial hemorrhage. I honored him for that by being there when he was on the mat years later.

Seeking any employment, I posted flyers offering handyman services. Thankfully, a woman called, almost a widow, for repair of her front door that wouldn't close. In forty-five minutes, I was at their home, making secure what had swung wrong. Her husband's left hand had the mark of the Japanese bullet that had passed through it, forcing his evacuation from Iwo Jima. The Second Lieutenant's contribution to World War Two was over, a Civil Engineer's career now begun, but he couldn't fix his front door from the weather that was to come. He showed me his Bronze Star for valor. I cleaned their gutters, raked their yard, and painted their basement pink and gray, just for grocery money. This captain feasted on humility.

A silver maple in our backyard that brightly brought forth fall yellows had a thick nearly horizontal branch that suspended a little swing. In its plastic seat sat my kid when she still thought I was funny. Twisties, double twisties, anything to make lots of giggles. I still have that in memory like a footnote. I took a job as a clerk for $15/hour at a local police department working second shift. It lasted until the last day of my probation, about four months in, when the city's Police Chief fired me. I just hadn't gotten the hang of it. I made mistakes all the time. It wasn't what I was supposed to do. I had failed again. At least I still had unemployment benefits left. At $300/week and monthly expenses over $4,000, I was a ship without a rudder or a sail. I only had to click the mouse and the indignity was over for another seven days.

I took a carpenter job in the spring. While I was placing 2X12s for concrete footings, my supposedly fixed abdominal hernia began to weep. I had had surgery years before for the bubble above my belly button. The physician assured me that the work he had done would fail in the years to come because I needed mesh, but he only used sutures. It was amazing that I didn't choke the shit out of this guy. Another surgery left me on the bench again; this time mesh replaced sutures. The Demerol was like a dream, but the Tylenol 3 I was sent home with had to be augmented with medicinal brandy. Listening to the Brewers on the radio while painting my house that year began a renewed passion for baseball, and I read Bob Uecker's litter-airy masterpiece, Catcher in the Wry. His baseball statistics were regrettable, but his broadcasting skills formidable.

I heard of a golden opportunity to go to Fort McCoy, to mobilize and to train soldiers to go overseas. It meant full employment, not too far away from home. To do what I loved to do—soldier. But it was months away until my application got approved. In the meantime, I drove to Florida to work as a carpenter. All I had to say was that I had gone through an apprenticeship in Wisconsin, and I was instantly hired. At $14/hour and no benefits, I appreciated staying with my wife's sister and her husband, Suzie and Phil. He was a carpenter, too. Eventually he had to have both knees replaced, but Phil kept on working in the field after recovery, a true craftsman

• • •

There is nothing else better than to soldier, for me. A few occupations require the kind of dedication required, because other people's lives depend on you doing your job—medical, cops, firefighters, first responders, are just a few. Uncle Sugar picked me up off of the canvas with a letter that in part read, "YOU ARE REASSIGNED TO . . . MOBILIZED IN SUPPORT OF OPERATION ENDURING FREEDOM . . . FOR A PERIOD NO LONGER THAN 364 DAYS."

The latter rain had finally come; not in a drizzle, but in a torrent.

# CHAPTER 15

# The Husky

Crunch, crunch, crunch. I broke the crystalline crust with every step of my Mickey Mouse boots, as the slightest squeak emitted between tread, twigs, and powder. As I pushed off again with a scrunch, the stillness couldn't filter the sounds of my steps. Breaking the beautiful white plane with my presence seemed a shame. Moving over the military ridge like a fool, alone, I plopped into a knee-high drift and passed toasty minutes in marvelous solitude, not concerned about my silhouette. My footgear was impenetrable by cold with its two-inch rubber sole and manual vent for when your feet got too hot, which they would. Solitude accompanied the still near glow of warm quarters and the knowledge of the Sumatran coffee I had freshly brewed for my big Stanley thermos. I didn't care about getting wet, as my Humvee was close by. Sunrise over Scott's Junction was almost two hours old. The steep hills through the dense Wisconsin forest slowed the Route Reconnaissance Engineers to a near standstill.

It snows deeply in Afghanistan's mountains, too. At each road and trail crossing, the lieutenant leading the twenty soldiers and seven vehicles probably felt a throbbing in his chest. The mission was to clear a road for the big logistical convoys to follow. Taking your eyes off of the road was to assume it had been mined again, and that happened every day at Fort McCoy with a wave of a pen and buried sheet metal that we observer/controllers would dig into place the afternoon before. The route would have to be cleared again and again. Welcome to searching for Improvised Explosive Devices through frozen tundra. The lieutenants and units changed frequently, but the mission did not.

Could they feel the ambush coming? The frequent twists in the white roads, the five-degree hills, and the switchbacks obliterated the platoon leader's line of sight. I hoped the platoon had rehearsed their MEDIVAC Medical Evacuation (MEDIVAC) procedures. That was really why we were there. It was going to be a bright, clear and calm fifteen-degree day. The observer/controllers had been with them since they woke up, and now hoped to feel the pulse and throbbing of the Husky's motor reverberating around the bend. Cardinals and blue jays waited to feed in the spring, hopping around bare branches, the wind being mostly still. I listened to the knocking of a woodpecker, but heard no rhythmic tune of a motor. A few chirps could be heard, along with limbs bouncing off each other as a few intrepid squirrels moved about the tree tops, inspecting their summer leafy nests above the snowy ground before retreating to second homes in the hollows of trees.

Three to five miles per hour can be too fast when you're searching for IEDs. The Taliban would bury devices for months over the seasons to catch soldiers unawares. The freeze/thaw cycle helped blend in the disturbance of soil from a dug-in device. They might think, "Was that pile of rocks there before? Why is it there at all? Is it a marker? An aiming point? What is different? We've been on this route dozens of times, clearing ahead of convoys dozens of times."

"Slow down, Stop! Damn it! This mission is going to take forever!" passed through many soldiers minds this morning. They wanted to hurry the laborious search. "Slow down, Stop! I want to make it home! Stay Alert, Stay Alive. Don't get complacent!" would pass between their ears on similar missions when they conducted them for real downrange. We wanted them to go slow, to take their time.

The Husky driver will find the Improvised IEDs before detonation. Or won't. But survival is based upon breakaway suspension and the V-shaped hull. It's a single-occupant vehicle usually staged two hundred meters in the advance. No reason to have others within the blast radius. Only those with more ovaries/balls than brains applied. Few of the volunteers got good enough to run missions in country. Some got blown up and volunteered to come back, running the gauntlets again. That's how intoxicating it was to have all that weight of responsibility behind ballistic glass and the most technologically advanced mine detector in the world. Concussions and traumatic brain injuries were quantified by the Army. Shock waves moving at hundreds of miles per hour deform soft tissue, like brains. Husky drivers were assessed after every explosion they suffered. Be too close to the point of detonation, and although without laceration, a body could become an instant rag doll to be shipped back home in a bag. Policy quickly developed for all soldiers in theater who had been exposed to detonations, becoming increasingly strict as the war continued. This eventually led to quick exits from theater when soldiers had several incidents, because the severity of injury always increases with subsequent blast exposure. It's like being more susceptible to heat stroke if one has previously become extremely dehydrated. Thus, leaders needed a bullpen of the trained and willing, in preparation for several getting hurt.

These incidents gave the NFL a big kick in the pants, too. The US started taking soldiers out of the game before they sustained unrecoverable brain injuries. The NFL adopted that same policy after several seasons. The myth that helmets protect both brains and bones was undone. Adult brains don't regenerate, but can compensate. Rehabilitation is possible. So is a change in personality after repeated head trauma—dementia, rage, depression, suicide.

Bobcats have roamed the Big Woods of Wisconsin for tens of thousands of years. Our little team took our name from these vicious predators and we became the scourge of the Deployables. We took them from their Home Station, USA, to bleed in the snow of Afghanistan/Wisconsin. My Motorola's volume was set high and I heard our non-commissioned officers crosstalking about the convoy's lack of progress. Each radio cost the Army $500, and the encryption codes within were another $4,000.00. No one could hear our internal communications. The Bobcat team of eight soldiers would be assigned a company (about 100 soldiers depending on the kind of unit) for their field training. Small convoys made up the Bobcat diet. Suited for glacially pocked terrain and hard changes in seasons, our big paws adapted against sinking in the snow, traveling alongside the vehicles through the forest, waiting, and trying to keep them from dying because of stupidity downrange.

The engineers were plenty nervous and going super, super slow. Every sharp turn towards Scott's Junction caused a pause. I had issued the platoon leader the Operation Order two nights before. The route recon patrol of seven vehicles left the wire an hour late. When I observed they weren't ready to leave the motor pool inside the Forward Operating Base Freedom, I was frustrated, like the rest of the team, about the apathy born from the trainee's inexperience. Being on time is professional and necessary, although having all your ducks in a row before leaving the wire is essential. Better to make your mistakes here than downrange. FOB Freedom could accommodate over one thousand Deployables, and often did during the middle innings of the wars.

I'd been spotted! The patrol jerked to a stop. Fifty meters past the intersection of a trail and the supply route, the Husky driver saw me sitting just below the next rise, two football fields away. She let everybody know that during the After Action Review (AAR) about 30 minutes later. I grinned in sheepish embarrassment. Kudos to her for an owl eye; she really wanted to make the grade.

The lieutenant communicated back to the FOB Freedom a few miles away, reporting an enemy sentry at Scott's Junction. It wasn't planned. I screwed up in reverse, again. The Route Reconnaissance patrol was now fixed, afraid to go forward or back. What would they do? Dismount a squad to force the enemy sentry to move off? Maneuver on foot through knee deep snow, across draws and thickets of frozen sumac bushes? Fire upon enemy they couldn't see? Maneuvering with the gun trucks was difficult with the multiple choke points between snow mounds and precipitous drops. I shot a few blanks with my M16 at the Deployables' vehicles and bounded down the hill, not wanting to be late for the show. The Bobcat team moved in on the double quick, as they were used to my fumbling and then needing another teammate to pick up the ball and run wild. Call it premature initiation. It happens to guys all the time, but never to me, except for that one time. Yeah, right. If you didn't tell the training audience that you'd made a mistake, they'd never know. It wasn't important anyway. Two of their training objectives from the Commander's list were: 1) React to an ambush; and 2) Evacuate a casualty. Both would be extremely pertinent to where they'd be in a month.

WHOMP WHOMP WHOMP WHOMP WHOMP WHOMP WHOMP WHOMP WHOMP! Fire from the machine gunner at the forward Humvee forced me to roll into a snowy ditch. That was an "'atta boy" to the gunner later. A staff sergeant from the Bobcat team unleashed multiple artillery simulators as we pressed the improvised ambush. Make-believe mortars screamed, as the Bobcats dropped multiple pyrotechnic simulators. WHISTLE BANG! WHISTLE BANG! The Bobcat observer/controllers "disabled" a Humvee due to a close blast. Our NCOs took soldiers from their now "disabled" vehicle into snow banks, and assessed three casualties as agreed upon beforehand—leg wound, head wound, chest wound. Our own machine gunners now swept the platoon, with the soldiers trying to perform first aid on their comrades. WHOMP WHOMP WHOMP WHOMP WHOMP! We ordered the wounded to yell! Turret gunners from atop their Humvees returned fire toward Bobcat positions high on wooded knolls. Hand grenade simulators screamed BOOM BANG, ringing between oaks and elms. Would the lieutenant use the radio to report the ambush? Report the casualties? Lots of fake blood from moulage kits (used to simulate trauma like fractures, burns, lacerations, and entry wounds) was poured about the ambush site and had a wonderfully appalling affect. Would the lieutenant see blood in the snows of Afghanistan?

What's the play, lieutenant? How are you going to get your wounded out? How are you going to recover your Humvee? Wait too long to get out of there and the Bobcats would start assessing soldiers as being killed in action or bleeding out, singling out the most likely to die like a hungry family of cats. We began snapping, baring our teeth, circling, trying to find the weakest to attack and kill. Freeze up and ignore your battle drills and the major might require the lieutenant to write a letter to the family back in their home town, due to their negligence, apathy, stupidity. Explain why their loved one didn't make it. Why you made a mistake. Write it down. It's going in the mail. You're the officer.

After the After Action Review (AAR) with the training audience at Scott's Junction, it was agreed to continue to run the mission. The Bobcats hissed their approval toward the progress of the troops. It was hard training. We all liked it, trainers and trainees. Of course we ambushed them again about a kilometer down the Supply Route. Their communications and reactions were better. The lieutenant even tried to call in artillery onto the Bobcat positions. "A" for effort, but I of course denied the request for fire. I told him later that target reference points had to be preplanned, but his thought process was starting to cook. At the next After Action Review (also known as a hot wash) we talked about their battle drills. During reaction on contact, can you maintain movement? Can the gun trucks maneuver? Would you ever dismount? This was complicated and dangerous stuff.

The Deployables had to have two hot meals a day or holy hell would shudder through the chains of command. Besides heaters in vehicles and the best clothing in the world, hot rations for breakfast and supper were the greatest control measures to minimize the effects of the frozen tundra. Early January's light started to fade by 1630. We'd train as long as we could. If a unit tried to leave a training event early and just return to the Forward Operating Base like they were taking a Sunday drive, we Bobcats would pursue relentlessly and maul the young Americans without mercy. We would catch whomever, assessing casualties in proportion to stupidity. They were made to treat casualties, call for MEDIVAC, then speedily get back inside the wire for another quick After Action Review.

• • •

Developed by the South Africans forty years ago, the Husky ain't your Grandad's mine detector. Not Grandad going to the beach looking for change and jewelry, an oldtimer sweeping the sand, shirtless, in sagging shorts, with a tan belly sticking out.

The driver enters the cockpit from the top hatch. The chassis can break off from its extended front or rear axles, as designed. The "V" shaped hulls are self-explanatory, designed to direct away the blast's energy. Production of the Husky was ramped up as fast as the US taxpayers could prepay contracts with foreign governments. By 2008, maybe thirty in the United States were available for training. Unfortunately, those were vehicles blown apart severely in theater, cannibalized, and eventually rebuilt, then sent to training platforms like Fort McCoy, Wisconsin, a relatively unknown premier training venue (see page 240).

The first variants had five-foot-long panels on both sides of the vehicle. When not retracted back to the chassis, they scanned with penetrating radar less than a foot above the ground. Deep scans could reach down through three feet of soil. Calibrating the system was tricky, so an operator actually making it work to detect objects on test sites became the MVP candidate on the team. But the team had to have several alternates in the event the operator got blown up or severely brain shaken. Surviving an IED strike right beneath you was built into the Husky's design. But what about the platoon's survivability? Who's next in line to operate? What happens when something is detected in the roadway? So glad you asked.

The Buffalo was a massive armored vehicle that could haul ten soldiers easily with a driver and vehicle commander. It was another vital piece of equipment to range over the plains and mountains of southwest Asia. In the family of Mine Resistant Ambush Protected vehicles (MRAP), the Buffalo brought a squad of soldiers to the Route Reconnaissance mission. The beast had run flat tires that rolled despite punctures, a V hull, and long range optics, but the greatest feature was a thirty-foot self-articulating arm with a claw that could investigate a possible IED. It looked like a giant spork (combination of a spoon and a fork) with a tongue on top. The spork would scratch and dig up whatever the Husky found. Failure meant blowing up the telescoping arm instead of a soldier. Unless the arm was broken; then some soldiers might have to prod the discolored earth or trash pile with bayonets and shovels. At over 25 tons and 13 feet tall, it wasn't a small target on the battlefield. It moved glacially over the unimproved roads of Afghanistan and the highways of Iraq. We didn't have one at Fort McCoy for several years. We just had to play pretend.

Smart people back in the States developed a remotely-controlled tracked robot called the Talon. It was brought on missions overseas and had cameras and claws that could place explosives on bombs. The Talon could move over broken terrain looking like a tracked coffee table with an arm growing out of the top. Getting close to an object to identify it was the first step in defeating an IED. Then the operator would move the expensive Talon away and the IED would be detonated. It was obviously far less risky than sending out a team to set the explosives. Unless the machine wasn't working, or you didn't have a robot.

Blowing stuff up has always been in the purview of engineers, so many construction units were transformed into route reconnaissance bomb hunters. Everybody wanted to be out front, alone in the Husky. Everybody wanted to use the Buffalo's shovel-size spork to dig out the bomb. Everybody wanted to drive the robot. The alternative was to be bored to tears in the back of the vehicles (aka window lickers), just waiting for something to happen, which terrifyingly sometimes did. "Everybody" means only the most courageous.

Up-armored Humvees were rare back in the States. All available models were sent overseas. But it did get better as time went by. Of course, specialized stuff went where the need was greatest. Designers developed vehicles to better withstand the blasts, with heavy doors, thick ballistic glass, and sturdier frames and suspensions. Turrets with rotating rings were placed into the roofs of Humvees with armored plates we called chicken wings, protecting the young gunners.

During the early years, we had to simulate having basic equipment, even the Husky. Soldiers walked in pairs with handheld mine detectors in front of convoys. Just like Pops did it in Vietnam. Secretary Rumsfeld was demonstrably correct. You go to war with the Army you have, not the Army you want. We pretended to have lots of stuff like long range cameras, wreckers, tow bars, binoculars, robots to disable IEDs, ambulances, and the latest secure satellite communication equipment. The training effect was minimized. The logistical train caught up eventually and the equipment improved, though never with enough of the right stuff.

Leadership is a skill that can't be purchased anyway. The missions didn't change because you didn't have what you needed or wanted. You had to gut your way through, always. The US Army Corps of Engineers is my tribe. In Medieval times engineers would tunnel beneath fortification walls to sap or undermine them. Later, explosives would collapse the castle walls from below with even greater effect. Combat engineers build and demolish. When IEDs came to the battlefield, USACE was given the mission to go hunt the bombs. The equipment was brand new. The battle drills were improvised from infantry tactics or developed from scratch. Units were re-missioned to provide Route Reconnaissance. Because of war, we Sappers have another impressive skill to bring to the fight. The intention was that these young'uns could keep the force safe when traveling.

• • •

Months later in Afghanistan, a young soldier who had barely survived a 50 kilo-barrel blast that she rolled over, said to herself after returning to her outfit, "You're all right. Best to get back through the top hatch and into the seat. You're the best the team's got. You've said it yourself. We all believe it because you've proven it in Qandahar. Two times a week you've pointed out an IED that could have killed. Every other day you save a life. Keep going until the end. You have to. You die/they die, you choose us. That's the oath. It is why blood is thicker than water. The Doc might see signs, but your headache and blurred vision is only your concern. Tell no one, especially not family back home. Not even your battle buddy. They could take your job if you leave. This is the most awesome job you've ever had. One in which you finally excel."

When the explosion tore the front suspension clean off, the V hull came to rest thirty feet away, just like a NASCAR crash into the wall. The Sergeant told herself, "Tell no one how you feel or you may get sent home to Charleston, West Virginia. Back to the National Guard to staunch floods along the Kanawha River before it spills into the Ohio. Before you have to have a celebratory luncheon with the quilting gals of the American Legion. Maybe you could figure out an undergraduate program if you didn't have a problem concentrating. Maybe you will find a nice country boy who DOESN''T chew tobacco and could still love a girl who will forever walk with a cane. If you ever get back home, other than inside a bag or a box with Old Glory draped over it."

She decided to get back into the seat, and the opportunity came soon. Back in Qandahar, Afghanistan every engineer on Route Recon was confident. They left the Entry Control Point after they test fired their weapons. On the radio she called with a totally flat and emotionless voice to the Lieutenant and the entire patrol, "Slow roll, slow roll, we've got to go." The Mountaineer was back after a week on the bench. The team stepped on themselves on the radio calling, "Wha-whoo." And, "You go, girl!" She was their best chance at survival, again. They'd heard her recite that instruction more than fifty times before. The Sergeant revved up the engine and purposely pushed through the first three kilometers in about 45 minutes. Not everything was as she remembered as her brain was flying through cloudiness. It wasn't like the first mission at Scott's Junction. Her mind was clear then. But at McCoy she was scared; now she wasn't. A logistical convoy followed behind the engineers toward a combat outpost too far away.

•  •  •

The Lieutenant had a hard time sleeping at FOB Freedom, Fort McCoy, USA, recounting his orders to the squad leaders an hour before. The Minnesotan prayed for just five hours of sleep, then four. His wife was 28 and their newborn, Laura, had the clearest blue eyes. Being a new mom, she dispensed with pursuing a career, instead taking a job with low pay and dismal prospects in exchange for a tolerable husband, and a child who knew only her. Now she'd be alone for a year. Relatives and friends said they'd help watch the baby, but she'd never let them.

"May I sleep a few hours? Please let me sleep," he muttered as a single tear rolled down his cheek onto a crappy, hard, ancient Army-issued pillow. The Lieutenant mentally rolled through the trip ticket again and again: personnel, vehicles, weapons, and the 0715 SP. They had to hit the 07:15 a.m. time hack, leaving the gate with their route reconnaissance patrol. He knew that no actual logistical convoys would be following, but in a month they would be. Where in Afghanistan would the big roulette wheel of fate place them? When their company came into the queue, where would the Combatant Commander need this precious asset? At Qandahar, the opium capital of the world? Or might it be Khost province, where men dyed their beards red and never ventured from their valleys in their lifetimes, but fought with their lives against anyone who entered. The Husky operator had better not let them down. He got some pushback for assigning her. But she had volunteered, the young Sergeant, for many work assignments. And the other leaders couldn't fault her. The Lieutenant didn't know if she had enough brains to have Point. But she had grit, and most of the time, guts are enough.

Looking at her watch in the dark metal hut, the Husky operator was pissed that six hours could pass that fast. She blinked awake at 4:00 a.m. and was unsure if she should stir. The warmth of her fart sack felt good. Placing the Husky in operation meant it had fuel and the systems would operate. She was savvy enough to know that since the electronics of the machine malfunctioned more often than not, that the Observer Controllers (they called themselves Bobcats) probably wouldn't care about her ability to detect actual metal in the snow pack. The trick was to maintain proper patrolling techniques and communicate, communicate, communicate. Civilians contracted by the Army had given hands on instruction on the Husky en masse for a half a day. In her case, thirty extra minutes of private instruction was invaluable. Those special instructors from General Dynamics would not be at FOB Freedom that early in the morning prior to heading out on the mission. The real technical stuff would be hers to figure out. What day was it, anyway? Oh yeah, Saturday. Time to pee and think about breakfast. Although she was a bit heavy, the idea of chipped beef, pancakes with syrup and sausage, tasteless cantaloupe, lousy coffee, and a few fruit bars for that post IED attack sugar rush sounded fine. Some personal hygiene and she was good to go. She was sweet on another sergeant in the platoon. He was more sugary than breakfast. A very quiet lad.

Just a stir of a wind through Fort McCoy ravines would meet the soldiers the day after a five-inch snow. The temperature hugged fifteen degrees on the 9th of January. The strange Arabic call to prayer sounded for the hundreds of logisticians, engineers, MPs and the IBUs (Itty Bitty Units, like laundry, postal, water purification, vector control, whom the Army couldn't do without and no movie was ever made about). At FOB Freedom, we purposely broadcast the Adhan, which means "to listen, be informed about, to hear." The plaintive call from an Imam in a foreign tongue reminded the Deployables where they were going and snapped them back into mission focus.

The glow of road lights ringing the motor pool helped the Bobcats converge. Some were hungover, most pissed off, and the rest dangerously psyched. I drove my bitching, metallic purple Camaro to the trainer's lot and met the team, then found my frozen Humvee, started the diesel engine, and failed to conduct pre-operations checks and services (PMCS) through laziness and the excuse of extreme cold. The log book was unannotated, wedged between the seats.

At 0600 I had already become highly agitated. I wanted to ring that Lieutenant's bell! Why wasn't his unit performing PMCS on their vehicles, getting ready to roll? I suppose warm chow was more important? Observer Controllers don't chow down with the Deployables. Bobcats eat them. I told my sergeants to call me on the Motorola, "Bobcat Six" when they'd hooked up with their counterparts. I entered the FOB Freedom's Tactical Operation Cell. I was a fixture there. I also helped build it. I tried not to get mean so early but the danger of not leaving on time is real. A sergeant I've known for a few years attempted to call the route recon engineers via tactical radio communication but got no response. The unit hadn't established communications yet, meaning the day had started very, very badly. Almost livid, I told myself, to "wait, walk away, don't pounce." Perhaps not being home on a Saturday has added to my frustration. Other units depended on the Route Reconnaissance Platoon to safely lead them, to get war material and soldiers to the fight. Soldiers should never be late. Leaving the wire an hour after it was scheduled is absolutely unacceptable. The unit felt no sense of urgency. Not yet. Hopefully, they'd get it before people start getting hurt. Discounting timetables could throw chaos into movement outside the wire for all traveling units. I pulled my thin fabric gator past my nose and walked off toward the motor pool. Better the lieutenant eats grits than have me right now. We had time, not much, but some. Tick tock. I held my peace.

Maintenance of the equipment means not just fueling it up the night before. When it's cold, cranking a diesel engine is dicey. And it is a supreme comfort when it does sputter and roar. Then you know movement, strength, and warmth will follow. The engineer unit played "mess around" for an hour after chow. After some stern one-way mentorship with the lieutenant about time management and the tradeoffs between timeliness and being ready, I split, swapping my Camaro for a Humvee. I went back to my bachelor quarters for fifteen minutes of CNN.

There wasn't really a reason to get warmed up, except to fill my thermos with fresh coffee and burn some time as the route recon crawled along. Staying ahead wasn't hard. None of us wanted to do this work, not hundreds nor thousands of miles from home. I grabbed my Mickey Mouse boots and drove the Army's Humvee towards Scott's Junction, mad as a hornet wanting to sting, or a vicious Bobcat wanting to bite.

CHAPTER 16

# The Woman with the Purple Finger

The battle of the dandelions continued on weekends for the next five years. My lawn slowly receded from a sea of yellow flowers, crab grass, Creeping Charlie, shoots from nearby bushes, and other species Ortho describes as weeds. Some dandelions grew unrestrained, their sharp broad leaves spread to the size of dinner plates. Abby became upset with my preliminary efforts to thwart the enemy because they were pretty, resulting in the effort becoming clandestine for years. With an eye for maybe having to sell the house, I endeavored to improve our "curb appeal" with a long handle spade shovel to pop up the weeds after it rained.

The Woman with the Purple Finger had more serious concerns. She held a common fear of losing her home even if it was only a cramped concrete box with a pair of toilets down the hall. Water scarcely dribbled in the few sinks on the fourth floor of the tenement she shared with another fifteen families. An even less desirable fifth floor rose above. Electricity worked maybe two or three intermittent times a day. Her memory of being violently removed from her home in the marsh, which had been home to the Shia, affected her tenacity to keep even what little she had. Her loss of home could come again in a moment, my own was a process.

Conditions actually got worse after the Americans had disposed of Saddam Hussein. Garbage collected in every outside corner and open space. Mules and horses rotted on the sides of streets and dogs feasted on their intestines. We called his ghetto Saddam City. More than two million people were forced into a concrete rectangle two miles by four miles. Because of its horrid connotation, the GIs renamed it simply "Square Town" because of its neatly planned square blocks filled with identical tenements. The ghastly slum was again renamed Sadr City in reference to the Shia firebrand cleric, Muqtada al-Sadr. From here he led militias against former oppressors, namely all Sunnis. He also violently resisted what he called the US occupation. His recruiting pool was bottomless.

When Iraq held a parliamentary election in December of 2005, the woman from the planned ghetto voted for a Shia politician only because of her religious affiliation. Death squads from both sects of Islam roamed the streets of the megalopolis for years, using the American curfew to their advantage. Neighborhoods closed ranks to protect themselves from the "Other." Sunni leaders had arrested men to be tortured. The prisoners were unlikely to ever see their families again, and now Saddam's police weren't present to protect the former ruling class from the wrath of the majority Shia. Americans were too few to prevent it.

The difference between Sunni and Shia in Iraq is sort of like the difference between Catholics and Evangelical Christians. If you lived in a country where the psychopath dictator nominally called himself an Evangelical (the minority) and only allowed other Evangelicals into government, and then brutally suppressed everyone else, especially the Catholics (the majority), to whom would you give your allegiance, if you were Catholic? After the dictator's overthrow by the world superpower, who would you vote for if given the chance? What would be the most important qualification for a candidate? Would you fear reprisal? Would you seek revenge? If your home was burned to the ground by Army officers appointed by Saddam Hussein, who were always Sunni, then the answer isn't hard to imagine. Iraqi Arabs voted their religious sect. Kurds voted for Kurds. The Iraqi body politic has remained extremely sectarian. No political parties span the religious and ethnic divide. Of course, Evangelicals don't bomb Catholic churches on a monthly basis. In America, a cycle of revenge isn't in play in which priests direct congregants to invade the homes of neighbors, raping daughters before their dads, and murdering husbands and sons before their families, simply to encourage people to quickly move away, or to get in the truck to the ghetto.

To prevent folks from voting several times, ink wells were placed at poll's exits. The women of her block proudly displayed their fingers and avoided washing the ink off, letting the badge of honor gradually fade away. She had participated in directing her future, and Shia politicians won in a landslide. Eventually, a Shia Prime Minister arose who would lead Iraq for the next eight years. Vetted to be a bulwark against Iran and hopefully allowing minorities to have influence, the new PM did the opposite. But the election was fair. She had a purple finger for a few days. The first freely-elected politicians never relinquished power again. American leaders gritted their teeth and reluctantly opted not to plan a coup.

Now, in her 39th year, of her 32 teeth she had lost four molars and three incisors through rot and pliers applied in the mechanics shop where her husband worked. His cousin Alim made him a perpetual servant. He looked for parts required for repair jobs, walking between shops in the human sea. The sweltering Muslim Shia majority stewed in poverty. A dentist of sorts, Alim also rebuilt carburetors at his bench, his shop no bigger than a two-car garage. He slept there on a cot and provided security at night, an operational roll gate in front of him. The woman with the purple finger was envious of Alim's medical training in Basra. If only her husband had some skill that could produce a better income. A couple of men scoured other shops and junk yards for the parts Alim needed. He attempted to clean his hands of grease before inspecting her mouth, but grime was soaked into layers of skin.

She had borne four children. The first was stillborn—a girl buried in the marsh, where her people had lived and died for centuries. Her husband worked between the reeds, finding fish and birds for the mat where they ate their meals, a rude adobe two-room house, a wedding present from his father. There, at peace, another boy clung to his mother too long, afraid to work in the skinny shallow draft boat with father until he was eight, when the mild man forced his son to learn his trade. This child had a curved spine; his jerking gait could be seen from one bend in the river to another. The woman with the purple finger raised chickens, spun cloth, and cursed Saddam and the Sunnis. The land was fertile and they farmed a sustenance living. These would prove be their "good times."

Her third child loved the marsh, and mended nets and cleaned fish as soon as he could handle a knife. His life was conscripted and eventually taken by the Iraqi Army, traded for a gurgling mustard gas death that burned his respiratory system like drowning in fire. He fought in the cataclysmic war between Iraq and Iran (1980-1988). Millions died with no territorial gains or strategic advantage, until both sides merely agreed to the war's futility, and then both claimed victory. The boy from the reeds fought against fellow Shia, but they were Iranian (Persians, not Arabs). The chemical shells were from Iraqi gun tubes; the wind direction mistaken by the artillery battery. The officers of her son's infantry division were embarrassed by the fratricide of hundreds of their own troops, but the loss was only of inferior conscripts. Saddam didn't care, except for the nominal cost of getting replacements from the reeds and the production of more poison gas.

Last came a girl, her mother's joy. She was too young to remember the forced relocation from their plot along the river. Soldiers packed people into trucks and stole their livestock prior to taking them to the largest suburb east of old Baghdad. The little girl never knew an existence other than the slum. But her mother told her stories about the beauty of the Marsh without end. The woman lay on an air mattress on the concrete floor with her smelly husband, her precious daughter between them forever.

• • •

It had rained the night before. I was home on a Saturday morning being fully awake at 5:00 a.m. It was time to dig out the dandelions, but first I had to let the furry cock-a-poodle muppet out to pee. She'd cock her head sometimes as if trying to understand. Ellen put drops in Daisy's ears when the dog would get an infection, smelling like a yeasty locker room. Taking a long spade, I popped the dandelions at their roots, filling a Home Depot, five-gallon orange bucket—a good dent in the sustained effort. In the afternoon I painted the house, listening to the baseball savant Bob Uecker call a game, able to clean my brushes quickly in order to accompany the girls to whatever activity they decided to pursue. A few times it included amusement park rides with my daughter, my wife too chicken to ride the roller coasters. Mostly it was errands to spend fat major pay on what Abby needed or wanted, what Ellen needed to have, or even a new garden hose for Dad if the price was not too dear. On Sundays, after Evangelical Mega-Church service, I'd drive my bitchin' purple Camaro back to the Fort, for another week of training the Deployables. I'd work five days, before another weekend back in Milwaukee. My weekend and husband stint lasted five years between deployments. In these years I plodded after unattainable goals.

• • •

The separation deepened between the woman with the purple finger and her husband. Darkening, due to stale breath and celebrations the couple would never want to attend together. The man in Sadr City waited patiently for the whistle of the one true God. An end to an awful existence.

There wasn't any love between them anymore, just a grimy resolve not to die hideously. How could he do better? Moving between vendors, hoping to find the correct brakes, hoses, belts, or bolts; bringing home lentils and flat bread, remembering when he was still a man. He was barely present for years, and stopped talking. What he said wasn't important anyway. The sing song of birds among the reeds was a memory. Just like sons who once loved their Papa. He moved with a purpose, afraid every day, and his daughter was shown his fragility, pointed out specifically for contrast to other males. Shoulders stooped, eyes diverted, the call to prayer the last refuge, his only solace. He hadn't the means to buy her charms for a bracelet or unclog the plumbing drains that other more established ghetto husbands accomplished for status.

In the marsh, he whistled back to the song birds with the same rhythm and pitch, a gentle man. His wrist was snapped and never healed properly when the Iraqi Army arrived. The woman with the purple finger was a strength he would never have again. His youngest son was lost to the war with Iran, the older slipped into the violence of the street. The sweep and buzz of flying things were gone along with his beloved river. His bride was embittered. And he hadn't the means now to buy meat, thread, or soap. Practically speaking, they had only what the government provided. Between garages he attempted to broker tiny deals, all to his wife's contempt. He lay beside her at night afraid to reach for her side; better alone than rejected.

Torturing former oppressors, the once shy, crippled young man came and went from the tenement, becoming a person of rage, willing to drill holes into men's knee caps. The screw gun spun at hundreds of rotations per minute with a "WHRRILL," spraying blood from the adjustable chuck. During raids of Sunni neighbors, before screaming families, the boy from the marsh become a dependable militiaman. Saddam's wicked constabulary was displaced by the Americans safely behind their fortifications and Entry Control Points until the sun drew below the horizon. Always, every night, hate displaced law. This way he would protect his mother. His father was broken and useless. But he brought home valuables that could be sold for bread, a wristwatch for a sheep quarter, a feast supplied through his guile and willingness to follow. Now he was head of household. The one his little sister looked in the eye.

# CHAPTER 17

# Big Daddy

B etween Range 17 and the assembly area where the Deploy-ables parked, was a 300-meter trail I walked alone hundreds of times, humming in my mind. In late September, puff ball mushrooms sprouted in the woods, growing like whitish fluff from the trunks of fallen silver maples. The big ones were the size of softballs and tasted like the forest air in a great big bite. The Big Wood canopy hid deer and soldiers alike. As the days shortened and the temps dropped, the elms and oaks stopped making food and swayed into shades of red, yellow, and orange. A breeze begged for flannel. Once, I saw a young wolf on a forty-five degree morning, trotting beside the trail. She looked at me and spirited away, seemingly annoyed at my intrusion.

When another platoon of forty Army Reserve soldiers had arrived at the assembly area, our cadre would introduce our-selves, then magically transport them to a Forward Operating Base in Southwest Asia just three football fields away, where for the next eight hours they'd be fighting for their lives. From elevated fighting positions, they'd protect the base from plastic target threats. They would run an Entry Control Point, keeping vehicle bombs from entering the FOB, or suffer simulated mass casualties themselves. Leaves were amassing between the towers and the company command post trailer. I wanted to bring a rake and jump in the piles, an act unbecoming a field grade officer.

At the assembly area, we showed them examples of the pop-up targets they would soon see from the eight-foot high towers. Silhouettes of a fighter holding an AK-47 or pointing a rocket propelled grenade (RPG) at you is a threat, and you fire at the silhouettes, or the simulated attack grows worse. Sometimes to increase the fear factor, artillery simulators would be dropped next to the fighting positions. WHISTLE BANG!

Seven little tree house-size positions in a line made up our defensive sector. Those silhouettes of unarmed folks or little kids would register if a bullet tore through the target. The civilian running the control tower would report the infraction immediately. Figuring out where the offending shot came from, the cadre investigated. It wasn't too hard since a Bobcat in every tower accompanied a pair of troopers within. Every pop-up was scripted. "Killing" a civilian could prompt a letter from your commander as to why you pulled the trigger, addressed to the mother of the kid or the mayor of the town. It depended on whether there were multiple shots, or on how pissed off the Bobcats became. The mock village facing the soldiers had vehicles on tracks, sliding across the hilly panorama two football fields across and up a small rise in the earth. The left and right limits of Range 17 were displayed by eight-foot-tall, orange, triangular range fans pointing towards the center. We told the Deployables that the locals weren't certain about their support for US forces; that enemy fighters had infiltrated their homes; that accidently killing a kid put all of us at greater risk. Good lessons within a counterinsurgency for getting the indigenous people to trust you. It was supposedly their country, right? The use of lethal force to defend them was as problematic and terrifying in Baghdad or Afghanistan as it could be in the streets of Chicago or Baltimore. A white Toyota pickup truck was on the BOLO list (Be on the Look Out for). A picture of Mahmoud Mahmoud circulated at the stations within the ECP. He was a threat that had to be detained upon contact here in the beautiful Indian summer of Wisconsin.

Once the platoon leader and platoon sergeant had sufficiently prepared their troopers with assignments and live ammunition, they marched up the trail. I always gave the Operation Order two days before to replace fictitious Americans units on the line. The platoon moved silently through the birch grove toward the culminating Range 17, white-barked sentries peeling its growth in the fall. The soldiers split into their initial assignments. We built the Program of Instruction so that soldiers would rotate through the several job assignments, manning the towers, the Quick Reaction Force, Entry Control Point and Aid and Litter. No soldier was ever injured by a live round at Range 17 by the grace of God and the professionalism of the cadre.

I had role players who would come through the Entry Control Point and have to be searched in order to "come to work" within the facility. They'd be local hires wearing too many clothes before the frost. Sometimes, I'd bring costumed women wearing the Hajib with a male elder to the lieutenant running the defense of the FOB so he could explain why his trooper had killed her child. The wailing would make the young officer quake. The act almost made me ashamed of myself, but he would remember. There is never a good answer as to why your soldier killed a kid. The point was written onto the soldiers' emotional core. We had to protect the people from the insurgents—not drive surviving sons to them. Just one of many teachable moments that sprouted from Big Daddy, Petraeus.

Trails between fighting positions continued to fill with crunchy brown leaves, rolling and flipping on soft breezes, rhythmically, like a very slow rain. The threat that the temperature would drop like a stone was real—flurries could mix with the terror we tried to create.

• • •

After the Golden Mosque was destroyed by Al Qaida's al-Zarqawi in February 2006, we painted the plywood onion dome of our "Mosque" bright yellow, amidst other plywood building fronts. It was smack dab in the middle of Range 17. NCIS-Baghdad still hadn't brought him down. We Bobcats did it to plant a kernel of awareness that Americans don't destroy places of worship. No pop-up targets were before it. It was sacrosanct. US soldiers would respect the cultural sensitivities of those we hoped to build back up after our own bombs had fallen. The Al'Askari Mosque built over a thousand years ago has been venerated by Shia Muslims since the tenth and eleventh Imams were entombed there. For them the destruction became a rallying cry. The effect propelled the civil strife that exists to this day to fever pitch. Al-Sadr built his Shia militias from the hate of the multitude. He blamed Israel and the United States for the bombing. Al Qaida had successfully spurred sectarian violence as death continued to meet fear; killing for the sake of killing just to prove the government couldn't protect the people, that it wasn't legitimate. The terrorists would cause chaos, then step into the void to rule. That was their plan.

Into the maelstrom of 2006-2007, General David Petraeus was assigned to make chicken shit into chicken soup; not a bowl but a swimming pool full. It seems strange to have affection towards one you've never met. America is deserving of him. And like another hero of mine this guy is spooky smart! Big Daddy taught US forces how to wage a counterinsurgency campaign in two separate countries. He coordinated the cooperation of many intergovernmental, host nation, and international agencies towards the rule of law. I hereby proclaim, upon the authority of no one in particular, that forevermore David Petraeus shall be known as Big Daddy. Big Daddy taught us that if the host government loses the support of the people, the war is lost, period.

The wars were going badly in 2006 in both Afghanistan and Iraq, when the President had his epiphany. Bush found Petraeus as Lincoln found Grant—bedraggled politicians and dogged fighters. Odds were stacking against the effort. Will was needed, imminent failure headlined—like the Union being chased back to Washington once again. The United States was about to lose the wars in Afghanistan and Iraq, the blood and treasure streaming into the void just like the old battlefields of Northern Virginia—killing others for perceived grievances. Visits to hospital rooms and graves gave both Lincoln and Bush pause and purpose. Years after he led the US from the precipice on two fronts, Petraeus tripped up by giving his privilege to his biographer. She was pretty, and the intelligence of troop distribution was old. A blemish proving his humanity.

Lieutenant General Petraeus, Lieutenant General James Amos, (US Marine Corps) and Lieutenant General Mattis oversaw the re-writing of the Army's Counter Insurgency Manual (COIN). And I lived it. The moment it was published by Barnes and Noble I had a copy and took a yellow highlighter to it. I ended up dedicating my military career to what this book taught me and hundreds of thousands of others.

In Afghanistan and Iraq, engineers built small and large infrastructure projects in conjunction with the host government to provide desperately needed services in the eyes of the people. Schools were built, police stations remodeled, and electrical transfer stations added to the grid. Artillerists traded in their gun tubes to help seal Iraq's porous borders with Force Protection techniques taught to their re-formed armies. Air Force Civil Affairs representatives were all over the map, providing condolence payments for injuries suffered and financial aid to media outlets. Once funding for agricultural projects were secured, federal employees from Virginia figured out what small planters needed, and bought and brought tools and seed. Marine veterinarians helped government workers provide programs for the care of livestock and cared for bomb-sniffing dogs. Navy nurses and doctors helped local medical programs with drugs and surgical supplies, while Military Police ran academies and tried to control the roads. The State Department sent Provisional Reconstruction teams to help build and teach budgeting and legal taxation processes. JAG lawyers from the Air National Guard assisted the fledgling courts. Massive amounts of money were pumped into Iraq from the American people to pick up the trash where IEDs could be lurking, and to ensure oil pipelines hummed with indigenous wealth. Infantry and Armor officers sought talented former senior soldiers from the Republican Guard to go to American military schools like the Army War College or the Sergeant Major's Academy at Fort Bliss, Texas. All this in order to stabilize the populace, address legitimate grievances, and take the wind out of insurgents' sails. It looks good on paper, briefs well, but is damn hard to achieve. Pitifully, all good work can be undone quickly; construction being hard, destruction being easy.

Since Saddam's socialist state controlled as much of the people's lives as possible, reordering society based upon process improvement rather than corruption was a mind-numbing endeavor. Working for the tyrant didn't encourage individual initiative within the government's bureaucracy. But the civil servants were educated and mostly willing, unless too wedded to the culturally acceptable level of graft.

The Field Manual, FM 3-24 Counterinsurgency, was in part employed along an unimproved, rolling, straight gravel byway we soldiers at Fort McCoy called "Burma Road." It was a testament to the British and Indian forces opposed to the Japanese in the Second Great War. We tested and taught lessons to keep soldiers from dying needlessly through discipline, intelligence, and an offensive spirit. If you were afraid to fire your weapon, this was the last chance you had to get over it before needing to do it for real. The Army needs soldiers who can think and act. In the northwest corner of Fort McCoy, at the end of the road, was Range 17.

• • •

Civilian role players during our counter insurgency training had badges and their names were checked against rosters as they were processed into the base by the Deployables. Men search men, and women search women, no exceptions. A soldier would have his/her rifle at the low ready observing the search, ready to lift the barrel toward the chest of the civilian. The role players' hands would be behind their heads, feet spread wide, with the soldier searching pulling them back to unbalance them, then patting and crushing pockets feeling for objects. They used the edge of the palm between the buttocks, called the "credit card swipe"; just business, nothing personal. Then, they'd pass through the Entry Control Point. Sometimes we'd plant a knife on a woman between her breasts. "Now what, Sergeant? What's the panic word?" "Baseball!" Vehicles were searched using mirrors beneath the undercarriage. Miss a bomb and the Bobcats would go nuts with grenade simulators and smoke grenades. Soldiers would be assessed with casualty cards. A mass casualty event meant four or more soldiers were hurt, known by the spine-shocking term, "Mass Cal." Vehicle Borne Improvised Explosive Devices (VBIEDs) were almost always planted in white Toyota pickups, unless it was a Dodge minivan with Wisconsin plates. The troopers identified and detained Mahmoud Mahmoud almost every time I sent him in. Holy hell rained down if they didn't.

The seven towers were each manned with two soldier crews. The Quick Reaction Force (QRF) practiced their drills, the Command Post established radio communications, the Aid Station prepared for casualties, the Entry Control Point was manned, the role players were waiting to attempt entry onto the Forward Operating Base (FOB), Bobcats covered all the Deployables, and a Department of the Army civilian checked the controls of the pop-up targets. Major Dupar as the Officer in Charge stood by. And a stable of deploying soldiers waited for their assignment to throw lead down range. The tasks were to identify your target, and save the lives of fellow soldiers if they're hurt. In essence, protect the Force.

God controls the universe, but McCoy is ruled by Range Control. Range Control was called by the Non-commissioned officer in charge, my battle buddy, Master Sergeant Thomas. Thomas requested a "wet" status. It was granted; live ammunition could now be fired downrange. A Bobcat drew a long tailing red banner up a pole by the Range 17 sign next to Burma Road, and it snapped in the October winds. The Range was now "hot." The temperature stayed at 43 degrees Fahrenheit, then dropped like a stone before the sleet to come that night. The soldiers felt cold, scared.

A plywood vehicle charged Tower One to test the soldiers' application of Escalation of Force (EOF) procedures. Now, imagine you're an Iraqi driving home when you see a US Army roadblock up ahead. From a thousand meters away, you see strobes flashing warnings, but you drive forward, toward the Americans. Horns sound, lasers point at your windshield, yet you continue, accelerating. Warning shots fire into the road ahead of you and you stop. Good thing to do, before their machine guns disable your white Toyota pickup truck and cut you to pieces. You turn around, thankful the American soldiers had their training at Range 17. It's always best not to test young Americans when they're halfway around the world and plenty scared themselves.

But in training, the kids manning the triggers were shocked by the plywood threat and sometimes fired at the "person" driving anyway, skipping most of the Escalation of Force procedures. Now trained to expect imminent explosions from vehicle bombs, their rifles loaded with live rounds, they didn't execute the proper visual or auditory warnings. The air horns we provided went unused, warning shots weren't fired, and the young soldiers shot at the target as it rapidly approached their position. The Deployables practiced what might come a month later in Iraq or Afghanistan. We reset the target and would try it again an unexpected time later. The second time they'd usually do better with life and death decisions. Heady stuff for those in high school just a few years before.

A mission got handed down to the Deployables' command post. An American Humvee convoy in trouble was just outside the gate (downrange), only 75 meters in front of Tower Seven, with "wounded" soldier mannequins filled with sand. The Lieutenant ordered the rescue, and the QRF (Quick Reaction Force) launched in only a matter of moments. They were overwound like an ancient timepiece, and unsure it'd work. Towers One through Four lifted their fire to the secondary sectors to the left, still engaging targets with live rounds. Soldiers in Towers Five through Seven took their hands from their weapons, Bobcats radioed confirmation, artillery simulators screamed on all sides "WHIZZ BANG Whistle Whistle BANG!" The Bobcat Cadre jogged beside the QRF vehicles as they drove out to render first aid to sandbag soldiers, "bleeding out" in front of the base.

Lifting the dead weight of the sand-filled mannequins provided the realism of an unresponsive comrade. Hand grenade simulators exploded, purple and green smoke canisters sent a pall surrounding the downed vehicles. Soldiers in Towers One through Four covered the rescue and continued to shoot live rounds at silhouettes. A member of the QRF was assessed as a casualty, hit in the chest with imagined shrapnel. Assessed casualties were encouraged to scream. If the Deployable reacted too slowly, another comrade might be told to lie down, a wound to her arm. The security elements of the Quick Reaction Force fired live rounds at targets from behind their Humvees. The patrol leader sent messages back to the command post. "Get the casualties back inside the wire," was the response. "BOOM BOOM BOOM," more artillery simulators whistled and exploded. "GET BACK GET BACK! GET THE WOUNDED! RENDER FIRST AID!" The Bobcats ensured all weapons were cleared and would jog behind the soldiers' Humvees as they drove slowly back inside the wire, a simple drop gate controlling the movement.

The leader radioed the command post and the order was given to re-enter the FOB (Forward Operating Base). Then the First Aid team descended, evaluating the wounded and giving IV sticks to the bleeding. The gate closed. All towers shifted back to their primary sectors of fire. We'd do in again in an hour or two. Mass adrenaline flowed, not dripped, at the northernmost point of Fort McCoy. Range 17's record for the number of successful IV sticks in one day was thirty-seven. Wrap the rubber tube tourniquet around the upper arm, find the vein, stick the needle in. Or not. Try again and again; lives of your compatriots are on the line. Quickly, quickly or soon they would "die." All-in training before the Deployables went to Southwest Asia in three weeks.

Gray clouds billowed, gathering ice. When the unit's roster had rotated through the towers at least once, the Master Sergeant eventually called Range Control for a "dry time" and it was over. As trainers it was sacrosanct that the Deployables got hot chow twice a day. We'd place them retrograde onto Burma Road before the storm. But while the training was still fresh, it was time to review the day's events in the classroom, where the Officer in Charge teased out strengths and areas to improve. After 200 such AARs I stopped counting. It was an art to have soldiers not be defensive while finding ways to get better.

Before the Bobcat Master Sergeant released the unit, he'd have the soldiers shake themselves down to find any live rounds which might have accidently found a pocket. You always checked at the conclusion of a live fire exercise, as you wouldn't want a young'n to trip and shoot another soldier in the chest.

Ain't that right, Big Daddy? Get down and give us fifty just to prove that you're OK.

• • •

A bubble gum bubble with a hair on it doesn't look like testicles. The Bobcats had run Range 17 for almost two years. I came down from the control tower one Friday afternoon to see three sergeants relaxing by the ambulance. Staff Sergeant Lyon had his "turtle" outside his buttoned fly. His majesty not displayed. I made eye contact with him, asking what his plans were for the weekend. I made no indication that his nuts were hanging outside of his pants. The other two Bobcats grinned liked Cheshire cats. They were clearly enjoying the prank.

A week later I had my revenge. Our outfit had mandatory classes back in cantonment (post buildings and infrastructure—not the wide-ranging Training Areas), which included a brief on sexual harassment. Staff Sergeant Lyon sat beside me. At the end, I asked the poor sergeant giving the class if it was wrong to show another soldier your turtle? The crowd erupted, everyone knowing what had happened before. The instructor was confused, taken aback. Lyon interjected, declaring that it wasn't his turtle but a bubble gum bubble with a hair on it. I replied that even if it wasn't, he should get it checked out because one of those freckles didn't look right. The class was in pandemonium and concluded without resolving the question.

Staff Sergeant Lyon was a menace to decent society. His field craft was excellent, and he needed to be overseas on a permanent basis. When back in the States between deployments, he trained troops, and exposed his balls to his Officer in Charge. I didn't mind, though. The bastard was worthy of his hire. This Bobcat was the one you'd want beside you when things went south. He'd be the one who'd win the fight, and drag your ass back inside the wire. He was in charge of training the Quick Reaction Force. Where the battle waged hottest was where he was at his best. Perverted, smart, rough like wiping your ass with an old corn cob, Staff Sergeant Lyon was a man worthy of mention. But take it from me, it's probably wise not to go out drinking with him.

CHAPTER 18

# Allah Akbar

M y driver and I we were reconnoitering routes for engineers
to practice; finding good places to bury mock Improvised
IEDs out of sheet metal pieces, when the message came over the
radio: "FLASH FLASH FLASH! STOP ALL TRAFFIC! ALL STA-
TIONS TO MAINTAIN IMMEDIATE RADIO SILENCE. FLASH
FLASH FLASH THIS IS RANGE CONTROL. STOP ALL VEHIC-
ULAR TRAFFIC. ALL STATIONS TO MAINTAIN IMMEDIATE
RADIO SLIENCE. FLASH FLASH FLASH."

The front gate shut down. All training on Fort McCoy, which
included 10,000 Deployables, couldn't move or communicate on
the primary radio network. Range Control shut down the post.
Everyone was to desist whatever they were doing. ALL STOP.
Someone must have been seriously hurt. I had only heard that
message once before, and a shiver ran down my spine, shimmering along with the brown leaves falling in late fall breezes.

The year before I'd heard the FLASH FLASH FLASH message from Range Control as a hot brass expended cartridge from
one soldier's rifle somehow flipped between the body armor
and tee shirt of his battle buddy. Reflexively, he fired a shot
into the belly of his compatriot. They were in a defensive tower

during a live fire exercise like the one the Bobcats ran. No cadre was standing behind them in the tower when it happened. That was a change implemented at Range 17. At the end of Burma Road, the Bobcats adjusted our techniques after the fact. The wounded soldier survived the shot.

"FLASH FLASH FLASH!" from the radio. "STOP ALL TRAFFIC! ALL STATIONS TO MAINTAIN IMMEDIATE RADIO SILENCE. FLASH FLASH FLASH. THIS IS RANGE CONTROL. STOP ALL VEHICULAR TRAFFIC. ALL STATIONS TO MAINTAIN IMMEDIATE RADIO SLIENCE AND MONITOR THIS FREQUENCY. ALL UNITS TO CONDUCT 100 PERCENT PERSONNEL AND SENSITIVE ITEM ACCOUNTABILITY. FLASH FLASH FLASH!"

All cadre and training units were again ordered by Range Control to stop and report that the First Sergeant and Commander knew where every swinging Richard and Jane were, along with all issued weapons, protective masks, encryption devices, radios, etc. This was going to take a couple of hours. My battalion's Motorola network quickly established cadre whereabouts. If you reported that you were "green," it meant that you were "good to go" in Army speak; you had accounted for your folks and all of their "sensitive items." Something bad had happened. Was a weapon or radio missing? We'd soon find out.

The two of us continued to wait in a hidden spot for further instructions from Range Control. Upon a knoll, attempting to find good ambush points to further train our sisters and brothers soon to go downrange, we had parked within a small clearing between the red sumac and both living and dying pines. The 55-degree sunshine felt marvelous that early November afternoon. My flip phone had rudimentary access to the Internet. I opened our cooler and asked the young man with me if he wanted a cold bottle of water. He did. It was silent except for the surging wind that rustled through the dry, calf-high grass, soon to plop over, blanketing the earth before the first few snowflakes fell. Gun-hunting deer season was rapidly approaching and it was fun to look for deer trails or where they bedded down upon mattresses of pine needles. On opening morning, intrepid hunters had already found their shooting lanes, and the crack of gun fire sent the scared does, bucks, and yearlings out of their usual routes, running confused, trying to hide. The CRACK CRACK CRACK of sporadic gun fire spread all around, just as the sun broke the horizon. Some deer stayed low; most ran madly, their routine abandoned, bellowing for their family, like a soldier screaming for a medic when someone got hit and pleading for first aid. But there were no medics for the deer, just a date to become yummy venison sausage sometime before Christmas.

I was peeing on a pine cone when I read on my phone screen: Massacre at Fort Hood, Texas. It was Blue on Blue. In the Army, colors mean things. When drawing forces on map overlays, blue is United States forces, red is enemy (for example, Soviet, a past threat), and green are allies (like Iraqi or Afghani forces – reference the "Green Zone" in Baghdad). Green on blue killing means that our sister troops have murdered their trainers, Americans. Blue on blue means treachery unveiled. A murderer was in our midst. Red versus Blue is what we train for, what we would expect.

One thousand miles due south from this lush hilltop where I spied for hiding spots was another Army Major screaming, "Allah Akbar," "God is great," while expending judgment on those in administrative lines. We found out later that he knew the routine of the Deployables, having worked as a psychologist at the Fort Hood Mobilization Station, ostensibly to help soldiers with their post-traumatic stress problems after they served overseas. Major Nidal Hasan knew their routes, where they might hide; where the few Fort Hood police were usually stationed. He waded among brothers and sisters and ignored their bleats for help as they gurgled in their own blood. The Major was about to deploy himself to Afghanistan in just a couple of weeks, but decided to destroy his own countrywomen and men instead. He corresponded with the firebrand Yemini cleric Anwar al-Awlaki, afraid of going to hell, and wanting to impose Sharia law. Hasan murdered for the Taliban, as he believed his religion demanded him to.

At Ft. McCoy, when it was established that the attack was at our sister post in Texas, Range Control released its headlock. It was time for evening chow. Everyone digested that our comrades were massacred by a fellow soldier. How could it be?

In 2003, when soldiers had rotten teeth, the Army paid for implants. That'd be about $1,000 a tooth for implants. You can't go to war without passing Dental. And that is just one station that could prevent you from going overseas. It didn't take long for the Army to figure out that it would be wiser for soldiers coming to Mobilization Stations like Fort Hood or Fort McCoy to be sent home before spending thousands to "fix" their medical issues. It's a common trip wire before National Guard or Army Reserve soldiers go downrange with their units. Some soldiers even arrive at mobilization stations with heart conditions, fretting. Some, like me, become suspect. I barely avoided being ignominiously sent home myself. Tremendous pressure was and is placed upon commands today that their soldiers be medically deployable. If soldiers end up not deploying with their units, other soldiers have to be found to replace them in their job. If not, the unit suffers. Not being medically ready to deploy affects everybody.

Optical is easy. The Army just gives you indestructible glasses. Brown frames, thick plastic, with quadruple barrel hinges. Guys called theirs "birth control glasses." Females' glasses were known as "rape proof glasses." Let's just say that the frames are not flattering. Bottom line is that no soldier should be subjected to unwanted advances by a comrade at a bar off post. The Army can fix your vision for cheap. Betrayal is different. We can hardly stop treachery, sexual or otherwise.

Soldiers married to another service member must have a Family Care Plan to provide for their kids, just in case both their units were called at the same time. Who would take care of their dependents? More commonly, a single Deployable who had sole custody of kids or elderly parents had to have a plan. Without a Family Care Plan in place before mobilization, you'd be forced to craft one under supervision, under the gun, with tremendous pressure and time constraints.

Finance is another station. You'd fill out paperwork declaring you were going to a combat zone and were therefore entitled to both a family separation allowance and combat pay—another $400 a month, or so. You'd be encouraged strongly to have a will in place, and make provisions for those left at home. A Power of Attorney was a powerful tool that could leave a soldier away from home penniless by the unscrupulous. Family members sometimes helped themselves to a private's paycheck, being legally able to sell property, open accounts, and even borrow money in the name of the soldier downrange.

Most of this pre-deployment activity was confined to square blocks, to ease soldiers' ability to walk to various appointments. Barracks by the dozens surrounded administrative buildings. This was where the pickings were best; where our dears bedded down—a target rich environment for a coward.

Many stations are required to "check the box" for each soldier. Audiology, Legal, mandatory classes like the Law of War and The Code of Conduct must be completed before the all-expenses paid year-long vacation to "Yourcrackistan." [I apologize sincerely to the Yourcrackistani people if they take offense here. They really are wonderful folks. They, like all folks, just want to live peaceably, provide for their family, work using their minds and hands as given the opportunity and talent, to pray as they wish, and not be terrorized with violence by someone next door].

A firearm is issued to American soldiers. It isn't theirs. Every soldier is required to qualify on an assigned weapon. That doesn't mean that you take an M16 rifle everywhere you go while at the MOB (mobilization) station. That's just an avoidable opportunity for a weapon to get left at the mess hall or on a bus. It is far better to have the government's firearms locked in a weapons rack, in a vault, or guarded 24/7. If you sign for it, you are accountable for it.

There is no such thing as an accidental discharge of a weapon. Pretend you had to walk around all day with a loaded weapon. Would that be dangerous? People are dumb, even the smart ones. We forget what we are doing. The issuance of live ammunition in the Military is strictly enforced for obvious reasons—safety. An errant firearm discharge in the Army is always negligent. Soldiers do not receive live ammunition until they are downrange, such as southwest Asia.

When you're in Iraq entering into a Dining Facility, there are clearing barrels placed by the doors. These are 55-gallon oil drums filled with sand, topped with plywood and plastic sleeves so you can place the barrel of your rifle into it and commence clearing procedures: placing the weapon on "safe," dropping the magazine, locking the bolt back to the rear, looking into the aperture to ensure there isn't a round in the chamber, placing the weapon on "fire," then pulling the trigger. If you didn't just stupidly send a round into the barrel, then you'd continue

228 | SCOUNDRELS IN IRAQ

to clear the weapon, slide the bolt forward, wash your hands, and get some fine Army chow. In the USA, no soldier has live rounds unless on a range. It is illegal to transport military weapons in civilian vehicles. It is illegal to transport privately owned weapons onto a military facility in the trunk of your car. It is illegal to murder fellow soldiers. The Major knew how to get guns and ammo onto the killing field.

"POW POW POW!" Heads exploded like rotten pumpkins at Halloween. Major Hasan walked behind the reception desk, where our family congregated, and began to shoot, not at civilians, but only at uniformed folks.

"POW POW POW!" His handgun's magazine emptied rapidly, targeting noses, emptying minds from skull cases like red softballs hitting walls. Dozens of soldiers sat facing the front of the room waiting for their names to be called. The individuals became targets now. Point, aim, breathe, squeeze the trigger; backs and chests gaped with vicious looking holes. The Major called them namelessly into an extreme pain they never knew before. Lungs deflated, sending blood into throats. Brain matter splattered and bodies scattered. Sometimes the red dot of a laser pointed toward the foreheads of civilians, but they weren't the Major's target. Unarmed soldiers yelled and screamed and maneuvered between carcasses pumping blood from veins. Seconds changed lives forever. His god not nearly satisfied, the Major waded into the midst of them, wanting not to die before completing the work. He had decided whom he would serve. One soldier rushed him with a chair and paid for the effort, silenced. The shock was severe; the blood everywhere. Moments etched into memories forever, before the sirens howled. Amidst the downed, scores rushed forward to help.

It was a cop from the Fort Hood Police Department who fired the defending shots, and the bastard was paralyzed, the apostate Major. But not to hear him tell it: While he had counsel and hot food each day, preparing his defense for his actions, we were told that we are the apostates. He grew a beard, flouting Army rules. The coward didn't go overseas, as was intended. The Deployables were worthy to die in cold blood before going to war against his people. But he wore our uniform, counseled our kinsmen, and cashed his paycheck in a Texas bank. Were we not his people?

The US Justice Department decided his crimes were merely workplace violence; not terrorism. The equal application of our laws and protection of our people were abandoned. It was decided that what it appeared to be, could not be, shown to be. The Deployables became deplorables after all; sacrifice ignored by political meandering between graves across our country.

. . .

We were able to move after about an hour and a half. The young soldier with me, who'd already had two deployments to Afghanistan, got back to cantonment because the next day was another day to train. The lonesome Cavalry trumpet wail signaled at 1700 across the post that it was time to get the horses to their paddocks. They eat before you do, always. He brushed the horse (Humvee) and after removing its tack, made sure the vehicle was topped off, and placed in the paddock with water and hay. The nose of the Humvee aligned military straight with the others, chock blocked against a tire, with an oil pan beneath the engine block. I did officer things, like check emails. Fort McCoy buzzed with the heinous news.

Scott & White Memorial Hospital in nearby Temple, Texas sent their ambulances. First responders reported to take the wounded from home ground, which was now considered a field of war. They picked up the dead from tile floors sopped with their compatriot's blood. Reporters for the next few days wrote community pieces about the families now ripped apart. Everybody wanted to know if their soldier was OK. Thirty-nine were injured for life. The butcher's bill tallied thirteen murdered.

He is in prison. Is man's law failing? I appeal for divine judgment to reckon the account. How he maneuvered isn't important. I won't describe it more. Which soldiers rendered direct pressure with their hands over pulsing gunshot wounds, and who covered a stranger's bodies with their own is personal to those that survived. Bits of bodies and grey matter were shoveled into leaf bags by the gloved handful. The streets around the building were marked off with yellow tape before the Fire Department washed blood into sewers. Mops full of treasure were squeezed.

These crossed the river that day at Fort Hood, Texas on 05NOV09:

Michael Grant Cahill, 62, of Cameron, TX.

Major L. Eduardo Caraveo, 52, of Woodbridge, Va.

Staff Sergeant. Justin M. DeCrow, 32, of Plymouth, Ind.

Captain John P. Gaffaney, 54, of San Diego, Calif.

Specialist Frederick Greene, 29, of Mountain City, Tenn.

Specialist Jason Dean Hunt, 22, of Tillman, Okla.

Sergeant Amy Krueger, 29, of Kiel, Wis.

Private First Class Aaron Thomas Nemelka, 19, of West Jordan, Utah

Private First Class Michael Pearson, 22, of Bolingbrook, Ill.

Captain Russell Seager, 41, of Racine, Wis.

Private Francheska Velez, 21, of Chicago. She was pregnant.

Lieutenant Colonel Juanita Warman, 55, of Havre de Grace, Maryland.

Specialist Kham Xiong, 23, of St. Paul, Minn.

These thirteen cannot speak past the waters or we to them. They rest beneath a canopy of the congregated. Evergreens sway upon soft blowing breezes, stirring through limbs in a gentle push and pull. Our departed rest in a place prepared, among beds of soft pine needles. Made to lay down beneath a staff, until after a time, times, and a half a time.

• • •

The General shouted out orders to imagined officers to bring up artillery against the Federals. His amputation was mortal, shot down by his own pickets before the victory; he had maneuvered his Corps brilliantly at Chancellorsville, Virginia 1863, in darkness. In a fever, upon a stretcher, Jackson pitched between battle and convulsive imagined conversations with his family and staff. His wife Beatrice hurried to his side in the early afternoon of his injury, as their home was close to his last battlefield, keeping vigil for the days to follow. She spoke soothingly, mopped his forehead, held his remaining hand and cleansed his body as it released its bowels. His fighting spirit tried to disobey death.

They had cleaved in life unto each other like two halves of dough. They were miserable apart, in miscarriage and in war. They wrote letters in hopeful postage before breaking bread again, yeasting into a single mass, almost joined unto a sovereign spirit.

When Robert Lee was told that Stonewall had fallen he lamented, "He has lost his left arm but I have lost my right!" The Confederate Commander had his ablest general cut from him.

At the small stone house where her husband lay writhing in pain, a soon-to-be widow tried to comfort an impossible Commander.

In a fit of clarity, he asked the doctor if he was dying, and was told, "General, you will not live the day."

"That's good. That's good. I always wanted to die on a Sunday," he replied.

When offered morphine Thomas Jackson declined, and said, "No, I'd rather have my mind clear." I think he didn't want to meet his Creator compromised.

Against echoing screams of wounded in his mind, a battle just won, another lost, his respirations became irregular, and then Jackson succumbed and said calmly to his love, "Bea, let us cross over the river, and rest in the shade of the trees." And was gone.

His wife remained to bury and persevere.

# CHAPTER 19

# The Call

Taps played only a block away from a loudspeaker, the sad and lonely bugle calling that the day was done. The boom of guns echoed in my quarters some evenings, as units conducted night live fire with their weapons. Usually I could hear the motherly PUP PUP PUP PUP of the Ma Duece, the M2 Browning air-cooled 50 caliber machine gun. It sounded like Auntie Sugar's heartbeat. Feeling safe and secure, I'd drift off to a wonderful sleep. You can't improve upon perfection.

Units of Deployables mobilized for years through Fort McCoy, at a peak of about 15,000 a year; the same number demobilizing. I was asked by surprised returning officers why I was still there, only training troops. Not doing my duty enough, I guess. This guilt weighed upon my neck like a millstone about to be tossed into the sea. I was fat, dumb, and happy that far away from war, and two-and-a-half hours down the highway from my girls. I just prepared young Americans for the abyss of war those years, not sacrificing much at all. The weight of duty to family, community, and nation eventually took second place to self. However, I did keep up the yard work, painted everything visible, and paid the bills. Exactly when I became a slacker, I cannot say.

I called my tribe, The US Army Corp of Engineers, and said, "Hey, you, this is me." That's all it took. I volunteered to become a Deployable. It had been over five years since I'd been down-range. This time I was coming out of the bullpen, the Sand Man. Ellen understood, or allowed. The Army was the best thing we had going between us. We didn't resist the calling.

Within four weeks I'd be a passenger nosediving in a C-130 Hercules transport plane making combat rolls to avoid possible ground-to-air missiles with REM's song "Orange Crush" playing in my head phones. The lyrics were quite fitting.

"Follow me, don't follow me,

I've got my spine I got my Orange Crush."

My daughter, now nine, had no vote as to whether she'd miss me for a year.

I had orders forthwith from the quasi-military organization, USACE (United States Army Corps of Engineers). "Place me on the roulette wheel," I thought. And they did. It was time to go back to war, to theater, to wherever. Iraq or Afghanistan, I didn't care which. I had to get my "street cred" back. One deployment wasn't enough. The mistakes I'd made were a bad taste in my mouth and in my heart. I hoped to avoid quasi-criminal undertakings this time. Soldiers were racking up multiple deployments and I had to keep up. Back in the States, active duty soldiers referred to it as dwell time. A year downrange, a year with a spouse and kids, then back downrange, repeat. I'd had too much dwell time personally. The force shuddered under the constant strain. Like a magnet, the booming of the guns drew me. Enemy videos showing IEDs ripping apart Humvees and those within them reminded me that we could still lose this war.

"Collar me, don't Collar me,"

I've got my spine; I got my Orange Crush."

I was fat when I got to Fort Benning, Georgia. In uniform I felt like a stuffed sausage. The six-day drill to get on the airplane overseas was a pain in the ass. Nobody wants the top bunk in case you have to pee at night. The wall locker was jammed with four duffle bags of gear you'll hopefully never use, like your chemical protective suit or your artic undies. I wasn't part of a unit; now I was an "individual augmentee." Soldiers filling holes in personnel organizational billets.

"I love you." I said at the phone bank. "We love you, too." I heard times two. Had I judged too hard too late? I was confused, but the die was cast. In another life perhaps, I'd be a better dad. You never get another chance.

You had to check the blocks in only six days when you became an individual augmentee. The process was abbreviated, thank God. Not that I have anything against Georgia, but what I wanted was to down a last few brews at Fort Benning, then catch a cramped flight to Kuwait. I was informed that my one personal bag couldn't be transported because it had wheels. Fatigue leads to submission quickly, and my new luggage was thrown into a dumpster.

Most soldiers were going to Afghanistan, but I was traveling to Baghdad, to USACE headquarters in Iraq, and then to Tikrit (Saddam Hussein's home town). I was quite pleased at that. Back in the world's biggest ashtray, a transient could grab a shower at the new Camp Wolf. It was just a prairie town when I knew it at the start of the war, but had evolved into a complex that hundreds of soldiers passed through every day. The chow was superb, with four meal times served for free in the desert, like a Denny's on steroids. Salad bar, made to order omelets, and clean as a whistle with Americans cooking and Pakistanis busing tables. Sleep is always the most precious commodity when traveling great distances. Getting to where you're ordered to go takes persistence and acquiescence to Army timetables.

You never wear head gear on the flight line. Your duffle bags are strapped onto Air Force aluminum pallets (the reason for the wheeled luggage prohibition). Yellow stripes mark your path as you walk into the belly of the C-130 from the tail end, after listening and waiting for hours, if not days, for your flight to be called or cancelled. The four ginormous props spin. In an orderly fashion, quickly, quickly, find a seat along the fuselage. This isn't a passenger plane, but it's free. Most prefer the bank of seats along the exterior of the fuselage facing towards the middle rather than the two middle banks of seats that face outwards. Strap in over your shoulders.

"We are agents of the free,
Single soldier augmentees.
I've had my fun and now it's time.
To take my place up on the line."

Now it's time for the big trick. All soldiers remain silent except for the few airmen communicating among their crewmates. There are no in-flight announcements. You're expected to know what to do. And you gotta' be cool. It's a cool contest before your compatriots. You have to have your earphones and shades, pretending not to notice leaving the ground, pretending to be asleep, pretending to not be nervous. Like nothing can rattle your cage, augmentee.

In only an hour-and-a-half from Kuwait, the pilot began his descent, which mirrored more of an assault. Called a combat landing, the pilots take evasive maneuvers as if dodging incoming missiles (which were rarely ever launched, but we practiced nonetheless.) Steep banks and wicked turns ensued and I played REM. It was like a roller coaster without the loop-de-loops.

"To serve our conscience overseas,

Over me, not over me.

Coming in fast, over me."

The C-130 dropped precipitously, sending out flares, as if to throw off heat-seeking missiles. I've got my Orange Crush, cool, Papa, cool. The pilots were just training, having fun, giving us a ride! Five minutes after the bottom dropped out, the cargo plane was parked, the ass end lowered, and we purposely left the aircraft. We pretended not to awaken to our new reality, Baghdad International Airport (BIAP). I almost didn't recognize the place, except for the 95-degree heat at 2300 hours. It took almost two hours for a driver to find me and take me five minutes to the Engineer HQ, where I got a dorm room and clean sheets, as the quiet set in. With the AC humming low, I slept well, thinking of calling home the next day. I guess it wasn't that important. I was exhausted. Ellen must know by now that the Army would take care of me.

The US Army Corps of Engineers had a wide range of projects in Iraq. Many were funded by the Iraqi Government, or at least, in part. The US taxpayers built waste water treatment plants, roads, schools, surgery centers, libraries, maintenance shops for the Iraqi Army, hangers for the Iraqi Air Force, prisons and police stations, government training centers, etc. Good job, America!

I was back in Iraq to conduct contract administration, to build stuff, nothin' but fun. It was a matter of professional pride. I was damn near a criminal my first trip downrange. This time I was determined to play it straight.

Don't give Beanie Babies to Iraqi Children

Major Dupar

Range Day

The Office Jewel

THE HUSKY (TOP), BUFFALO (MIDDLE),
TALON (BOTTOM)

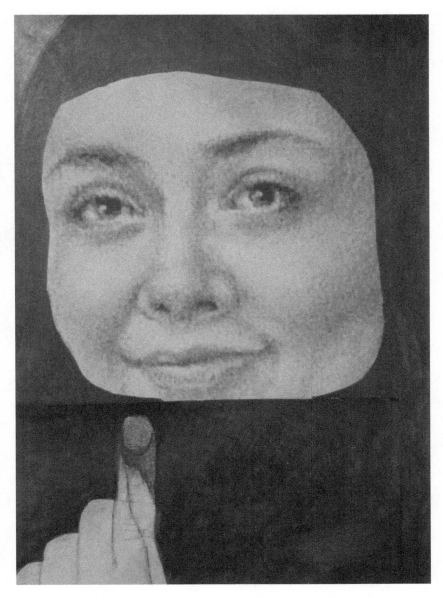

The Woman with the Purple Finger" by Hank Molina

# PART THREE

# Retrograde Movement
# TIKRIT 2010-11

CHAPTER 20

# The Office Jewel

"I'm Shaun. We'll be taking you to Speicher today, yeah?" The former British soldier shook my hand, his smile beamed past the tiny microphone besides his lips. "It's close by, only a hundred and twenty-five miles or so. Probably get there in two-and-a-half, three hours." He helped throw my duffle bags into the back of a big up-armored Land Rover. "Ever been there before, Major Dupar?" He didn't pause enough for even a stammered response. "It's absolutely fucking splendid. OK. Buckle up and we're out, right? Make sure you get the shoulder harness strapped tight in case of a rollover."

Four vehicles made up the convoy. I was the only passenger, which felt weird, like I was the Queen of England being conveyed between her possessions in the Middle East in the 1950's. This tactical movement was conducted by a private security firm the Corps of Engineers contracted with to take our folks anywhere in Iraq we needed to go. The fellas were paid well. The least paid gunner could expect almost $180,000 for a year tour. But you had to be willing to die or get seriously hurt in Iraq. Many stayed on for years, and they had their "shit wired tight." Money was no object for us Americans and the contract was supposedly over $100 million a year to transport the Corps throughout the country. Yeah, the US Army Corps of Engineers was everywhere in Iraq via British Convoys.

Ten former UK soldiers bristling with automatic weapons treated this movement in every way as a tactical convoy. Shaun took the passenger's seat in the second vehicle. He was the commander. "So, Major Dupar." He turned around in his seat to look at me, "I want to orient you to our vehicle and discuss emergency procedures quickly, yeah?" He kept leaving his sentences with a question but wanted no answer, which was good since I had none. It was kind of like the pre-flight safety briefing you get from an airline attendant. But instead of ignoring the instructions in case of a water landing, I listened to Shaun as he explained gently that if we were attacked, and everyone else was unable to place an emergency call for help, that the secondary radio he pointed to was always set to the correct frequency. "All you'd have to do is talk." Barring an IED or a rocket-propelled grenade attack, it was time to sit back and relax.

I thought I could hear an attendant's voice over an intercom, "Thank you for traveling British Convoys. We will be leaving Baghdad International Airport shortly. Please have your ammunition at the ready as we are about to leave the wire." Those Brit boys drove like proverbial bats out of hell. Traffic cops can kiss your ass when we have turret gunners that can pop up out of their hatches with 7.62 millimeter standard machine guns at the ready. But clogged roads were the norm—the population of Baghdad alone was seven million. They even had a modified rear vehicle hatch to engage any threats from the six o'clock position (the direction of travel of a military movement is always to twelve o'clock). I wouldn't see the engineer headquarters again for six months until I traveled back through Baghdad homeward to Disney World during my mid-tour leave.

Baghdad International Airport had changed some in the six years since I'd been there, but it wasn't like I could ask Dad to take out the car to have a look around my old stomping grounds. Too much was familiar anyway, like the oppressive July heat, dust-covered vegetation, and young soldiers cruising to objectives outside "the wire." I recognized the large pyramid-shaped ammo bunkers (like the one that stored the former President of Iraq, Saddam Hussein Al-Tikriti), the palaces, the same air traffic control tower. Then out onto the raceway, out of Entry Convoy Point One, out onto Route Senators and past the interchange that would take you to the Russian Embassy or Baghdad Island. We proceeded to the Forward Operating Base now named after fallen United States Navy pilot, Captain Michael Scott Speicher, the first American killed in action in 1991 during the Persian Gulf War. Operation Enduring Freedom reached back to Desert Storm in homage to a warrior.

The airbase was home of the Iraqi Air Force, just west of the city of Tikrit, on the edge of a vast desert wasteland. The US Air Force blew up the planes, hangers, and support buildings in 2003. Only infrastructure required for use by US Forces were repaired. Razing worthless structures took time and money; they were usually were left to rot and remind. The Corps was building a seven-story state-of-the-art air traffic control tower beside the two 10,000-foot runways in 2010. I was assigned as the Officer in Charge of the Speicher USACE office. And this tower was the office jewel. All the team had to do was make it fully operational now that the concrete skeleton was completed. We had a year to complete the handover.

The compound the Corp had built since 2003 would seem like Shangri-La to an average soldier if allowed entry by our hired security. The US Army Corps of Engineers doesn't do things the way any other Army organization does. Within the

USACE compound was a huge gazebo for parties and two small sections of perfectly groomed Bermuda lawn with a baby palm tree in the middle. Our digs were the envy of all who passed by our Ghurka guards, the most feared mercenaries in the world.

From the Himalayas, the Ghurka tribe's most lucrative occupation for many generations past was soldiering for the British. When the Brits took back the Falkland Islands from Argentina's invasion in the early 1980's, they let loose the Ghurkas at night with their long knives and black fatigues. The Argentinian infantry absented themselves from their positions forthwith as the rumor of their impending silent doom spread. Once a Ghurka's blade was drawn from its scabbard it could not be returned until it drew blood. For the Ghurka warrior, if it meant his own, then the shame was his. The war-factory wage passed unto tiny villages high above the clouds. These slight men were always on post at the entry to our Speicher compound, desperately bored by western standards, with a language foreign to all but them. No one ever attempted to enter our compound ringed with ten-foot-high Texas barriers and a self-sustaining electrical grid; they would breathe their last if they tried to bypass our Ghurkas. They treated me like I was the Queen of England and gave me a brass representation of Nepal when I left. Theirs was no small service for a man from Milwaukee. It looked cool on my desk, but it has been lost to many, many displacements.

Luckily, I had adult supervision at Speicher, as my boss was co-located with me. The Northern Area Office was led by Ben Watson, Lieutenant Colonel extraordinaire. The Corps divided Iraq into three zones of responsibility, North, Central, and South. Ben had the North, which included Tikrit, Mosul, Balad, and Kirkuk all the way up to the Iranian and Turkish borders. His daughter had muscular dystrophy and was his center of gravity, half a world away, with his wife nursing the child turned young woman. He was firm in leadership, mournful not be at home helping. He was a be-spectacled, white- haired, former Marine, heart-of-gold type guy. He hated any sort of violence and couldn't even watch American football, as it upset him so. Ben chewed tea leaves and released printed email correspondence from his hands to his office floor, like leaves from trees, his photographic memory making a filing system of its own. His mind leapt ahead in earnest, despite initial observations that he was a slob. The Hindu workers knew better than to sweep his office. Ben knew everybody, and like a politician, he kept everybody close. I don't remember our initial interview except to say it was like slipping on an old soft shoe that had been re-soled many times. He called everyone either "Sir" or "Ma'am," and laughed at his own folly when it occurred.

Rush, rush, rush. Everything in the Army is done as quickly as possible and then you sit idle indefinitely. My predecessor introduced herself the moment the Land Rover door opened. Boy was Major Tamarra Artois happy to see me! Another soldier, Master Sergeant Gibbons just said, "Hi." She was a dear, quiet, another experienced solder.

"Let me take you to your CHU (Containerized Housing Unit)," said the Major, grabbing one of my duffle bags. I struggled to keep up. "Boy, am I glad to see you. I leave in just a few days."

"Where to?"

"North Carolina, back to Bragg." Tamara was an Ordinance Officer in an Engineer Officer's billet (job position). She was a no-nonsense Active Army Officer who looked upon me as Moses coming to free this Hebrew slave from the oppression of Pharaoh. After a year I would feel the same way towards my imagined replacement. No, make that after a month. I mean a week.

Into the luxury of the Engineer utopia I was ushered to my room. "Your office is right there," she winked. "I'll be in there packing my stuff. We should go on a tour of Speicher when you're settled. 20 minutes OK?"

"Are we going to go see projects, Tamara?"

She looked at me oddly as MSG Gibbons handed me my key on the porch beside my bungalow.

"Oh sure." She looked at her fellow soldier. "We can do that. But wait. Are you hungry? Chow's about to close for lunch. We should hurry." Everything in the Army is in a hurry, and then you wait, as I've said.

The bungalow CHU (Containerized Housing Unit) had a queen-sized bed, refrigerator, private bath, cable TV, rug, dresser, etc. The phone on the night stand had a Virginia area code associated with it. I could call the States whenever I wanted to, free.

India was once referred to as the Jewel of the British Crown. It was queer to learn that Indian contractors were present to clean our offices, rooms, and compound from all dust and grime. A houseboy? The short, gaunt, Indian man was always genial in outward appearance. He was from the sub-continent. I did my own laundry, although others paid a trifling for such service. These brown men spoke little English and had a funny wag of their head in assent to questions. They were always at the ready with a broom. I couldn't pronounce the name of the man who cleaned our office and vacuumed my rug once a week in my CHU. I never saw any of them grow frustrated with their work. They were always extremely polite and smiling. It always gave me an uneasy feeling that they were there, but at the end of my tour, when everyone had to leave, the compound deteriorated rapidly without them to maintain the buildings and the grounds.

Despite being nervous in this strange and dangerous land, I felt like I might be getting my mojo back. And I didn't even know if a pinkish/white guy from Wisconsin could have mojo. So far so good on deployment #2. If you have to go to war, go to war with the Corps. Remember that.

The Chow hall could serve several hundred soldiers at one time. Everyone cleared their weapon into barrels outside and stepped into air-conditioned bliss inside to wash our hands and have our ID cards scanned. The cornucopia of chow was impressive. Salad bars, fresh fruit, surf and turf on Fridays, mango juice, desert bars, OK burgers and fries. The pizza was subpar but the stir fry station was outstanding. It was the line I almost always headed to. I'd pick my veggies onto a plate, pick my meat and then spice it up as best I could. I swore off white flour for a year and that in conjunction with no beer and running several times a week led me to shed forty pounds in the next year. My mom again sent me a variety of hot sauces, which combined with copious amounts of jalapenos in my stir fry made the Hot Mama pickle episode of 2003 seem like a grenade compared to regular nuclear events. On the weekends, soldiers performed Rock n' Roll music during evening chow, on a little elevated stage. Banners from professional and college sports teams hung from the roof trusses and I eventually wrote to the coach of the Badgers for a Wisconsin, big red W. After winning several Rose Bowls recently it was our due. And the sacred flag and a nice letter was received in just a few weeks. It was hung with pride in the front, next to the hated Ohio State, Michigan, and Iowa banners.

I was in charge of a couple of folks. Fourteen Iraqis were on the payroll outside the wire, locals who helped monitor the projects. Five Department of Army civilians, which included two gentlemen born in Iraq and two other soldiers, were part of the Tikrit Resident Office of which I was the Officer in Charge. British Convoys were their own entity, but more than 25 former soldiers from across the former empire hung their hats each night at our Engineer Shangri-La.

The office had a real civil engineer, a brainiac named Neal Darrow. Just before we swept up, turned off the lights and locked the door, he was sent to help wrap up the projects in Mosul. Short in stature and big in humor, he managed the crown jewel. The design was that of others, but he made it work. An engineer, a true builder, Neal did the quality assurance for the systems going into the building, such as the fire suppression and electrical backup systems. When the Iraqi Air Force officers demanded that the Corps build bathrooms on all seven floors of the air traffic control tower, it was Neal who said, "Hell, no." Not only was it out of scope, but as Neal said, "We do that and the Iraqis will turn it into a goddamn hotel." Male and female designated bathrooms were constructed on the first floor. The elevator was the last thing to be built, which is usual in buildings. With no temporary elevator, a trip to the top meant a little cardiovascular workout up the stairs. The glass observation deck itself was built right before I arrived, but the Raytheon and General Dynamic contractors had yet to appear. Stepping gingerly around the catwalk, I observed an awesome panorama. The terrain was flat, brown and dusty, stretching into a vast desert looking west towards the horizon. Aviation units clung nearby. The big post was completely observable, almost touching the outskirts of Tikrit. A mere 15 kilometers from the Tigris looking east, the former home of the Iraqi Air Force would have a new headquarters. That is, if they would fight and defend their own air traffic control tower gem.

The insignia of the Third Infantry Division has broad diagonal blue and white stripes. It signifies the efforts of the division at the river Marne in northern France in 1918. The "Rock of the Marne" held when others retreated. They were young doughboys not experienced enough to know that it wasn't dishonorable to withdraw when being overrun. That shocked the attacking Germans trying to get to Paris. Thousands paid for that moniker with their lives and life-long disabilities. All at a time when no health care pledges or pensions existed. A modern brigade of the Marne Division spread out across Speicher, with their motor pools, barracks, and admin buildings. They secured the roads and kept their presence felt in Tikrit and throughout Salah Ad Din province. They trained Iraqi soldiers how to use their new equipment and employ basic Infantry tactics.

Shipping container yards occupied dozens of acres. Support facilities like massive fuel tanks and hangars dotted the facility. An ever-present plume of noxious black smoke rose from incinerators at the southwest corner of Speicher, drifting away, hopefully. Toxic chemicals rode the wind and blew back upon those who set them. The ring road around the ten thousand-foot runways took more than twenty minutes to circumnavigate. There were camps for foreign contractors, a decent sized 5,000 square foot Post Exchange (PX) with commissary. Burger King and Pizza Hut made brave attempts toward authenticity. Silver and gold jewelry were abundant as well as Persian rugs and other goods to expand your wartime souvenirs at the continuously held bazaar.

"Hey, Tamara, of all the projects the Tikrit office has, what's the total contract amount?"

She barely moved her chin toward me from the front seat. "Over $50 million I guess."

Holy Shit! That was 50 million times more than anything I'd ever been responsible for before. I let that sink in as the tour continued past the million-gallon aviation fuel tanks. US forces didn't destroy them, for good reason. "So, are most of the projects off post or on?"

"That's a good question."

Either she didn't know, wasn't going to tell me, or I was like a baby trying to feed himself the first time with a spoon, messy and ineffective. Isn't Kenny adorable with all these stupid questions? Bits and pieces of project details fell from Tamara's speech like pearls. She reminded me of another officer of few words, Diana Berry, my commander from deployment #1. On the way back to Engineer Nirvana my confidence finally cracked, "I don't know. There certainly seems to be lot about all of this. I hope I can keep up."

From the front of the Humvee: "Are you kidding? You're a carpenter! You're one of them!"

Cool. Thanks. She was right, as it turned out.

I didn't think I'd see Tony during deployment #2, but I sometimes wondered what he might have to say. I wasn't nearly as stressed out as my first trip to beautiful Iraq.

# CHAPTER 21

# Rock Stars

"Tomorrow we're going to visit three of the modular schools. The contractor is having a hard time getting started. He's a Chinese guy out of Virginia. I think he's a chiropractor or something. He has promised to send a project manager but he hasn't shown up yet." This was the most Tamara had spoken to me in one breath.

His primary subcontractor was Turkish; their subs were whoever they could appeal to locally, not including their traveling assembly crew. The takeaway is that anyone can bid on a government contract to build overseas, even a Chinese chiropractor from Virginia who didn't give a shit except for the money.

"OK. What're the names of the schools?" I was looking at a map on Tamara's office wall of Salah Al Din province (which is the size of Massachusetts), and the eight schools my office now had to build before I could leave Iraq. The three we would visit were Al Basserah Elementary, Abu Hanitha, and Al Rassoul. All were northeast of Samarra, in a place so violent in its politics that even the President of Iraq avoided going there. That was like a Republican campaigning for President not visiting

255

Chicago, or a Democrat avoiding Lubbock, Texas. An ancient ziggurat in Samarra built in AD 800 rose in association with the Great Mosque. It was at least the height of The Office Jewel. It looked blurry with a dusty red hue in the bright sun. I wanted to inspect how it was built but I wasn't a tourist. Unauthorized stops would make the British Convoys seethe.

We arrived at the Combat Outpost around lunch time on the 4th of July in an environment of extreme heat and tension, waiting for a Samarra police escort through the city. We may be representatives of America, bigger than old King Kong, but they were from Samarra, and meaner than a junk yard dog. We waited a couple of hours, counting the sweat beads rolling off our individual noses, trying not to blanch at the smell of rotting food and waste next door. If you were an experienced soldier, you'd pooped prior to convoy movement. Unregulated, gastro-intestinal excursions into a fly-filled latrine were a hard lesson learned.

Independence Day wasn't celebrated that year; neither were anniversaries, Sweetest Day, Thanksgiving, Christmas, all Federal Holidays, birthdays, Valentine's Day, you name it. Pay day looked good on paper—too bad I had nowhere to spend it. If the Army wanted you to have a family, they would have issued you one.

A short jaunt through a massively dense population, inactive in mid-day and poverty stricken, brought us back into somewhat arable fields. We rolled onto a "jobsite" of Al Basserah, where I witnessed sandal clad men mixing "concrete" in large bowls in an attempt to place footings onto which a pre-fabricated building would be erected. Tamara got out after the Brits secured the site and started taking pictures of a bunch of jack shit. I wondered if the three men working had ever seen a work boot. As a union guy, I felt bad that safety just went out the window.

Who'd protect these guys when they got hurt? Perhaps, if they worked slowly enough, that wouldn't happen. I asked a security member rhetorically if the workers had ever seen steel- toed work boots before, not to mock, but to mark. He looked at me oddly: "Not bloody well likely." The safety of the people building the schools became a bridge too far, a foray into nothingness. But I was determined to continue to try.

Then I got pissed. "Where's the foreman? How does anybody know at what elevation these footers are being placed?" I asked to no one in particular. "Where's the transit?" Who the hell knew? Certainly not the contractor. I hated the asshole already. If I ever find that bastard chiropractor in Virginia, I'm going to choke the shit out of him. You'll see why later.

The other two sites, Abu Hanitha and Al Rassoul, had no workers at them at all. This was unfortunately a normal situation, exposing ourselves to risk outside the wire, even if the odds of something bad happening was very low, for very little gain. "Bad" meant one of our own getting hurt. It became frustrating over the course of months that schedule wasn't important to the chiropractor from Virginia. At least perimeter walls had been started at all three locations the day Tamara and I recon'd them. I documented current status and sharpened my knives for the next conference call.

The locations were approved by local politicians or tribal leaders, to be put beside adobe shacks that now served as classrooms for a few. The concept for these modular schools was simple: build the school in panels in Turkey, ship them to Iraq, and assemble. The contract for my eight was $5.5 million. I'd pick up another ten to finish out as the Kirkuk and Balad offices started to close up in preparation for the big drawdown in US Forces. Two long buildings would parallel each other, providing six large rooms. Classrooms 25-foot-long by x 18-foot-wide, with two bathrooms and two offices, AC, and running water were leaps ahead of what the kids had now. Each school would have a back-up generator, water storage tank, septic tank and leach field, basketball court, and large, swinging double gate to secure the school inside, and nine-foot-high concrete block walls covered with plaster and painted a nice earth tone.

In 2010, the US President was planning the complete removal of American combat power in Iraq and almost all of the civilians helping their government. It was like he was visiting colleges with Big Sister (USA), and little sister (Iraq) was going to have to fend for herself soon. I thought we would keep a residual force of 10-15 thousand troops to provide a backstop, but that was a wrong assumption.

This time, construction had to get completed or not at all. There wasn't going to be anyone to hand the project folder to. Getting electricity to the sites became an earnest undertaking, with such spoils strictly controlled. A few times I would convoy to a politician's office to express The United States' appreciation for his efforts. Permits aren't free. Americans stroking Iraqi egos were cheap applications.

Our Tikrit Residence Office would visit each school at least every six calendar days, in order to mix up the days of the week we'd show up. You could never, ever, coordinate with a contractor, or anyone else, when at a location. Physical security concerns of course were paramount. As in, not having an IED rip apart your vehicle or getting shot at. But we took lots of pictures, had weekly meetings with our chiropractor-turned-builder, and held the local guy's feet to the fire. My several Iraqi quality control guys gave half-assed coverage of the projects outside the wire, but their labor was cheap. Only a few days after Tamara left, I met my Turkish partner on the ground. Thank God, he had professional pride. He lived on Speicher and had a small office there. The Turkish boss, Derin, came to the Engineer compound regularly just to say "hi" and keep us informed about upcoming work. I met his right-hand man, Derya, by happenstance, at a planned school. He was about thirty years old and knew no English. I came to appreciate his work for the schools. He ended up paying a very high price.

The school at al-Zamamkshari was far off of the beaten path near one of world's largest man-made lakes. The few dozen families tried to subsist in the desert beside a dead body of water, forced by Saddam's Ba'ath Party officials pushing Shias from their native homes to where no one else existed. When the Euphrates River was diverted and dammed, lake Tharthar grew large as the marsh Arabs were forcibly settled upon its dead banks. You can see it on maps of Iraq. Its northern tip is only a few dozen kilometers from FOB Speicher, where the road ended and a winding track began a short distance to the hamlet of al-Zamakshari.

A sole electrical line stretched to the hamlet; that was good. Houses were close by the new school site. Trenches were being dug with pick axes, about eight inches down into what seemed like virgin soil. The idea was to place something like concrete into them to make footings. I was happy the site was apart from the residents and that workers were actually there. A pantomime ensued with my new Turkish friend Derya about how to establish a consistent elevation for the corners of the modular buildings. I met with his boss two days later at my office.

I began, "Derin, I don't see how you plan to place the buildings out at Zamakshari when your footings aren't the same elevation." Back in my office my partner had tried to draw his idea on a white board. About 35 years old, and engineer-trained, he began to draw a series of built-up rows of masonry to create a level platform to build the school's footings. He liked to snap and roll his big gold watch along his wrist. Derin smiled easily, and was one hairy bastard.

One of our office's Civilian Construction Representatives was with me during the meeting. Like Mike had said earlier in the day, "It's not our job to instruct the contractor how they have to build. Just as long as it doesn't mess up the rest of the project."

"Well, OK, my friend," I began. "Show me your concept, Derin. I don't get it, but it's your project." With an erasable marker in his hand, he dubiously said, "You see, Major, if we build up to the proper elevation then it won't matter if the footers just run at the ground's height." At least we had one good partner. We'd help each other mightily to build those schools. The affection on my part was genuine. This part of the COIN (Counter Insurgency) doctrine had to be successful—to show the local people that their leaders could provide services for them. Working with the Americans, the ribbon cutting ceremonies were always a big deal with media present. I think I was on Iraqi TV once. Only in the background, of course.

I called my furry friend (his chest hair stopped where the razor started to shave) to ask why he wasn't building the school at Al Rammalah.

"We are there, Major Dupar. The walls are going up. We have started the footings." It took me another recon to finally figure out the trouble. Again on the phone, I asked the important question:

"Hi, Derin. The location of Rammalah. Are you getting the coordinates from latitude and longitude or from military grid coordinates?" He cited the same document I was looking at. Latitude and longitude.

"You're about 20 kilometers from where you should be building."

"It is not possible; the coordinates I get from my GPS. It is correct."

"I'm sure that you're positive of where you are building, but it's not the right place. The title deed that the Corps of Engineers obtained a year ago has the correct location. In military grid coordinates. You're off by 20 kilometers."

His voice grew thin, "but what about the expense of the work we have already completed?" he whined.

"Look, Derin." This was amusing to me. "I don't know whose land you're building on. But if I were you, I'd get the hell out of there and not say anything."

The work began at Rammalah about two months later. I had to bitch and complain for him to start. Maybe Derin didn't like my attitude? Well, that's construction. I'm an American; you know, the bill payer.

• • •

Besides having our own private security forces, electrical grid, and telecommunications system, the Corps also had our own IT infrastructure. Our computer guy on site was a kid named Johnny. He'd been a federal employee for only a few years, and was amused by how the Army did stuff, especially now that he swam in "our" fish bowl. The US Army Corps of Engineers is over 30,000 strong, nominally run by 600 soldiers, but the bulk of the workforce were Department of the Army civilians. In the States, the Corps exists in a civilian fish bowl. Theater is much different.

Johnny was campaigning for class clown and I didn't have time to compete. Once a quarter I'd have to inventory IT equipment, having no idea what it was or how it functioned. When a civilian representing the Speicher mayor's cell (the post headquarters) had to get into our IT room, he was so giddy at its organization and cleanliness I thought he was going to cream his jeans. Johnny knew what he was doing even if I didn't.

IT is like that. Either they are ignored 'cause everything's working, or they're pieces of shit worthy of nothing but normal stupid people's scorn when you call them. "Why isn't my computer working?"

"Did you try to turn it off, then back on?"

"No."

"Try that."

"OK." A minute later. "OK. I think it's working now."

"Is there anything else, Kenny?"

"No. I guess not."

"Have a nice day." Which is a euphemism for "you're a stupid idiot."

One morning I was having a frustrating time with our internal Motorolas, and said so with a stream of profanity. I was standing next to the printer in the office hallway while Johnny, calmly stirred his fresh mug of coffee and offered, "Gee, Kenny. You seem somewhat frustrated this morning." At which I grabbed the back of his head and faked giving him a knee to the balls. Coffee was on the floor tiles, walls, some on him as I walked away. Johnny was gasping for breath he was laughing so hard. You got to get your giggles when you can.

I amused Johnny with my frustrations and contractor difficulties. We ate most meals together. He got hammered during his mid-tour leave and called me on my office phone, just like he said he would. Through his slurred words I heard him yell at his girlfriend, then tell me how much he loved me and everybody else back in Tikrit. Johnny didn't remember the more salient points of our conversation upon his return. I guess that's the effect I have on people. They tell me they love me only when they're drunk and don't remember afterwards. It's something. I shouldn't complain.

Early on in deployment number two, the sky turned an eerie orange hue in the late afternoon. A black wall of cloud was approaching from the west although the air was very calm, not moving at all. I remembered Tony teaching me the correct term—"dust storm." I almost bumped into him en route to the Dining Facility, trying to get a meal before it hit. "We better hurry up." he said.

"Yeah. I'd better wrap my computer in a garbage bag."

Pointing to the horizon, Tony grimaced, "This is going to get nasty." He had his goggles with him already, and I wished I had mine on the short walk back from the DFAC to my office. By then the wind had picked up to 30 miles per hour. The big goof walked into the storm with me, like a specter alongside.

• • •

A Beanie Baby craze in America swept the country sometime after the turn of the century. The kids in my daughter's Christian elementary school thought it'd be considerate to send boxes of gently used ones to me in Iraq. It was a bad mistake. Not good.

There was an anecdotal phenomenon in the Arab world we American soldiers commonly referred to as, "Man Love Thursday." Christians' weekly Sabbath is Sunday. For Jews it is Saturday. For Muslims it is Friday. For each, the tradition is to take the day off work, and contemplate the righteousness of God. Maybe you ask for forgiveness for awful sins performed during the week. Sometimes, living with a painful transgression before absolution, days go by slowly, unless your guilt can be absolved the next day.

But what does "Man Love Thursday" have to do with Beanie Babies, you may ask? Nothing at all, except for awful demonstrations of human nature revealing itself only moments apart. I took a box of Beanie Babies on a recon of the three Samarra modular schools, Basserah, Abu Hanitha, and Al Rassoul. Derin had solved the foundation problem by creating a factory near Kirkuk, where he'd make hundreds of footstool-size concrete piers for the buildings to sit on. Very smart. Most of the time the ground was extremely level and compact. Structurally, it made sense. Some shimming between the structural steel and the top of the pier and we were in business.

At Al Rassoul the kids gathered near us begging for some sort of handout. I was mobbed when I produced the little stuffed animal toys. The bigger kids, meaning the boys, grabbed, yelled, and fought for the stuffed animals I passed out like they were hundred dollar bills. I handed a few to small girls who beamed with delight, and then cried with horror as the fuzzy Beanie Babies were ripped from her hands by a boy twice her age and three times her size. The bedlam didn't end until the box was empty, when my popularity vaporized. Never again would I submit myself to the creepiness of such overt bullying, or subject little ones to such meanness of heart. I couldn't wait to split.

The convoy of up-armored Land Rovers sped down narrow flat straight roads at 50+ miles per hour to the next school, past an empty guard shack. Or at least I thought it wasn't manned until one and then another Iraqi soldier sprang from it to watch the Corps zoom by. A third soldier followed and was pulling up his shorts when he and I looked each other in the eyes. He was trying to button his pants with the sling of his AK-47 weighing down his wrists. What a predicament! Oh yeah, I thought with a smirk—it's Thursday. I guessed absolution would come the next day.

• • •

My continual bitching during the weekly phone calls to Virginia included the Senior Project Engineer DA (Department of the Army) Civilian for the Northern Area Office. Carl was in his fifties, with graying curly hair, and really knew his contract administration. For more than 25 plus years he had mastered all of the Army Corp of Engineers systems. Several deployments to Iraq made him a total pro. Mr. Carl Harding was the adult in the room. I sat in his office a few times, but despite his generous mentorship, the sweet stink inside was oppressive. He had an automatic air refresher which sprayed once an hour, once onto the back of my head. His office smelled like your grandmother's bathroom. I soon arranged for the meetings not be held in his office.

Via conference call, Carl prodded for a direct representative of the contractor to be present immediately in order to get these modular schools completed. We were promised, lied to, and deceived about passports and licenses—all manner of bullshit to avoid responsibility and expense. We cared about schedules because we were there. The contractor was already getting paid for the work performed. The situation stank, but we had no leverage. The Chinese chiropractor from Virginia couldn't be fired. Although they were slow, they had performed somewhat, and finding another contractor would take a year. A year of delay the Corps of Engineers didn't have. And everybody knew it.

My Turkish friends made the mistake of emailing me pictures of three bullet holes on the outside of the newly plastered wall of the Al Rassoul site. This they claimed was why they were behind schedule. The workers were scared. This was so delicious I almost couldn't stand it. We had a sit down the next afternoon, and I couldn't wait to ask Derin and Derya to tell me the story.

"When the workers got to the jobsite they found bullet holes outside, near the gate. Did you see the pictures, Major Dupar?"

"Oh yes!" I smiled. They looked nervous.

"The, uh, workers won't come to work," he shrugged, "because they don't know who might shoot at them." Derin snapped and rolled his big gold watch around his hairy wrist. All they had completed thus far was the wall around where the modular school would be placed. I beamed at them and leaned forward in my chair. I excitedly asked, "So, what happened next?"

"When?"

"After they found the bullet holes?"

"They tried to work, but a man with an AK-47 came up and asked if they had any security guards on site to protect them."

"What did they say? What did they say?" My eyes lit up.

"I don't know." The two cross-talked in Turkish. But I was so jumpy I interrupted.

"Did you hire him?"

"Who?"

"The man with the AK." I plopped back in my chair and waved my hands. "That's the best application for a job I've ever heard of."

My Turkish friends were confused by the American Major. How did I know if the workers didn't shoot the school's wall themselves? It didn't matter if they did or not. The only thing I cared about was getting the damn thing built. And the building panels hadn't even started trucking from Turkey yet, so my "give-a-shit meter" about their problems was at zero. Less than zero. They pushed back with a litany of petty difficulties. I wanted to ask Derin to pour me a nice, fresh, steaming mug of "shut the fuck up." But upon consideration I thought that might be rude.

"Haven't you visited the locals, Derin, and donated to their local charities?"

"Well, yes. We have." Pregnant pause. "Donated."

"Do you think that the man with the AK-47 shot at the school?"

"Yes, most definitely." Derin had to shave twice a day. Probably since he was nine.

"Why didn't you hire him? He is your security guard!" I didn't like the dumbass routine.

"Fix the wall and get back to work." I stated. "I don't see a problem." And my face went blank like Al Capone's mug shot.

If they thought the Major was crazy, maybe it was better to give them what they expected. People sometimes will do what you ask only because they think you're unhinged. It's a method.

"I, I, I don't understand, Major."

"The next time the man with the rifle comes around, the same guy that shot at the school (I agree with you on that point), hire him. He's perfect. What? 50 or 75 dollars a month?" Dramatic pause. "Hell, I'll hire him. Get me his name and I'll put him on my payroll."

After a pause my Turkish friend asked, "Where did you learn about construction, Major Dupar?"

"Chicago."

Even to a Turk in Iraq, that made sense.

• • •

The right rear tire blew out, causing the driver to lose control of the up-armored Land Rover. Down the ditch from the narrow road it rolled onto its side, then flipped onto its roof, turning, crushing, snapping the neck of the young gunner, cutting his spinal cord. Momentum flipped the vehicle again, glass broke into myriad spider webs, smoke and dust started to suffocate the Brits within. It rested finally. One dead, all injured. The choking gurgles led their compatriots to them, gloved hands pulling them out of the hulk. Others sprayed it with extinguishers. Thank God no fire broke out.

During another seemingly worthless mission to a school one month later, two other men perished in a similar wreck. One of my office's Construction Representatives, Mike, was in a vehicle ahead, when another right rear tire exploded on the vehicle behind his. The Marne Division's Quick Reaction Force launched to the spot fifty kilometers northwest towards Kirkuk. The site was secured into the night, while MEDIVAC choppered the injured back to Baghdad. A lament was sent to Birmingham, England. Hoses sprayed the blood away before the wrecker hauled the mass back to Speicher. The second and third to die building the schools. The Corps and British Convoys continued the investigation into the cause of two tire blowouts leading to losing control at high speeds. It could have been any one of us in a vehicle that rolled, which is the reason the up-armored vehicles had shoulder harnesses for riders.

We had to visit the schools frequently because the US contractor wouldn't send a field superintendent to run his own job. Often there would be no progress since the previous visit six days earlier, but we wouldn't know that if we didn't drive there. There was no other way to keep the pressure on. I had Iraqis who would visit the schools in between times, but their value was limited.

• • •

Tall and lanky, the full bird Colonel had a bad wheel. He ran for enjoyment and stress relief. The Colonel in charge of United States Army Corp of Engineers in Iraq traveled incessantly, along with his Sergeant Major, from Baghdad to all projects. He took a run from our compound the evening before we visited schools. I met him resting at our big gazebo and asked if he needed some ice for his ankle. He said he was OK. They visited with me at the place where we were truly American Rock Stars—AL Warka.

My boss's boss rode with me the next morning in silence, past oil refineries and combat outposts. The secure convoy embraced the western edge of a rocky spine before heading east over a serpentine highway and its 1000-foot climb. I couldn't stand the quiet, and inadvertently blurted out when passing a shepherd with his flock, "What a horrible job!" Might my senior rater think that I meant my own job? I looked towards him: "It's boring. I mean the shepherd. Not my job. You know, shepherding? I love my job!" Oh, boy.

Paternalistically, Colonel Johnston merely said with a smirk, "I know what you mean."

Atop the mountain was a good place to take pictures and pee. Before us was the narrow Tigris Valley, lush green strips less than a few hundred meters on either side of the river. Ancient fortifications still clung to the slopes that protected this pass. Driving down the switchbacks toward a reedy marvel of green with cows dotting the pastures, we saw adobe homes, some two stories and freshly white washed. Houses became more numerous as we approached Al Warka, home to a few thousand. I imagined the higher up the slopes a family lived the poorer they were, away from the river and its wealth. But even here a view commanded pricier digs. It was cooler now in November and the temperature might not even hit 100. The street corners were filled with garbage and men milling about.

We followed the twists and turns through the little hamlet's streets, more like alleys, with the Brits taking corners like it was a Grand Prix at ten miles an hour. Although I'd been here three times before I couldn't have driven the route back to the mountain road on a bet. One kid ran alongside my window. Others started to shout and took off to hail more neighbors. I saw the boom of the crane and knew the crew was setting panels. The already gathered crowd grew. This was payday for the Corps of Engineers. The half-acre footprint inside the walls had both buildings' floor panels set, pinned together, and the walls were getting hefted into place by the crane. The kids and parents buzzed, most scolding fell upon deaf ears. I climbed up three feet onto the floor of the school, using it like a stage, and quickly greeted the crew and found the foreman. We talked process. Sergeant Major Peters took pictures. The Brits pulled security. Colonel Johnston observed mostly, but he may have asked one question. I discussed methods and asked when the 5-K generator would be on site. Do you know when the leach field will get placed or is your crew just erecting the building? Do you have the water tank or is that a local contractor? And then I stopped asking questions he didn't have answers to and let him get back to work. They were making good progress and would complete it in only a few more days, and then head south towards Samarra where panels lay stacked inside the perimeter walls, protected by local security with fantastic interview and marksmanship skills.

Upon leaving I high-fived a few kids and took a few pictures myself. Upon extending my hand towards a girl about ten, she raised two fingers, snapped her wrist while spinning her back to me, declaring in English a loud, "No!" A grown man should never address a young lady. Despite being the man of the hour, I was still an infidel. And an extremely rude one at that!

Pardon me, miss. I guess I was acting like an arrogant rock star.

• • •

The part of the drawdown plan created by the Baghdad office of USACE concerning the Northern Area Office based in Tikrit was that my office would get all of the Kirkuk Office's projects around February and all of the Balad Office's projects come March, 2011. That was about another $20 million in contracts to wrap up. We even got three modular schools from the Mosul office.

The progress on the schools was slow. My office now had eighteen of them spread out 100 miles in all directions to bring across the finish line. No one from the States ever came to represent the contractor. My Turkish friends were it. I lost all professional bearing with the chiropractor from Virginia during one conference call. I linked our wasting time visiting sites with lack of progress with the risks of traveling in Iraq, with three of my men having lost their lives. His dithering had contributed to the tragedies. "Three of my men are dead, six others injured, for no reason. And you can't even send a damn Superintendent, which is a stipulation of your contract!" I was livid and shaking after my tirade. Mr. Carl Harding, the Senior Project Engineer for the Northern Office, pressed mute on the phone speaker and gently said, "Major Dupar doesn't get to talk anymore," with a smile. Mike's face was grim through his goatee, but his head was nodding. He was a dead ringer for what I thought Tony would look like. I went outside to smoke and cool off. What were they going to do to me? Send me to Iraq?

I thought to myself that I may not be the one to take out the chiropractor from Virginia, but sure as shit somebody was going to. It was just a matter of finding him. That wouldn't be hard. All somebody needed was the will to take a baseball bat to a kneecap.

# CHAPTER 22

# Aircraft Simulator at the Gym

When it comes to construction, it doesn't matter if you're American, Turk, Arab or a chiropractor, it always comes down to money. Through that lens all motivations become clear.

The biggest problem the Corps of Engineers had in theater was never enough time. Having too much money actually worked against us, because our quality assurance was to US standards, which meant we wouldn't accept poor construction. Our open projects in Iraq numbered well over 150 in 2010. Closing them out before everybody else went home and turned off the lights became of enormous strategic importance. Because we were backed by the American taxpayer, our contractors knew if they eventually did a decent job they'd get paid. They weren't going to be penalized for coming in late. However, for some Iraqi contractors, quitting a job halfway through didn't matter, as they had been paid handsomely, and might just be cashing out, already the richest guy in the village. It was time to wrap up all the projects and leave Iraq. The tradeoff for the limitless greed of our contractors is that they had to deal with unstable assholes like me.

The processes that the Corps brought to Iraq were those created in the United States. When they have a contract, firing people you don't like (or those who refuse to perform) takes a lot of time. It takes more time to find three other contractors to bid, negotiate, award, mobilize and finally pick up the pieces where the other guy left off. There had to be a great deal of "kissy face" on my part in order to get some projects completed. And the smaller the project, the bigger the pain in the ass it became. My favorite refrain was, "Well, then you're not getting paid." Or, "I won't be able to pay you unless..." That last one sounds better, more kissy-face.

The Arabs have an expression they use frequently—"Insha Allah." It means "God willing." Here are some examples of its use:

1) Major Asshole: "When will the windows arrive on site?"

Iraqi Contractor: "It is two weeks on the schedule and they will be here. Insha Allah."

2) Major Asshole: "I need you to come to my office on Speicher immediately to discuss the project. We have to talk about the timeline. The contract may have to be awarded to someone else (big bluff)."

Iraqi Contractor: "Yes, we will be there tomorrow or the next day as the roads are bad and there are many problems with the check points, but we will be there. Insha Allah."

It is a superb dodge. One that I couldn't figure how to overcome. I mean, if the construction effort is truly in the hands of God, just like everything else is, how can I get mad if you don't do your job? Sweet Jesus! My Iraqi interpreter and dear friend, Aabid, eventually explained it to me this way. "If a Turk says, "Insha Allah," to an American, it means "I will try very hard to accomplish the thing in question." But if an Arab says the same thing it means, "No way! Ain't happening. Maybe it'll work out or maybe not. I might try or I might not. You Americans are always uptight. Why don't you just relax and enjoy your stay here in Iraq? Everything is going to be fine."

I think the Bronze Star Medal I received for my second deployment was for NOT killing anybody. It was for Meritorious Service (NOT valor – big difference). "Meritorious service," meaning I accounted for lots of stuff and supervised people. "Valor" means saving people's lives directly, courage under fire, calling in a MEDIVAC, rendering first aid, engaging the enemy, winning the fight.

In the cruel world of construction, lying is like breathing. But don't ever, EVER try to point out his falsehood to an Arab man. His pride is sacrosanct and an ugly situation will only get worse. And there won't be any apologies. Lying to a Christian, however, is like driving five miles over the speed limit. What's the big deal? All I could do was stick to the facts and adjust the schedule back, again. I never lied to my contractors, much.

It was in this atmosphere that we built two state-of-the-art F16 Fighting Falcon aircraft simulators in a brand new, never used gymnasium in a back corner of Speicher. Lockheed Martin had the easy part of building multi-million-dollar machines, dismantling them, shipping them across the world, and putting them back together. The building was truly remote and designated as a gymnasium only because it had never been used. It was a great shell in which to build. My office, unlike Lockheed Martin, had to get our Iraqi contractors onto post (they didn't always show up) and build to blueprints that had plenty of hidden flaws in them. Thank God for George. The effects of dust storms and temperature/humidity fluctuations had to be mitigated perfectly for the pricey simulators.

George showed up at just the right time. He was a tall, well-built, geeky black guy. He had his degree in Mechanical Engineering from Florida State and had worked for the Corps in Georgia for more than ten years. He was a good family man who deployed to enhance his career. It took several months for George to break down emotionally from "normal standards" into the world of building in theater. I immediately gave him the thorniest of issues to decipher. Figuring out electrical requirements amid patchwork spaghetti was his deal, and it stressed George mightily. Welcome to the party, pal. The contractor ain't going to do it; the team had to. I put him in at short stop and made him play every day, injured or not.

I became so upset with the aircraft simulator project after a few weeks of the contractor refusing to start that I finally demanded that the owner of the company present herself to my office in Tikrit. That's correct. A woman won the contract. She said nary a word at the meeting. Her husband talked incessantly in decent English, and her company, I was to learn, was a shell game of musical chairs. I asked how many employees the company had, and the response was thirty, which actually meant five. Their email addresses and phone numbers were bogus and kept changing. But they had an acting point man, or actually a sub of a sub of a subcontractor of the woman who had the affirmative award.

My Iraqi counterpart was a devious well-spoken bastard who wore a prodigious amount of cheap cologne to mask the stink of continuous travel. He took far fewer showers than a germophobic American. Faruq's business acumen was superb. I helped him make a lot of money and he took us over the finish line. He started with the aircraft simulators and a renovation of a mess hall for the incoming Iraqi Air Force cadets. Both Speicher projects were awarded to someone else, but his guys did the work. We had a huge strategic interest in getting the Iraqi Air Force up and flying again, as you could easily imagine.

Faruq also built for us a Technical Center in central Tikrit from the ground up, but under the auspices of his own company. The purpose of Tikrit Technical Center was to train local government workers on new processes to collect taxes, acquire resources, hire/pay personnel, and administer budgets. That was a $1.1-million-dollar project. The biggest project his company had with us was the secondary school with 19 classrooms at the city of Halabja. But that's a chapter in itself. Faruq messed up a lot, but I was very forgiving since I had no choice. His name was Ghulam Faruq, which I think means dickhead in Arabic. If he wants to write his own book and state that Kenny means a dog's butthole in English, then great! Even so, I hope I meet him again and that he has done well for himself.

The one Entry Control Point into Speicher had 19 speed-bumps and was almost a half-mile long. A transient camp sprang up along Route Tampa at the turnoff into the base. The first fighting positions were three hundred meters inside. It was a decent standoff distance to measure intentions. Convoys were channeled into large lots for searches, individuals into other lanes. The vetting, identification, credentialing and escorting sometimes took hours. Getting contractors onto Speicher took all morning on a bad day. That's if Faruq's guys showed up at all. I had one junior enlisted soldier who seemed to spend most of his deployment just babysitting them. I pitied the young sergeant his duty, and spelled him sometimes just to share the escort pain.

• • •

Everyone who had run the Iraqi government in 2003, from military officers to petty functionaries issuing permits and contracts, were Ba'athists. They had to belong to Saddam's political party to get their jobs. Paul Bremer was the HMFIC of the Coalition Provisional Authority in the beginning of the war. All Ba'athists were canned by Paul Bremer soon after the invasion. It was a major mistake that significantly led to the rise of the insurgency.

The Tikrit sniper was a total pro, part of a small cell. Her targets were those of well-planned opportunity. Her brother owned a small electronics store in town and moved weapons for the Sunni insurgency in the back of the house. Observation of American activities in the city was collected and analyzed for months. Ba'athist sympathizers within the fledgling city government passed information about projects the Marne Division, the US State Department, and USACE (United State Corps of Engineers) had started. Not all the bureaucrats had survived new vetting; some did. Recruiting drives at police stations could be a wonderful target, but a bullet through the head of an American Military Officer was the gold standard.

Her father received a small pension, at irregular times, for his service in the Republican Guard and as a former construction inspector for the City of Tikrit. From young ages he trained his progeny to shoot and the manual of arms. When, she finally had a proper rifle and scope she demonstrated her proficiency at more than 500 meters. From rooftops pointing towards desert openness, her marksmanship gained notice. Baby brother provided enough ammunition for practice. But it was her ability to mask herself among her neighbors and her quick vision of shooting lanes that sold an Al-Qaida team leader in Iraq to take a chance on her. Al-Qaida in Iraq was the precursor to ISIS (Islamic State in Syria and Iraq). Upon his recommendation a shoot was finally authorized.

Intersections where new traffic lights were to be built were leaked to the insurgents/freedom fighters. Although the schedule was undefined, the six locations in Tikrit were legitimate. Planning such service improvements in cooperation with local authorities was just the kind of low-hanging fruit the Americans loved to pick. The Tikrit sniper would have her shot.

Determining the perch wasn't difficult for her, but gaining access without undo notice was. The exact apartment she wanted would have to be vacant and available for rent. Another conspirator did just that, only to have the sniper reject the lane because of electrical lines close to the intersection. Money was tight, so greater detail and planning was needed for the rental of the next sniper platform. The police would be under intense pressure to find out who made the shot, the locals would be arrested, questioned, and probably released. Escape routes were the next element to be planned. The cell observed American convoys moving through the city and tried to watch them at the halt, to see how they'd disburse and occupy busy places. Where did the officer ride? Contractors began to excavate for new poles at several locations. More intelligence provided information that the poles were delivered to Tikrit.

Another apartment was rented, pointing toward another intersection, and she and her spotter camped with several days' worth of food and water, with plastic jugs brought for them to piss in. They played a young married couple moving from another part of town. No one saw her bring the duffle up the two flights of stairs. They waited. They had to be resupplied a few times in the two weeks they waited for the Americans

Luck was on their side as the American convoy came to observe the construction where the team hoped the poles were to be placed. A First Lieutenant from the Signal Corps was the Project Officer. Wanting to demonstrate US presence and resolve, she would have Arab men shake her hand. The morning was warm; everything was fine, nothing but green lights for the shoot. The traffic was busy, the comings and goings of a large compressed city. She reached out her gloved hand to a worker she didn't know, remembering to remove her sunglasses just before...

The spotter gave way to the Tikrit sniper as she again sat in her shooting position behind the 50-caliber bolt action rifle, its bipod steadied by a small table just beside a window. The site picture in the scope cleared, exhalation and the smooth squeeze, just as she had practiced since she was a kid.

The young officer wore a black vertical bar of rank on her Kevlar helmet. The round ricocheted off of her head and skimmed the neck on the soldier standing beside her, a slight spray of blood following the trajectory.

The first shot of a career. BANG! She thought she had killed her quarry, seeing the spray through the scope. Calmly, the team packed the equipment, descended the stairs, and walked two blocks to an awaiting car. The Tikrit sniper covered her grin with a scarf. Although a "miss," her intent hit the mark. No American soldier was safe in Saddam's hometown. She wouldn't try another shot for three months. Like I said, the Tikrit sniper was a total pro. She was active for many years. The first shot was her only missed fatality, a black mark in an unhealthy record.

• • •

I kept my appointment with the Deputy Governor of Salah Al Din province at the Tikrit City Hall to find the weirdest office I've ever seen. The politician kept me waiting, of course, and I was stunned when I was escorted in by the purple back lights in the soffits that wrapped along the wall. It was decorated like a fraternity president's dorm; I was expecting him to grab a remote and watch a bar revolve out from a wall. It only needed a water bed and a thumping stereo to complete the scene.

He painted a picture of his work effort before I could I broach our need for juice at the modular schools. The velvet pictures made me homesick for Elvis. The chia was fair and I could feel the cameras already rolling at the ribbon cutting. I left and he came through with the provincial electrical utility. The Deputy Governor just needed me to kiss the ring, which I was happy to do.

A few days later terror cells assaulted the City Hall without hope or plan of survival. Spectacular attacks demonstrated an earnestness nothing else could. More than 12 armed men gained control of the building after murdering almost two dozen security officers, politicians, and office workers. By 2:00 a.m. the shooting stopped. The counter attack killed all the insurgents and several more soldiers. The butcher's bill totaled 38 souls. In 2010-11, during my deployment to Saddam's hometown, such spectacular attacks occurred twice more, all against local government targets. And we were building a potential target ourselves, the Tikrit Technical Center.

I had to drive by the City Hall to a school just over the Tigris a few days later, and was shocked at how nonchalant the security forces were. Two armored personnel carriers flanked the inside of the main gate. One soldier stood behind his machine gun hands off, the turret hatch popped open, his entire midsection exposed, instead of being ready to fire and scanning his sector with his shoulders behind the weapon, thus providing a minimal target. The gunner was relaxed, unconcerned. Insha Allah, I suppose, if he dies in the next attack. Others slept at their fighting positions, helmets off, or smoking and joking, not paying attention, bleating absurdities to each other, not prepared to defend. Like sheep before the slaughter. Why wasn't a sergeant berating them? Where was the officer putting his boot in someone's ass?

We crossed a small busy bridge and just before a traffic circle I observed a butcher's stand, with sheep quarters hanging from the joists of a small open shed. A half dozen animals were penned beside, bleating, waiting for their turn. Women bought sections of meat for their family's supper while the cleaver worked among the flies, ascending and descending rapidly. The 100-degree heat meant shopping in the morning.

• • •

"Oh, hell no!" I spoke to no one in particular. I was making a quick tour around the back of the Tikrit Technical Center. The crew was applying stucco to the concrete block above the second floor. At the top of the fourth ring of scaffolding (twenty feet above the ground) I saw a man work off of only a single plank, a large bowl of material beside him. There should have been at least five planks to make a platform. I started looking for an interpreter when I noticed that the scaffolding wasn't attached to the building. The only time I'll yell at a jobsite is if something is really unsafe. Who's going to care if that poor guy falls? Is it his fault? I was boiling when the foreman finally came around the corner. "Stop what you're doing! Just stop!"

"Why, Sir? Why?" I began to spit out the safety violations. My security detail was getting antsy. Shaun called out to me, "Bad place to have a conversation, Major, yeah?" We were stationary in the open. He was absolutely right, but I continued my circumnavigation of the building at a decent clip, continuing to curse at no one in particular. Inside, I moved between the six or so classrooms on both floors, making sure not to silhouette myself in front of windows. I looked to ensure activity ceased at the scaffolding. Later that day I sent Faruq pictures of the worker on one plank twenty feet up.

He responded immediately that I was impeding progress, although I was the one who was always complaining about the schedule. The workers had to stop because of me. "Goddamn right they stopped, and that poor bastard didn't get hurt today either. I'd better see a proper scaffold set up next time." This time my threat was serious. The next time I saw improvement —they added more planking. But it was still only a gesture. I never had a lost time incident cross my desk in the year I was at Tikrit. A few dozen jobsites and no one got hurt. What does that tell you about our safety program? It was both a dereliction of duty and a bridge too far for Iraqi contractors in the field.

High-ranking government employees kept asking about our progress at the Technical Center when we were about 75% complete. They were chomping at the bit to occupy, and had to budget for furniture that could be ordered immediately. They had visited the site, but had no sense of when features such as windows and doors, plumbing fixtures, and electrical stuff would be completed. The planners needed a tour, so I ignored my intuition and made a date for a few days in the future.

I let it drop to the Brits that we had an appointment just before we left for Tikrit Technical Center. Not cool. Not cool at all. They pulled me up to the front of the building, which was finally getting stone veneer, and I was hurriedly whooshed inside. The bureaucrats arrived just before me. The meeting was productive and I convinced them of a pretty firm date they could begin to move in. It wasn't ten minutes after getting back to our compound that our Master Sergeant Gibbons found me in my office. "Sir, Colonel Watson needs to see you right away." She paused, "I guess it's really important." I had just taken off my body armor and my uniform hadn't wicked out the sweat in the dry desert heat.

Like I mentioned previously, my boss was co-located with me at Speicher and had the northern third of Iraq under his Area Office. The meeting started off strangely solemn.

"Please, Sir, close the door." This was odd. There must be some secret squirrel shit he needed to tell me about. Lieutenant Colonel Watson got right to the point. "Major Dupar, did you coordinate with the Iraqis to meet them at the Technical Center at an appointed time today?" Ben looked like he was about to be sick. Oh crap! The enormity of my error in judgment rushed around me like a wave. I could feel my blood pressure spike and my pulse began to race.

"Well. Yes, Sir, I did. I was desperate to turn over the building and they needed to be shown where we were in the project so that they could make their plans to occupy." I said this knowing in my heart I'd put everybody's lives at risk because I was impatient, lacked creativity, had used poor judgement.

"It doesn't matter." His tone remained intensely still. "We never tell anyone outside this compound where or when we are going anywhere." Another agonizing pause. "Ever." He could have been irate, but he wasn't. It was gentle mentorship from a gentle man, an approach I didn't deserve.

"I understand, Sir. It won't happen again." My eyes stared at a spot on his desk. I wanted to be sucked down past the floor boards. "I apologize. There's no excuse."

"Then we understand each other. Thank you for your time." At that, I slunk away.

• • •

"Do you believe in God, Major Dupar?" The Iraqi Air Force General asked me.

I was stunned. We had just finished a lunch on paper trays at the renovated Air Force Academy Dining Facility. The stew contained wretched mutton, but the vegetables, something like okra with cumin, coriander, and cardamom was tasty. The flat bread was passed around, hand to hand. And I thought that the bugs these guys had in their guts had to be a lot tougher than mine. I'd seen how the Iraqi Airmen prepared their food. Let's just say that sanitation, proper food preparation/refrigeration/ storage and hand washing wasn't their strong suit.

The discussion I only listened to was between two other Iraqi Air Force officers and Colonel Johnston about funding. It was a vague explanation of how money ebbs and flows from Baghdad to projects their Air Force wanted. The subjects under discussion were in conjunction with Corps projects at the new Air Force Academy. The runway repair for instance.

Amazed that he addressed me, and thinking that I was about to have a theological discussion with this man, I finally stammered out, "Why, yes. Yes, I do."

"Can you see God?"

This was getting deep in a hurry. "No, I can't see Him."

"But can you feel Him?" His English was spot on, His smile paternal.

I took a moment to consider and answered, "I can feel his presence through the works and actions of others around me."

The General's chin tilted, "That's a good answer." His hands clasped over his chest, in a comfortable pose, he said, "Getting money from Baghdad is like our relationship with God. You can't see it, but you can feel it."

Either this was profound or some eloquent bullshit. He was a general after all.

"I see what you mean." And the short conversation ended with a lap around the facility, thank God. I didn't understand at all what he meant. Still haven't figured it out.

The Iraqi officers didn't want me, the Project Officer, to explain the construction. They just wanted to wander on their own accord, like generals do. At the renovated chow hall, per Iraqi building practice, black water (poo poo-pee pee) didn't have to be contained within a closed system, which meant that at 90-degree junctions, right angles could be created out of small concrete boxes, the incoming pipe higher than the out-flow, gravity fed. The concrete lid sealed nothing but the sight of the inside of the microwave-sized box, not being a closed system. The 150-foot run from the new bathrooms to the new concrete septic tank and leech field produced a smell like a ripe, un-serviced Port–a–Pottie in August heat, times ten. It was like having a water treatment plant and landfill next to an outdoor farmer's market—nauseating.

The kitchen had all new appliances delivered before any other construction began. The Dining Facility had the capacity to feed hundreds. George from Georgia assured them that the electrical contractor wouldn't start any fires when he tapped into the one-megawatt generator a block away. He was nervous about it, which made me nervous about it. The load calculations were just a guess, since other buildings close by also tapped into the big machine.

The grease trap I fought with Faruq and his gang to install was the last piece of the puzzle/project for the new chow hall. When I watched the young Iraqi Airmen simply throwing food scraps into the large concrete holding tank made for gray water (food preparation, washing, non-toxic), I just walked away. "Good luck, fellas." It was disgusting in more ways than one, wasting precious effort. The plumbing system would be fouled soon, the Airmen perplexed why their sinks wouldn't drain anymore.

Did I mention that George was a godsend at the gym? Getting Faruq and his crew to install new generators with diesel tanks properly plumbed to send juice to new air-handlers (de-humidifiers and chillers) with controlled climate pushed through new ducts took only seven months of wrangling, four months late. A large rolling overhead door was cut into a side of the gym to get the aircraft simulators inside. Two small rooms sat almost dead center in the space that could have been used as a basketball court, but wasn't. Lockheed Martin had both F16 simulators on Speicher for two months before they agreed they could begin the install. You can imagine the pressure to complete. Although late, the construction was acceptable. Getting Iraqis able to control their own skies meant that we could depart home without everything going to shit, maybe.

For months I'd bothered Faruq to go to the Mayor's cell, (Speicher's Military town hall) and request Port-a-Potties delivered to the gym. He refused my demands. I thought his workers would appreciate it. I suppose comforts like that cost money. One day I circled the vicinity around the gym, (we must have been waiting for the contractor to show up), when I came across the dry detention pond near the facility. For drainage purposes, when rains came, this 75-foot-wide depression would hold water before flooding adjacent buildings. And lo and behold I solved the mystery of where the workers were going number two. Among dozens of empty water bottles were dozens of little black sun-dried poops that looked like the twirled tops of chocolate soft serve ice cream cones. Iraq never stopped shocking sensitivities.

The T6-Texan is a Raytheon built single-engine turboprop aircraft used for basic pilot and combat systems officer training.

They were often flying in pairs in the Speicher airspace. The Iraqi pilots were getting stick time in a cockpit similar to the real deal. US Airmen co-piloted. America wanted to sell F-16 fighter jets to Iraq. By 2015, they finally received (for a lot of money) their first squadron of Fighting Falcons. But not before the Iraqi Government bought Russian, British, and French aircraft as well. That was smart, keeping their options open—not solely relying on fickle America.

# CHAPTER 23

# I saw Santa in Kirkuk

Kirkuk is a particularly unhealthy place in terms of air quality. Approaching the city from the southwest, rolling barren hills give way to oil wells as the prominent terrain feature. The pall from natural gas burn off chokes out the sun. A place without suburbs—just a big, sprawling, polluted city with cargo trucks and tankers moving continuously. Fifty kilometers northeast of the confined city begins Kurdistan, unofficially. The Kurds made Kirkuk their forward bastion when ISIS aka Daesh aka ISIL threatened from Tikrit. Perhaps when Iraq is partitioned, Kirkuk will be inside a modern Kurdistan, defended by the Peshmerga, or as they are affectionately known by GIs as the "Pesh." However, most of the inhabitants of Kirkuk are Arabs.

Grim blocks squeezed together stretched for miles, with a few scattered evergreen trees between houses. Nearly a million people densely packed. Oil refineries and cell phone towers dominated the skyline. Devoid of agriculture, rich in oil money, it surrounded Forward Operating Base Warrior, the military airport.

A sight I'd never seen before came into view upon the final approach to the base. Like four massive jet engines placed on end, plumes of natural gas flames shot sixty feet in the air, full blast, cooking off the gas they hadn't the technology to reap, and wasting precious energy and filling the sky with a greasy, smelly, smoke. I could feel the roaring through ballistic glass from a mile away.

Through twists and turns and a large Entry Control Point, our convoy reached its destination, the Kirkuk Residence Office inside FOB Warrior. A handover of its projects to my office, Major to Major, was set to begin. Project folders, blueprints, basic face-to-face downloads, and visiting jobsites were a thousand times more insightful than digging through USACE (US Army Corps of Engineers) computer data bases for project reports. The Brits brushed and watered the horses/Land Rovers. Cooper, a Construction Representative from our office, and I really wanted to see the prints of the 18-classroom school at Halabja and of the Chamchamal Prison sanitary lagoon.

The Major wasn't in when we arrived at the Engineer compound. Cooper and I waited nearly an hour, interrupted briefly by a Staff Sergeant who quickly unlocked his office, closed the door, reappeared with a white cardboard box, and relocked the door and quickly tried to leave. I engaged him about his "part of the puzzle." The Sergeant stopped for a moment, his hands full.

"You'll have to ask Major Jingus about the projects, Sir. I'm leaving in two days." The Kirkuk office had nearly ten open projects, all behind schedule.

"Going home?"

"Well, first I have to get to Baghdad and clear the hand receipt there, and then come back and clear our buildings with the Mayor's cell." Which meant USACE really was leaving Kirkuk.

Curious about process, I asked, "Doesn't Major Jingus have to clear HIS hand receipt?" As the Officer in Charge, he would be personally responsible for the station's property and equipment. Delegating this important task to a junior subordinate was revealing. That kind of shit really pisses me off. You can delegate authority, but never your responsibility. Major Jingus was just trying to get out of doing his job, a dereliction of duty.

The NCO was getting impatient, "No, I'm signed for everything." He shuffled his hands under the box, "but you'll have to ask Major Jingus about that."

"Uh, thanks. Safe travels." And that's the last time I saw him. OK, I'll ask Jingus. But where's Jingus? What's a Jingus? I was about to find out. And he wasn't no Santy Claus.

Major Jingus entered the building and without saying a word went straight to his office, unlocked it, entered briefly, and then responded to our presence, reappearing.

"Hi. How are you?" I introduced myself, "I'm Major Dupar from the Tikrit office. This is Cooper. He's the Senior Construction Rep from our office."

"Hey, how are you guys doing?" Chris Jingus still hadn't looked me in the eye even while shaking hands. It was as if he wasn't expecting us. "Come on into my office."

I never understood people locking their offices. I mean, if you want the paperwork, take it, it's yours. But don't steal my Swingline stapler or I'll burn the building down.

The first thing I noticed on his desk was a Victoria's Secret catalog. Cooper saw it too, and we looked at each other in disbelief. Before the age of porn on your smartphone a terrific deal was to buy a pair of socks at Victoria's Secret and sign up for the catalog via the US Mail. It was like free soft porn before Al Gore invented the internet. But on top of your office desk? It was distracting. Maybe Major Jingus was nervous. But he was about to rotate home. Now I knew why he had a lock on his door.

"What're you going to do when get home, Major?

"Chris. My name is Chris."

"Where's home for you, Chris?" I asked.

"San Bernardino."

I cut him off, "California! That's where McDonalds started." I was proud to be quick witted.

"I guess so."

Cooper was done with the idiocy, "Major Jingus, if you have the blueprints for Halabja or Chamchamal I'd like to look them over while you and the Major chat."

Thanks Cooper, I thought, right to business. Major Jingus rummaged through some file drawers in the outer office, before exclaiming, "I guess we don't have them anymore. I can burn the prints on a CD for you if you want." Not good. WHAT DO YOU MEAN YOU DON'T HAVE BLUEPRINTS! It is like going to your doctor and being told that they don't keep patients' medical records. But the mountain of stupid was just beginning to rise.

"When do you want to go to the prison? Tomorrow?" I asked Jingus. Cooper walked away as if in a daze. I just wanted to salvage this bad first impression, as I needed this man to throw me the ball.

"You can ask the convoy guys."

"Where's their office in the compound here?"

"They moved a few months ago, but I think it's near our gym." YOU THINK?

I didn't know what to say except, "OK." The transfer of projects to the Tikrit Office would get worse. Major Jingus didn't know where the gym was either, by the looks of him.

"My last Project Engineer left two weeks ago so it's just me and Sergeant Olsen, and he's clearing the hand receipt for our stuff."

It was like rushing to the bridge of the Titanic and seeing that Homer Simpson was at the wheel. He'd look at you and say, "Just because I don't care doesn't mean that I don't understand."

"So what have you been doing," I wanted to ask, "besides overpaying lazy contractors, and putting me in a bind on every one of your construction projects?"

"About what?" He'd probably ask. Thanks, Homer Jingus. We got it from here.

• • •

The Russians were contracted to build a prison in the 1960's that could have been constructed two hundred or even five hundred years earlier. Solitary, massive stone walls appeared on a rolling barren plain. Only 60 kilometers northeast of oil rich Kirkuk, the village of Chamchamal lent its name to a prison. It was just inside Kurdistan. We would take off our body armor and helmets upon crossing the unofficial border. There was no danger of roadside bombs or ambushes where the Kurds lived. The four-story square fortress, with roundhouse towers at the corners, was imposing. The low hills bubbled up from the scrubland where a few sheep grazed. Except for one unimproved road stretching for many kilometers off the highway, there's no entry or escape from the prison of Chamchamal.

The Kurds are a people still without a nation. There are many such people, but the Kurds may be the largest and certainly the oldest without their own borders maintained by war. Almost completely autonomous, the Kurdish people skip from rebellion to revolts, fighting Arabs, British, Ottomans, Mongols, Muslims, Romans, Greeks, Persians, Babylonians, and Assyrians throughout recorded time. They fought with Coalition

Forces in the recent wars with Saddam and ISIS. Americans in Kurdistan are as safe as newborn kittens nuzzled by little kids.

The prison kept many people who resisted forced migrations of Arabs to Kurdistan and the removal of Kurds, Turkoman, Yezidi, Armenian and Assyrian Christians, in a fiendish effort to influence parliamentary results for the Ba'athists. The socialist political party champions were the Assads of Syria and the inner circle of Saddam Hussein al-Tikriti.

• • •

Out of Forward Operating Base Warrior through the only Entry Control Point, the armed escort wound its way through the choked boulevards of middle-class Kirkuk, where I saw Santa Claus in a store front. He looked like the Coca-Cola cardboard cutout inspiration of Madmen advertisers in 1950's New York, with white beard, red suit, pot-bellied, with the alcoholic rosy nose of affluence. It was just before Thanksgiving and I hadn't thought of the fact that there have been Christians in Iraq since Christians existed. The Christmas ritual was as confused in Iraq as at home. The birth of Christ versus presents. In Northern Iraq, Christian refugees would flee from the horror of ISIS into Kurdistan a few years after America left.

In an hour, I spied small cranes dotting the art deco village of Chamchamal and spotted several contractors' construction projects. These people thought they lived on Miami Beach with peach, pink, and lime green paints. The little hamlet was prosperous. Once it was in the rear-view mirror, the continuous rise before us seemed to lift the prison skyward. It made me feel like I was going to fly off of the earth. Our scope was to fix the sanitation problem at the fortress prison.

The awful stench of flowing raw human sewage quickly overtook all other senses. I never got inside the prison yard. I was never invited in, thank God. Since Saddam was dead and his regime cohorts removed, political enemies must have been released by 2010-11. Real criminals (not like those who merely appropriate bulldozers), were over-crowded inside. Perhaps the water was turned on for only an hour a day, at which point the inmates clogged toilets that could barely flush. It must have smelled appalling in there, making the prisoners even more frustrated, angry and dangerous.

The Corps of Engineers had contracted years earlier an onsite wastewater treatment system that was both too small and built incorrectly. Or so we thought. The reader, by now, understands that one facet of my humor resides permanently in the fifth grade. Nonetheless, I am forced again to talk about poo. I'm an Army Engineer, so I am needed for shit like this. It was like a crap crescendo, standing next to the nastiest, gurgling, cesspool ever. I felt much luckier than the men on the other side of the walls, in this symphony of bubbles, shudders and burps.

From huge plugged-up underground concrete tanks containing socks or whatever devices the prisoners chose to disable the plumbing system, the black water fed into open concrete pools that were supposed to strain the big stuff at the top, thus allowing the bacteria to feast. Those pools were overflowing into the first lagoon. Imagine how your coffee percolates through the grounds and filter. The pools were supposed to have big rocks on top, smaller rocks beneath them, and so on until you got to sand and drains running from the bottom to the first lagoon. The system is gravity fed, so there's a second lagoon containing lots of reeds, until eventually the runoff enters the ecosystem as pure as an artesian spring.

That's the theory. Except that wasn't what was happening. Since something was messed up, the Corp simply decided to build the same system again, but this time twice as big. Then, if that worked, they would drain and repair the original system and find out if the material to strain out the nasties and give our bacteria friend adequate time to munch had been reversed; in other words, the sand on the top and big rocks on the bottom.

The contractor wasn't there working when we showed up, but two bulldozers, a scraper, and an excavator were on site. Some survey stakes laid out future cuts and fills (earthmoving), and the job trailer had a schedule and plans laid out on a table. A phone number was written on the white board. Cooper called the number and a man and his interpreter came out in about a half an hour. I came on strong as usual, telling him he was behind schedule and that he needed much more equipment on site. He complained about the winter rains and that he couldn't push mud, which was true. We shook hands, and sure enough the rainfall tables showed that the deeper you got into Kurdistan, the rainier, greener, and more beautiful it became. He said he would make up for lost time when we got to February.

Dirt plus water equals mud. Dirt plus mud equals more mud. You had to let earth dry in order to move and shape it, and that means no significant rain for a few days. I liked him. At least he had a plan. He told us that the previous contractor wasn't any good. And that a local farmer was bitching about the contamination and threatening him with possibly seeking monetary damages. Farming? Where? I asked myself. The new guy was worried about proceeding under the current conditions. I said, like a tough guy, "Don't worry about it. We'll take care of it. Just keep working."

I thought, "Maybe I should visit my Peshmerga General contact?" I didn't want any more trouble than I already had. Maybe he could fix that new problem for me.

• • •

Crossing through foothills, I could see the earth slump toward the plain. Coming back toward Kirkuk, leaving unofficial Kurdistan, the poplar and willow trees gave way to date palms and then just dusty brown aridness. Helmets back on, body armor restored, the war resumed.

Winding through neighborhoods and busy boulevard's traffic jams, I looked for Santa again and there it was— the cutout! It was late November and I saw the holiday symbol several more times before Christmas. And then in a dignified sort of way he was gone by mid-January. Not like in America where folks leave the colored lights on their houses until Easter; where Christians don't have to flee from their homes.

FOB Warrior had a fabulous main chow hall, the best I've ever enjoyed or encountered. As I mentioned before, the worse the place, the better the food. Gourmet salad bars with various nuts and cheeses. Pies and cakes. Steaks were regular fare, as were crab legs and thin crust pizza. Stir fry bars were standard at dining facilities across Iraq, and they had two of them. Five hundred could sit comfortably, and you faced the cooler night air with the satisfaction that you couldn't have had a better meal.

In the Engineer compound the trailers were divided, and although you got your own room and a decent bed, the dusty yuck of ill-maintained premises reminded me of the old Army adage, "it can always get worse." This was a long way from the worst, but pretty tough by Engineer standards. I brought my own linen, fluffy towels, and down-filled pillows.

At 0500 I was awakened by a distant "THUMP THUMP THUMP" of incoming mortars about to impact.

The juvenile voice of a southern boy having his fun thundered, "AT-TENTION ON THE FOB."

"AT-TENTION ON THE FOB." I could feel this kid trying not to grin and pretending to be some sort of Wizard of Oz.

"BOOM." No vibration. "BOOM. BOOM." The explosions were far off from where I slept.

"THIS IS THE BIG GIANT VOICE!" Why weren't there any sirens?

"INCOMING, INCOMING, INCOMING." I jammed on my shorts and t-shirt and ran outside in my flip flops. But there wasn't a soul in sight.

"I SAY AGIN. ENCOMIN ENCOMIN ENCOMIN." A slight lilt in his voice on the last word—so surreal. The Sunni insurgents reminded us of their ability so regularly that US Forces fell into complacency before our withdrawal.

Everything fell silent. The soldiers treated this more like a morning alarm because it happened so often. I didn't know where a bunker was. Nobody around. I never found out if any damage was done to personnel or equipment. I smoked a butt, wide awake now. The next time it happened on subsequent visits I fell back to sleep. I suppose it wasn't my turn to cash in my chips. Or was I just lazy-sleepy like everybody else? There were never more than five or six mortars when the Big Giant Voice broadcast.

One morning we visited the open projects on post with the Major. All were incomplete, with contractors overpaid and absent from the job. We had to drag them over the finish line, as fire suppression systems and aircraft hangar doors had been begun, then abandoned mid-contract. Frequent phone calls and follow-up pushed the work to proceed, long after the Officer in Charge at the Kirkuk Residence Office left.

"What are you going to do when you get back, Major Jingus?" I asked.

"I'm resigning my commission and am going to teach English in Japan." That was a shocker!

What's your commissioning source?"

"West Point." Really? He was Active Duty, not a silly Reservist like me.

"How many years do you have in?"

"Over ten." I was astonished he'd throw that away. No pension, no nothing.

"Why?"

"I just don't want to get deployed again. This one was too much."

It didn't make any sense. He was away from the proverbial flagpole, with the best boss in the world two hours away, Lieutenant Colonel Watson. He could do (or not do) anything he wanted. "It's tough being away from family," I said. I knew I was pressing but this man fascinated me? "Are you married?"

"No." I was confused and wanted to shift direction. I should have stopped asking so many questions but I couldn't.

"Well, that should be really cool living in Japan. What made you want to go there?"

"I just always wanted to go there."

"Do you speak Japanese?"

"No." Great plan. Good luck. "I'll pick up the pieces here by myself." I thought. I had to walk away, I just grabbed my duffle bag and ruck sack and waited for British Convoys to take us back home to Speicher.

• • •

From the Resident Office in Balad, we got another five modular schools, but they were wrapping up quickly, administered efficiently. Diyala Province had many poor people, side roads were filled with garbage, the government services dicey. I was psyched knowing that we would stop on the handover tour at Ba'Qubah, the birthplace of Aladdin (you know – with the magic lamp, Genie, and the flying carpet.) Diyala was the land of the "not quite right."

Bombings within that city were frequent. Five civilians this week, then the next week ten more blown up, destroyed. Dozens would be injured with an IED detonating on a busy street or neighborhood market or a mosque. We reviewed the intelligence reports weekly, snapshots on a storyboard made by Power Point rangers in the Divisional Staff. They were crucial to plan routes toward our nearly finished hospital addition in downtown Ba'Qubah; the birthplace of Aladdin, a classic Disney tale.

Major Diaz was an experienced, traveled man, with a beautiful family somewhere in California. I saw a picture on his desk. He had three kids between the twelve and six-year range. His wife was smoking hot and his athletic body must have served him well throughout his life. He was a long-distance bicyclist and couldn't wait to ride a century (100 miles) through the Sierra Mountains on his Wisconsin- made $5,000 Trek, and be with the fam of course. There's nothing like the feeling you're about to go home. The sense of urgency is fantastically painful.

You could get a really good tan in Iraq if you worked on it. It's always good to avoid looking like a raccoon-eyed soldier with windblown cheeks and white rings around your eyes. Major Diaz had spent much time in the sun, both in Cali and Iraq. It was a night versus day comparison in competency from the Kirkuk Office where I was wrapping up projects. It was Major Diaz who coined the phrase, "If you have to go to war, go to war with the Corps." He was a proud Engineer. And absolutely correct.

The FOB in Balad had a lot of amenities. The pool was in operation most of the year. A theater was established seven years before, probably one of the first things that got going and of course, the DFAC was excellent. The proverbial Burger King was on station, and a few other restaurants served a variety of Middle East and American fare, Tex Mex and pizza.

A new four-story hospital addition had been built, with just a few finishing tasks in order to be able to walk away. The heating/ventilation system and an elevator that still had to be completed and commissioned, but the contractor had demonstrated function; now it was the tasked to energize the HVAC and balance out the air flow in the new building. I met these contractors on the roof despite a warning by my British brethren. Those guys went everywhere, and advice from them had to be taken seriously. It was brief, but we walked through the pieces yet to be functional. Ba'Qubah inspectors had green-lighted work thus far. The construction was 99.9% complete. Administrators waited on equipment for their surgical suites, technical departments, and patient floors. The third-story bridge between old and new only needed a temporary partition to come down, and a river of hurt and sick people would gush into a much-needed space.

The one-megawatt generators were the sore spot. The new medical facility could have uninterrupted electricity for the heavy price of thousands of liters of diesel, to the tune of more than ten thousand dollars per month. From what quarter of Iraqi governmental administration that money would come from was unknown. That wasn't America's problem or concern. Going home was.

# CHAPTER 24

# Disneyworld

It was my turn to go home on mid-tour leave, January 2011. I had heard of a place called Shades of Green on the grounds of Disneyworld in Orlando and made the reservations. They catered to military families with sweet deals. My daughter was ten and not too old to race Dad from the elevator to the room. She was quick, and although I could accelerate and close the gap, my daughter always won. Sometimes I'd take a lead by cheating and starting to run on two instead of the count of three. Cheating, like in baseball, was tolerated in my little family, reminiscent of board games like "Chutes and Ladders," in which accurate counting was an accident. Fourteen days of paid leave started when my boots hit Atlanta.

I became a failure at playing Barbies, as it always resulted in car crashes with the Barbie mobile home and kidnappings at the hand of stuffed animal kingpin "Earl, the Squirrel." I had his voice down pat, with a gravelly baritone like James Earl Jones. It is a crisp memory from days I could still play on the floor despite spent carpenter knees. It was upsetting to me, not being able to play; some causes lead to lonely effects.

To my tremendous anal retentive frustration, Ellen hadn't kept up on the snow removal, and ice compacted by winter tires remained until spring—only one reason why we eventually broke up. Everyone knows you have to shovel as soon as the last flake falls. But I did get to push the white stuff once that season. On the other side of the world it was a pleasant 85 in Tikrit. But don't think that the deployments or military service led to the dissolution of the union. The Army probably kept us together longer.

Immediate family had dibs on our limited time, as we had to visit relations and friends. That's the thing—obligations don't end even when you just want to be let be. We weren't special per se, but when Dad or Mom comes back from the war, everybody wants to give you a hug.

Ellen could have been an editor, her nose always in a book. She never forgot a name or phone number; it was her brain that always attracted me most to her. Remembering those brief days of paid leave now fills me with fondness and loving kindness. I was actually home, not worried about a thing except the hours that kept slipping by without profound meaning. Sleep was like wasting time, the mundane being interesting, like the Cock-a-Poodle's ear infection and the gross yeasty smell it produced. Overindulgence of adult beverages from habit, nervousness, and stupidity wasted more time.

My girls grew beyond any patterns, me on the outside looking in. Like all families of Service members, they serve while staying in the US. Avoiding the news and videos of IEDs exploding underneath the vehicles of those they love, they imagined those on sleepless nights and exhausted mornings. Their duty is worry of the unknown, while reality is boredom between missions, video games on cots, austere living conditions, and infrequent racing of your heart when you heard the "BOOM BOOM BOOM" of mortars. We are part of the meager 1% warrior class in a society full of armchair generals, and those that couldn't be bothered to care.

The night before flying to Florida we went to Sesame Street Live on Ice at Milwaukee's arena. I thanked God that it wasn't Barney the purple dinosaur, but something from my own childhood. The Muppets skated out to the lyrics of, "Can you tell me how to get, how to get to Sesame Street?" Their band then began playing a jazz funk. Cookie Monster was always a favorite. The cerebral Muppet had introduced my generation to big words like EN-CY-CLO-PE-DI-A but now teaches kids how to use GOO-GLE. Bert, and Ernie, who never stopped messing with him, floated in from opposite entrances. Grover, who seeped love and always ended skits with hugs, pushed the scary Oscar the Grouch in his grimy trash can to center ice and spun around. Even the massive, unsure, elephantine Mr. Shuffleupagus lumbered out, skating on four big hairy legs. We could see him, but no one else could. He was the imaginary best friend of the star of the show.

Kermit and Miss Piggy had their duet. Elmo was laughing, gauging tight circles in the ice, laughing. But something was definitely wrong. Suddenly, a man in a costume with yellow feathers skated out on orange and pink striped legs, with his right arm held straight over his head. Everyone roared as the tallest Muppet stole the performance. His presence forced open a plumbing pressure relief valve I didn't know existed, and the tears flowed furiously. I remembered his soothing tones. He always gave comfort to kids from the ugly speech of playmates and parents. I always keep a handkerchief in my left back pocket. You never know when something cathartic might happen. Like a hymn, a bit of prose, or Big Bird skating on ice.

Milwaukee to Chicago to Orlando was like a trip to the bathroom compared to getting out of theater, which took several days of the Army's paradigm of "Hurry up and wait." My wife allowed our daughter to pack her own things and immediately on the first evening the lack of a swimsuit became a MAJOR crisis. I ventured to a Disney shop via monorail and bought a Tinkerbell suit three sizes too small. What did I know? We would have to try again. Dinner surrounded by a jungle motif, beer, wine, and ice cream calmed the tropical storm, and the kiddo eventually fell asleep in an adjoining room. Another pressure relief valve opened during our own duet.

Space Mountain was a fun little coaster. I paid homage to the statues Walt Disney and Mickey Mouse inside the Magic Kingdom. The park wasn't crowded in late January. Ellen was increasingly fearful, so my daughter and I rode together. Spinning the wheel as fast as I could on the teacup ride, I couldn't make my daughter scream, "Stop!" Abby always was a tough kid. A spectacular display of fireworks and parades topped off the evening.

Epcot Center has America's biggest golf ball, with a rollercoaster inside. We strolled past Restaurants of the World around a man-made lake. No one could make a decision among the twenty or so places to eat. I was up for German, with the requisite dark beer; but oddly, neither Korean, South American, Moroccan, nor Indian food sparked my daughter's interest. Ironically, we ended up having cheeseburgers, American fare, halfway around the pond. We watched an entertainer juggle lit torches while balancing from seven tilted chairs, twelve feet in the air—quite the act. It was all worthy of the admission.

A water park, an animal park, more rides, and a hurricane barreling towards the east coast of the United States, and our adventure's end was pushed back another day. I tried calling the airline from the landline at the hotel, while Ellen changed flights with her smart phone in minutes. I was still on hold with the airline when I decided I had to upgrade from my flip phone. "When I get back to the States in another five months, June, right after my birthday," I told myself.

I watched the mighty, mighty Green Bay Packers narrowly win Super Bowl XLV with Mom, Dad, and Sis at the house where I grew up. The dreaded Pittsburgh Steelers got close in the 4th quarter, but the Green and Gold scooted away. Our banner was already displayed proudly in the chow hall so I didn't write to the coach, Mike McCarthy, requesting another. 2011 was starting off great.

Rewinding, getting back to theater, was a chore. It took all of three days to get back to Tikrit. This time, though, nobody cried at the airport. We had become a rugged little family.

CHAPTER 25

# Happy Place

There came a time when I realized that US Forces really needed to get out of Iraq.

Across Route Tampa, just east of FOB Speicher, was the largest contract under my office's purview, at over $22 million. It was always on schedule. I wish I could place many emojis here, because this was my Happy Place. The headquarters for the Iraqi 4th Infantry Division was huge. An American outfit supervised the building of the complex, and construction reps along with me—Lieutenant Colonel Watson, all VIPs—went there to see what "right looks like." No problems, only the hum of correctly completed construction tasks.

Just next door was another similarly huge complex that had been built the year before as the logistical hub for the Iraqi 4th Division. That contract was another massive $22 million. At least some of the costs were covered by the Iraqis themselves, instead of only the US taxpayers.

Both installations had nine one-megawatt generators that guzzled diesel from massive tanks nearby. An inconvenient truth about construction in Iraq is that placing generators anywhere was like putting a pressure bandage on a hemorrhaging wound. The electrical grid, no matter where you went, was inadequate. Power interruptions were the norm. Placing big generators by new facilities really just obligated administrations for big budget expenditures for diesel. You'd think that in an oil-rich country that energy would be abundant. But there was never enough refinery capacity for diesel production, and it was expensive. Often, a project's operational expenses got lost in the fervor of new construction.

The headquarters had offices and barracks, and a dining facility with as yet unused stoves, prep tables, giant mixers, walk-in freezers, and the like. Beautiful stuff if you're a cook. For the mechanics, shops were built with tool cages, vehicle lifts, garages, and hydraulic lines ready to be plugged into pressure tanks. A water treatment plant processed the black water, and a lagoon was ready to eat up the nasties filtrating out into the desert. We encountered a hospital, laundry facilities, a shooting range, vaults for weapons and ammo storage, motor pools, and raised guard towers behind berms, with tall fencing topped by razor wire. Everything needed to resist ISIS when they came down route Tampa from Mosul except the will to fight.

Prime Minister Nouri Al Maliki, a Shia, purged the military of Sunni officers, attempting to create an institution loyal to him, and not the nation. The Officer Corps became extremely politicized and alienated the Sunni people of Iraq even further, sowing seeds for future rebellion. Besides, the Shia officers might think, "why should we fight for Tikrit? It is a Sunni city, and Saddam Hussein's hometown?" America put a lot of resources into training officers to be apolitical, just to have Maliki end their careers because of their religious affiliation.

With only two weeks before the ribbon cutting at the huge facility shepherded by my office, an Iraqi Colonel came to inspect the premises. I just happened to be there. He was very angry and demanded we go to the General's office.

"OK. Why?"

"Where is the General to sleep?" He sputtered.

In the barracks? There are single rooms there. In a bed? I gave him the deer in the headlights stare. "What do you mean, Sir?" I asked through my interpreter. That put his balls in a twist.

"This is no better than where we are now!" What was really happening began to become clear. "At our headquarters now, the General has his quarters in his office. And doesn't go down the hall to use the common latrine."

Ohhhhh. The perks of office weren't built into his office. It wasn't big enough. The accommodations weren't commensurate with a man of his apparent status. Now I was starting to get mad. The Commander needed his own private bath. It was common for folks to want to have their hooches next to their desk, I get it. But let's get this one thing straight—in the last two wars, who kicked whose ass? But he outranked me ostensibly, and was the "customer," so I had to wring out all the military bearing I had. The blueprints are the blueprints, though; I have to build to them. Maybe I could place a hook on the wall for the Colonel's kneepads for when he wasn't servicing the General. My blood began to boil.

"Sir, we built according to the plans, which I'm sure were approved by your government." I gave his balls another half twist. He was just lashing out before the ass reaming he was preparing to receive himself, trying to figure out whom to blame. How about that cocky Engineer Major? The tongue lashing continued. The latrines were too small. Go piss up a rope then, I mused, although my face was grim. "Come with me," the Colonel snarled and gestured triumphantly, turning his back. He walked quickly to his car and the tour continued three blocks away. My interpreter and I had to run to catch up at the sparkling mess hall, as my vehicle was too far away to be useful. I hoped that his putting me in my place made the Colonel feel better, the bastard.

"There must be a private dining room for officers." The Colonel's hands were on his hips, his face sweaty. He asked, "Where's the officers' mess?" His English was passable.

"This is it. This is for everybody," I panted. How egalitarian! I waved my hand sideways across a hall that would feed hundreds at a time, and beamed back. I thought, "Fire me, bitch; fire me."

We went to the hospital, where he proceeded to complain that the concrete didn't extend out into the drive, so that rolling litters could meet the ambulances. That was somewhat valid. Perhaps they could place concrete on their own? There wasn't the needed medical equipment in order to be operational. A true statement, but that wasn't my problem. The laundry facilities were too small. Now that had occurred to me as well. Too bad, I'm going home in a few months, and there's nothing I can do to change the plans now, even if I wanted to.

Eventually, the Iraqi Colonel just stormed off, disgusted, got in his car, and was driven away.

I walked out into the plume of dust the tires kicked up and waved high into the air and said," I love you. I'm going to miss you." Yeah, like a hemorrhoid.

• • •

A few weeks later, my good friend, Captain Dmitri Fletcher from the US Air Force, took us across the road to the logistical hub with his security detail. I needed to close out a maintenance contract. He needed to meet with the Iraqi Garrison Commander, if he was there, to discuss plans to finally complete the occupation of the facility. I didn't envy Captain Fletcher's role of mentoring an older senior Iraqi man. The Tikrit Residence Office had built this installation in 2009. The Corps decided to pay a contractor (two guys) to maintain the facility while the Iraqi 4th Division Loggies (soldiers specializing in Logistics) moved in and figured things out. These two fellows were underworked and overpaid. But a contract is a contract, and it was coming rapidly to a close. I met them briefly and asked them what they were working on.

"We have to replace an exhaust fan in the bakery," he told me in very good English.

I observed one man leave to go get a screwdriver, while the other waited. Their gravy train was almost at an end, probably the most money they'd ever receive in their lives. $300/week in Iraq could make you king of the village for a while. But hey, at least they came to work every day and kept the one-megawatt generators humming. Although operational for a year, not a single loaf of bread had been baked there. The stainless steel mixing vats were pristine, the sinks never used to clean out a pan. Why did the Iraqis pay the US to build these facilities if they weren't going to use them? They could have made more than a thousand loaves a day easily, if the need arose.

The logistics hub had its own reverse osmosis plant to clean its water, lots of maintenance shops, barracks, and offices and other support structures—much that had yet to be used. Captain Fletcher and I peeked into a couple of buildings before trying to find the Commander. I was impressed with how tidy everything was, such as the grounds, inside living quarters, the latrines. At least the sergeants were doing their jobs.

The Colonel was extremely angry when we finally sat down with him. I had just recently seen the same movie.

"Good afternoon, Sir," Dmitri said when we were settled in. I noticed we weren't offered any chairs. "Major Dupar is here to discuss the maintenance contract, and I wanted to ask about your timetable to complete your unit's move here."

"Do you know, Captain, how much diesel we will need to run the generators? It costs $10,000 dollars a month, maybe—probably much more." He leaned forward over his desk, "Are you going to give me the diesel?" The officer's English was superb, his tone as snarky as a teenage girl.

"Well, no, Sir. That is supposed to be within your budget. But when we finish the transfer station off of Route Tampa, your electrical needs should be satisfied, and the generators won't be used all that much." Dmitri told me that the Colonel was at work maybe two weeks a month. Not unusual for senior Iraqi politically-appointed officers. The problem was that in autocratic leadership structures, subordinates are often afraid to make decisions, so progress towards organizational goals comes slowly. Delegation and knowledge of what the boss's intent is fosters better results.

"We both know that will never happen!" He considered his tone and throttled back, "Even when the transfer station is operational, we don't know with the budget uncertain when we will move the entire unit here." The Colonel scowled patronizingly.

He looked at me. "Can't you just continue with another maintenance contract? If the generators stop working, then it will be a disaster. Then we will call you and you will have to fix the problem."

Oh, goody. It was my turn, "No, Sir! Can't do that. I have no way to pay these two men after next week," I whined. It felt like Dimitri slapped my hand and exited the ring. I flew across it, did a sling shot against the ropes, and gave the Colonel a clothesline smash across his chest. "And that's why we trained ten of your maintenance soldiers on how to keep the generators running." I wanted to ask why they were dragging their feet in moving in 100%. Usually customers are right on your butt to utilize vastly better facilities.

Having anticipated the antipathy of senior Iraqi officers towards working and planning, my predecessor Major Tamara Artois tasked Mr. Darrow to develop a small program of Instruction to include both classroom and hands on training to avoid such a disaster as the Colonel now acknowledged could/would occur. But as for calling on me to help after they screwed the pooch, he could shove that up his—you know. We'd done enough. I had him in a headlock, figuratively, then spun, grabbed his upper arm with my left hand, hooked my right arm under his crotch, picked him up and spun again. But I had to ask this question, "Sir, what was your plan to maintain the facility after the contract ran out?" BODY SLAM, BITCH! BOOYAH!

He stammered about things being unfair to him and then eventually dismissed us both. On the short walk to our awaiting vehicles, I looked at Captain Fletcher and said, "Dimitri, we've got to leave this country."

"You're goddamn right about that, Kenny." He was fuming too. Unfortunately, he still had to babysit for a few more months before he got to rotate back to the world. The more America gave the more that was expected. The cycle had to end sometime. Even Uncle Sugar had a budget. There was an option to extend the maintenance contract another year, but both of us, Army and Air Force, agreed it'd just postpone the inevitable. Little sister had to step up and stop whining, now that big sister was leaving for college.

• • •

The efforts at the schools continued and we visited each one every six days. In the crossroads city of Tuz Khurmatu, the city itself intervened and prevented the school from being built. I didn't believe my contractor at first—"just another dumb excuse" I thought. The factory in Tukey delivered all the panels and piers. But it took a few weeks to finally speak with a city councilman, who had thankfully safeguarded the air conditioners, lights, and other pilferable items. It was one of the four schools my Tikrit Office had inherited from the now closed Kirkuk office.

I had met the principal during an earlier visit. The modular school was to be built in the middle of the city of 50,000 people, so I had to be somewhat circumspect in terms of just walking around willy-nilly. After a bad cup of chia, he gave me the tour of the grounds, and sure enough, the coordinates placed the new structure behind the old school, into what basically was a bowl. It always flooded there, he explained to me. That's why it was just a place for the kids to play, if it was dry, but today it had mud puddles. He showed me how the rainwater was ushered from the school's roof and towards the storm drain, and I instantly realized that someone in the Corps had screwed up royally, probably without making a site visit.

But the title deed given to the Corps through Salah Ad Din Province was specific. Trying to change it now could take months. New site surveys, politicians, and bureaucrats gumming things up. And the contractor needed to start building immediately. What to do? How about some nefarious not-so-legal type shit from the mind of an ethically challenged major? I went back and forth with the city councilman a few times trying to explain my predicament. The panels for the modular school were sitting out in the open for a month, then two months. My Arab politician friend was equally in a rush to secure the pieces of the school.

"We can build it ourselves. We want to move the school about two hundred meters when we have the new deed." It always impressed me how many Iraqis spoke English; how well educated and well-meaning local leaders were.

"I don't know. I guess we could take a credit back from the contractor for not building it." At this point in the spring of 2011 the other seventeen schools were being completed in rapid succession. He continued, "We have to have the contractor bring the panels to our warehouse." Where? "Then, when we can, we will build it, no problem."

Tony suggested that I ask headquarters for permission. "You never know. They probably don't care either," he said. It was getting so late in the game that a desperation play almost made sense. I quietly pitched the idea through channels and it met with no objections. One smart Project Engineer in Baghdad said I should get documentation from the City of Tuz. Documentation! Of course. Why hadn't I thought of that? My politician teammate, whom I never met, had the plan in my email Inbox in four working days, signed and stamped.

Darren, my contractor, arranged to have a crane onsite and the panels were moved. It was off our books. Everybody was happy. I wish I could go back and see if the kids got their school. I'm sure they did, as what politician wouldn't want his picture in the newspaper, beaming at the opening.

A few years later I saw a story on CNN about a spectacular terrorist bombing in the city of Tuz that killed more than 20 people. ISIS continued to cause chaos and murder families. Why? Because girls got to go to school?

• • •

"WE'VE GOT A RUNNER!" There are fewer funnier and ass-puckering phrases in the English language than that. "We've got a runner!"

Within our Tikrit office family was an Iraqi poet who worked for the Corps of Engineers as an interpreter. Aabid's poetry had won international prizes. He gave me his work translated into English. It was primarily about the anguish felt by Iraqi women due to the tremendous and needless loss of their husbands and sons during the eight-year Iraq/Iran war. It started when Saddam Hussein attacked his neighbor. The butcher's bill to these women tallied in the hundreds of thousands of souls. No territory exchanged hands, no national goals were reached, just wanton destruction. His poetry to me was lost in translation but extremely emotional stuff.

Aabid was devout and kept the fast of Ramadan faithfully. Sun up to sun down, not even water passed his lips. During that month I often couldn't find him. I leaned upon him mightily for cross-cultural stuff, like what "Insha Allah" means in actual context—"God willing." He had moved his family to Dallas years earlier and although his pay was low, his circumstance was better now than at any other time. Aabid had multiple deployments to his credit, which to him was like coming home. He was a slender, short, dignified, and well-groomed man. The type of guy you know has fifty IQ points on you and who thought and breathed righteousness.

If he wasn't outside the wire on a mission, or at his desk, the poet was in his CHU (containerized housing unit/bungalow) praying. The few times people looked for him, that was where he was, and Aabid wasn't shy about saying he had been praying. I guessed things at home in Texas weren't great. Would he have liked to get back immediately? A man with his exemplary record could have been given emergency leave. Or Aabid could just quit.

My Senior NCO, Master Sergeant Gibbons, couldn't find him after a day of inquiry.

"Sir, I checked the airport terminal like you suggested, but finally found out this morning that he got onto a convoy with the Brits going to Baghdad."

I cocked my head a little, "Does he have a mission down there that he didn't tell us about? Or forgot to maybe?" Please, not Aabid. He was my favorite Muslim in the whole wide world.

"I checked with headquarters in Baghdad and no one has seen him so far."

"You know what this means?"

"Yes, Sir."

"We've got a RUNNER," I shouted with all the due emphasis that this demanded!

"We got a runner," she repeated, and kind of smiled.

"HARD TO STARBOARD! BATTON DOWN THE HATCHES. SOUND GENERAL QUARTERS! CANCEL ALL LEAVES AND PASSES! ACCOUNT FOR ALL THE GUARDS! DIVE DIVE DIVE!" And I started to make that shrill horn sound when a submarine in the movies descends as fast as possible to avoid the depth charges from the destroyers above, "AARRUGGA, AARUGGA, AARUGGA!"

Master Sergeant Gibbons, who had known me for nine months, calmly, gently said, "Sir, I think you need to calm down."

I was starting to slap myself in the head and spin around like it was feeding time at the chimpanzee exhibit. Her suggestion helped. Now, Auntie Sugar doesn't take kindly when a guest absents himself without proper leave. But then, this wasn't a prison, exactly. He was a civilian, after all. She'd just wait until he finally popped up, and then hopefully, kindly, simply send him home. No reason to waste good talent. Aabid was just under a lot of stress. I prayed he got back with his family OK. Insha Allah. If God wills it.

# CHAPTER 26

# Poison Gas at Halabja

Getting to the secondary school at Halabja always meant running through Kirkuk. It was a lot easier to stay at FOB Warrior two nights, one coming and one going. I had to check on the ankle-biter projects still not finished on base. We'd leave Speicher after lunch. It was only a 90-minute ride. Major Jingus had rotated back to the world. The stupid idiot paid the contractor $400K for concrete work not yet completed. I guess fouling up the project was his parting gift.

When I checked with the Mayor's cell at FOB Warrior about the building handover, a Department of the Army civilian told me that the post had almost the entire Engineer footprint assigned to units leaving Iraq for good, without another unit handing off.

She was a rare breed in Iraq, an American civilian, and female. She didn't have a wedding ring on, I noticed. But I had no time left to flirt with a pretty girl. I didn't want anything at that moment, anyway, as if that would've mattered. It never hurts to be friendly, though. The American presence withdrew as soldiers traveled back to Forts Bliss, Hood, Benning, Dix, McCoy, Hunter Liggett, and Leonard Wood, then finally home.

British Convoys did not like the fact that a fog the next morning hindered our mission heading into Kurdistan. We delayed 30 minutes for a little burnoff, and then spit out of the ECP and whizzed past the storefront where Santa had been standing inside a women's clothing store. I haven't seen him since. I have remodeled a Victoria's Secret in the States around Christmas time however, and can report that they indeed sell X-mas undies just for the holidays.

We bypassed Chamchamal Prison and the big hills between it and the awesome Metropolis of Sulaymaniyah. Mountains began to grow all around. We sped past a university that hugged the eight-lane freeway through a city with a skyline much like Salt Lake City. Many tower cranes punctuated the downtown, and building was prosperously ongoing. We moved at the lawful speed, too fast for me to gawk; in only fifteen minutes the roads narrowed outside of Sulaymaniyah, then followed into neighborhoods with old but well-kept streets. The convoy continued on as more fog piled up onto the road from the valleys and crawled up one mountain, then the next. Sedimentary giants vaulted at sixty degrees. We wound through natural serpentines 600 hundred feet below their peaks. The Brits unwillingly slowed down. Suddenly, the chatter through their internal NET communications was that the lead driver and movement Commander wanted to pull over in order to turn around and head back to Kirkuk. Halabja was only 65 miles away.

The visibility sucked, to be sure. I completely agreed that slowing down was prudent, as the view of the mountains was partially obscured. Hearing this, I forcefully chimed in. "If you want to stop for an unscheduled halt, in order to let the weather lift, then that's fine." Between clenched teeth I added, "but we are getting to the school this morning!" This wasn't my first trip to the school, or my first rodeo. Besides, no one would shoot at us deep inside Kurdistan. Practically no chance of encountering IEDs along the route. More plausible was the risk of a tire blowout, overturning the up-armored Land Rover and tumbling into a ravine.

As senior leader I had my employees' attention. They worked for me at that moment. Not that I was shrill or thought myself to be the Queen of England, but because it was the right thing to proceed. The convoy commander was risk averse, but I wasn't bluffing. We continued the march. None too soon it became sunny, and the topography was gorgeous. A Heineken sign appeared in a restaurant's window, and spots of civilization continued to amaze with neat little farms with modern equipment.

I hoped my vague emails would produce a rare, outside the wire, scoundrel-to-billpayer meeting. It was another risk taken to coordinate in a hostile environment. A talented young Iraqi businessman versus Major Dupar; place your bets. The same contractor who was building the Tikrit Technical Center, the renovated mess hall for the Iraqi Air Force cadets, and the aircraft simulator at the gym had the project to build the school in Halabja. I nurtured a love/hate relationship with Faruq.

Big, rolling hills like perfect sine waves floated pasture for nibbling sheep, replacing the mountains. Five miles further was a hard-fought border dividing the land between Iraq and Iran. After Iranian forces briefly captured territory north of Halabja, in the waning days of the eight-year cataclysm between the Sunni Arabs of Iraq and the Shia Persians of Iran in 1988, Saddam Hussein al Tikriti murdered upwards of five thousand Kurdish civilians on a bright March morning, just like this one. The beleaguered fort north of town wasn't attacked, but the neighborhoods of the town were. The Ba'athist government punished civilians for past uprisings, and justified murder of supposed "sympathizers of Iran," blaming them for losing a battle. Iranian doctors recognized the effects of mustard gas on thousands needing treatment afterwards. Tens of thousands of their countrymen had died similarly during that war. Saddam believed Iranian agents hid in the town, so gave the order to murder as many Kurds as possible.

Creeping things and flying things froze or dropped to die on Kurdish earth in unknown numbers. Crops curled brown; all food and water were rendered unfit. This greatest recent unprovoked massacre upon civilians was enough to stir a momentary, international, unresponsive rage. The wanton cruel acts at Halabja, with its 11,000 people injured, many to die later from their burns, turned our collective stomachs. And the world quickly turned the page.

Helicopters directed fighter bombers to drop a combination of nerve and respiratory agents. People smelled rotting garbage and fresh cut grass, laughing before choking up bright green vomit tasting like sickly sweet pears. Trucks squished bodies as panicked families fled, crushing skulls like melons. Women pushed their children, seeking shelter into cellars where the heavier than air gas sank into low lying spots, to persist and to blister. Ranting people screamed, "GAS, GAS!" Then dropped dead. A regular patter of bombs thudded onto streets, raining shrapnel and billowing out yellow clouds. The murderous sorties ended by the late afternoon as the sun sank low. Cattle and sheep strangled. Pets and people convulsed and moaned. Those who could move from the center of the town used the night to crawl away, leaving whole families to the dark. Children's death masks with wide shocked eyes questioned the star-filled heaven; their froth-filled lips and bile-flecked chins quieted forever. All was silent. Many things were dead or dying in Halabja.

Lights turned on along the streets for no one. Survivors sheltered in their homes, terrified the attack would start again.

Chemical weapons to a tactician are useless. They render the zone in which they are employed "off limits." Only a madman would send his own infantry into the poison. It disperses depending on the wind, uncontrolled. People survive chemical attacks because they are in a pocket where concentrations are low. Just lucky. The next morning photographers documented mothers clasping babies and toddlers strewn about the streets like rag dolls in brightly colored wraps. Faces were planted into holes in a rough last attempt to breathe. The world knew in a few days, well after neighbors dug mass graves for thousands, too fast to get an accurate count of those murdered.

The US Army Corps of Engineers struggled for several years to build a 19-classroom, two-story school there; to make a mark. Or better yet to say that we remember what happened. That Halabja was not forgotten and left all alone.

• • •

"We're going to need the scaffold plan immediately," I bullied. It was a bluff, but my contractor didn't know it. "How are you going to build the tower for the water tank, Faruq?" Mr. Darrow had been asking for the scaffold plan for two months, and now we couldn't wait any more. Even if Faruq was ready to start, he hadn't given us any submittals on what the scaffolding was going to look like, or how they planned to build the tank. I showed frustration despite my glee that I had Faruq on site. The Corps of Engineers, Mr. Neal Darrow, the smart guy from the Tikrit Resident Office, an honest to God structural engineer, required knowing how the contractor would build the three-story water tower, so it didn't just collapse during construction, and would actually function.

"We can't go forward without that. We have to plumb the whole building next and how the system gets pressure has to be figured out immediately!" Dramatic pause. "That means we're screwed!" Dramatic pause. "Do we have to review the schedule again?" I asked Faruq, turning away grinning, trying not to giggle.

The concrete structure for the school was almost completed. Two stories of stairways, corridors, bathrooms, offices, foyer, lunch room, kitchen, and 19 classrooms were itching for electrical rough-in (placing conduit), rough plumbing (laying pipe – very exciting), then windows, roofing, siding—and the list of critical activities to finish went on. It was unfortunate that Faruq was paid ahead, all leverage lost.

"I do not understand why you need a plan for scaffold? We will build the parking lot next, Insha Allah." My blood ran cold when he said that—"God willing."

"NO. No no." I turned to hide my smile. "Let's go to where you have to tie into the electrical grid." And I started to walk toward a corner of the school property.

The Brits gave up on "securing" the jobsite during my inspection here in Kurdistan and watched the goofball Major roam around. Kids kept flocking and neighbors came with advice with better English than Ghulam Faruq. He didn't like being advised by local Kurds, but when another man drove up stating that he was from the building department of the City of Halabja, I beamed with the fortuitous meeting of the minds. Electrical, well water, and sanitary sewer plans were confirmed as to where the school would connect to these utilities.

A member of the school board and the appointed principal even showed up to ask me if the US tax payer could help furnish the school, too. I said I'd check to see if that was in the scope of work. It wasn't. "Will the school be ready for the fall semester?" they asked. All I could say is, "I hope so." If God and Faruq wills it.

Faruq didn't like it when I chronicled his manpower over the past two months. It was woefully inadequate. We visited our projects every six days in order to monitor the work. He tried telling me about his problems with getting people from Baghdad to travel to Kurdistan to work. "Why don't you hire locally?" I asked.

"NO, No no." He responded that he must have people from Baghdad to work here. "We Arabs don't like to work in Kurdish area." Many centuries of reasons lay behind this.

"Right. Why don't you hire a local subcontractor?"

A ten-story apartment building was going up across the street and Faruq claimed that all the local workers were there and couldn't come to work on our project. It was a dubious statement at best. But I couldn't force his hand too much, so I returned to the subject of the water tower. It had to be built high enough in elevation in order to provide water pressure for the structure. I reminded Faruq that the tower was on the blueprints and we had asked him about it every week. He didn't like me. But the poor bastard was seemingly lost in the sauce. It was hard working with the Corps of Engineers, especially since we didn't want people to die during construction. Weeks earlier I had the bright idea to place the water tank on the roof instead. Mr. Darrow said that if they could demonstrate that the concrete roof could take the load, then it was possible. Yeah, man. To hell with the architect!

When I suggested this approach to Faruq he seemed happy, but also a little confused that I was trying to help him. I just wanted the school to move past just being a concrete shell. We needed all interior and exterior features of work to begin, and unfortunately, I couldn't withhold payment as a carrot or a stick. All features of work were past their scheduled starts, as if my contractor cared about time. The US Army Corps of Engineers would always pay and never penalize for lateness. Placing the parking lot should be the last of his concerns. But it was something he could do quickly and easily.

"But only if the math works out. Structurally. For the tank." I said.

Now he got it. "Of course," he wagged his chin, "we will show it will support the tank. No problem." I bet he would make the math work out. Although Neal would check his figures for sure.

"Maybe you will have to build another internal column to bear the weight." I paused to think. "But you can really put it where you want. And then you can start to run your plumbing throughout the building." We had just eliminated a feature of work that had been delaying the project on paper. If the architect wanted to argue with us, she could travel from her cozy office in Virginia to the border of Iran to speak her peace.

Upon the roof, I again admired the natural beauty of the place, inspected the bituminous roofing system to be used to make the school watertight, and reluctantly descended down the ladder. But first I took a picture of Maggie Moo with the Iranian border as the background. She was a black and white little stuffed cow with a pink dress that a friend of my daughter's had sent me. It was for a contest to see who could chronicle the toy's travels the most. (Something fun for fifth graders to do.) And I thought this picture a slam dunk for first prize. I mailed Miss Moo along with the picture back to Wisconsin a few days later. I don't know if she won.

Faruq and I shook hands. We were now "besties" again. A couple of kids ran alongside my ballistic glass window as if I were a rock star, and I waved. British Convoys drove away toward the museum commemorating the poison gas attack.

I had seen the bubbly museum roof from the school's roof a few blocks away. It sure was weird looking. At the center, what appeared to be a pole was pushing up a white masonry tent. On the edge of the circular museum at the roofline were concrete clouds, tumbling over themselves like soap bubbles about to snap with yellowy poisons. I learned inside the exhibit that it was built to represent the clouds of gas that billowed over the town. The curator opened the doors just for us. It was as solemn as a funeral. Hundreds of photographs of thousands of dead people strewn about Halabja's streets and fields like brightly colored matchsticks tossed about, some alone, some in clusters. All the ground was hallowed in this town.

A life-sized panorama greeted you at the entrance of the museum with plaster bodies of families dispatched in their own front yards. An elaborate hall of peace centered the building, with carved teak chairs and a large round table. Flags of neighboring countries were displayed on the walls, while sheets of white linen stretched upwards at the center towards a large circular skylight, reaching towards righteousness. Poetry and pictures of survivors adorned the walls of the museum. I was glad to depart. The curator gave me a DVD to take home to America. It contained many pictures of dead bodies; evidence of the massacre by poison gas at Halabja.

I've asked myself if the war was worth the sacrifice of blood and treasure. The US military made certain that Saddam Hussein or the Ba'athists would never order such horror again. And that was something to be thankful for.

• • •

Just south of the city of Sulaymaniyah, the Brits regularly stopped for a meal. One man guarded our weapons as we entered the equivalent of a Kurdish fast food joint. We did this to pay respect to the Kurds and demonstrate our comfort while in their midst, not wanting to appear to be a threat ourselves. Besides, we were hungry. The Kurds use silverware to eat, but the ubiquitous flat bread was passed from hand to hand to hand to hand as it was torn and dipped into the sauce and relish of choice. Lamb and chicken dishes, reminiscent of fajitas, with coriander and cucumber dressing were quite tasty. We uniformed men wiped tables clean before flopping down to gobble our orders.

The bathrooms were appalling by American standards. A plate was brought to the weapons guard, and I dug deep in my wallet to pay for everybody in US currency, about $60. The chance of introducing your gut to a bug it'd never experienced before was 100%. After our quick stop, British Convoys got back on route to bring me to my next appointment. Passing through the modern city always brought about American hubris. As in, "I thought only we had tall buildings and universities."

Through one of my local construction representatives I was able to gain a meeting with a Peshmerga general near the hamlet of Chamchamal. Through the fast work of Nawroz, whom I paid weekly, I had to wait for the General only about an hour or so. It was always a pain not being able to make firm meeting times, but the man was flexible and willing to see the American major only knowing the date. I met Nawroz for the first time that afternoon while waiting. For his ability to make hasty arrangements, I recommended his continued employment to the anonymous major soon to replace me.

The chia was sugary with the two lumps I added. His office was big. It was in a plain building beside the artery connecting Sulaymaniyah and the Arab part of Iraq. The rugs, couches, and furniture were old but in good repair. The General was cordial and wore a blazer without a tie.

I felt privileged and he may have felt so as well, as the Pesh love America and most Americans. Two leaders rubbing elbows to make things work. I told him all about the prison project and our efforts at the school in Halabja. The General knew all about them. I felt out of my league but quickly told him about my problem with the local man complaining about the toxic goo leaching into his fields from the failed sanitation ponds at Chamchamal. Looking back, I hoped I didn't buy that farmer a bloody nose. Time was running out and US Forces were leaving in a big hurry after a nine-year presence. I wished his people well and good fortune. The Kurds lived in a very tough "neighborhood" to be sure, Baghdad being the worst offender. The General reassured me like a gray-haired uncle. Such good people deserved a reliable patron.

Or would America simply walk away again once its immediate interests were served, as in Afghanistan after the Soviets departed and our armed Mujahedeen filled the void, to blend with the Taliban? Would America abandon the Kurds to a Turkish genocide next?

We continued the road march towards Kirkuk, and then home. Past a ridge 30 minutes east of the oil rich city of Kirkuk, we donned our Kevlar helmets and vests. Once again IEDs were a possibility in the Arab part of Iraq. There was no insurgency in Kurdistan.

The next morning at 5:00 a.m. the alarm went off as usual, "Boom, Boom, Boom." Then landing somewhere on the FOB, "BANG! WHIZZZZ BANGBANG!"

The same wimpy-voiced southern drawl warned through the loud speakers, "AT TENSION ON THE FOB; AT TENSION ON THE FOB. INCOMING. INCOMING. THIS IS THE BIG GIANT VOICE! ENCOMUN' ENCUMIN'!"

I hoped that nobody got hurt. The impacts sounded far away. I rolled over, pressing an imaginary snooze button.

CHAPTER 27

# Closing Up Shop

The best boss I'd ever had was already gone—Lieutenant Colonel Watson. I had been without adult supervision for two months in the early summer of 2011. Leadership now became a premium as the quick exit of American Military Forces accelerated, tugging at our elbows with a Presidential order. One by one, individual augmentees ended their year-long deployments. It was like the band splitting up. Department of the Army civilians planned their movements. Our brightest, Mr. Neal Darrow, was ordered to Mosul, to finish re-construction of police stations in the midst of bombings and bulging, load- bearing walls. Units gave up their digs to whoever would sign for them or not, formed convoys, and headed south. The USA had given itself until Thanksgiving to un-ass its position in Iraq.

The structure of Iraq was as it was, America's commitment at an end. Big Sister was leaving for college. Little Sister was going to have to fend for herself, starting right now. President Obama had signed a piece of paper.

The US Army Corps of Engineers exit plan was in ever-changing development for a year, as there were many unknowns within a vast number of competing demands. A small contingent of a few hundred souls would actually stay behind to support the State Department projects and clean up the last of ours. I was to brief the exit plan of the Tikrit Office of USACE to a general from 3rd Division. I didn't understand a lot of what was going on. Many good questions were asked for which I had no answers. Making stuff up as you go along is okay for oneself, but when responsible for several dozen others plus millions of dollars of property, it gave rise to panic. The Baghdad headquarters was about as helpful as tits on a bull. My counterpart in Mosul was even worse off than I was. At least we weren't being mortared and shot at while we tried to close up shop.

America at home was tired of war, unwilling to sustain the effort. Those in the field kept opinions to themselves. Both blood and treasure were expended in devotion to a people we had freed from a tyrant. The Iraqis were aided by the US, within our own national interests to control their borders and maintain the rule of law within.

The heavy lift completed the crush and destruction of Iraqi roads by overweight tractor trailers. The Turks wouldn't allow their NATO (North Atlantic Treaty Organization) allies to transit through their country, so it was a laborious retrograde movement to the world's largest ashtray, breaking pavements with tens of thousands of loads of personnel and equipment. Friends that we now somewhat understood watched the US go by and knew the highways and streets would not soon be rebuilt. Some were jubilant, everybody fearful. That included we Americans.

This is when I was the most scared. I was apprehensive about getting home.

The Mayor's Cell at FOB Speicher set the date for the exit brief by its tenants before the Deputy Commander of the Marne Division. All planning was done at either the confidential or secret level of security protocol, as troop movement was as sensitive as information could get. The Power Point slide deck didn't readily fit the US Army Corp of Engineers' plan. Others might leave, but the Corps was going to stay as a tiny, former slice of its nearly decade-long presence. Some support to the Iraqi government had to continue, despite everyone else "popping smoke." The term means concealing one's movement, especially for a retrograde movement off the battlefield, like using smoke grenades that pop when they ignite. The logistical tether rewound, increasing in momentum. The Engineers were going to help cover the withdrawal, the end of the counterinsurgency effort.

It had been a long time coming. This iteration of the conflict was at an end. I was at low ebb. With a hiccup and burped-up nervous reluctance, I recalled a friend I'd had during my first deployment. What would Tony do in a situation like this? I needed someone to tell me what I was doing was OK.

I had pushed those memories back for a long time. But I was in Iraq, after all. Maybe I could listen for a while and leave him behind like before? It wasn't a hard step, just a conversation in my head, like writing fiction. I wondered what Tony would look like seven years later—less hair, maybe fatter? It was a very comfortable feeling, taking a trolley to make-believe.

• • •

I was still able to buy New York strips at the big PX on Speicher that early summer, and cooked out often as a way to say goodbye to those leaving. The IT guy, my friend Johnny, who had called me drunk when on his midpoint leave to tell me he loved me, left. One by one the team broke up. Johnny was the sound system in front of the stage, and God help those remaining when the computer equipment hit bad patches. We were told that the few military personnel who remained in Iraq would be wearing civilian clothes and not permitted to carry weapons. It seemed pretty dicey, if not downright dangerous.

But who was I going to get to sign for our beautiful compound? Our stand-alone telecommunication network, the dozens of bungalows, the little gym and the patch of grass with the diminutive palm tree? I walked over to the Mayor's Cell blind. There wasn't a blueprint to refer to. I had only two weeks before I briefed a general on our plan to get the hell out of Dodge. A lot was unknown. Advice rang in my ears that I should "brief what I knew." Guessing was an invitation for the reviewing officer to drill down for answers to thorny issues. I felt that any uncertainty in my presentation could lead to public embarrassment. Shaking like a dog pooping razorblades behind a lectern wasn't my idea of fun, especially while the General Officer chased rabbits down a hole.

"Look. This really isn't that big of a problem. No matter what, you're leaving. Don't worry who's taking over after you. The first thing is to get someone to sign for the compound. Get over to the Mayor's Cell. Remember, you're about to sell Boardwalk and Park Place for nothing. This is easy."

"Thanks, Tone," I thought.

I walked in there like Donald Trump trying to find a buyer for his namesake Tower in New York City for pennies on the dollar. And I found Tonia.

She was the Senior State Department Representative in Northern Iraq and when I told her my need to shed the most valuable real estate on FOB Speicher her marvelous blue/green eyes gleamed. In her early forties, Tonia was easily the prettiest girl I had spoken to in months/years/forever.

"You mean the Engineer Compound by the dining Facility?"

"Yep. Where are you and your staff staying now?"

"Third ID has us staying in a dorm with bunk beds on the other side of post."

"How many folks do you have now?" I asked.

She tossed her long raven black hair to one side and said, "Only five. But I have another five coming next week. And I didn't know where I was going to house them." Tonia stood up from her desk and came closer to me. She was wearing a skirt and her bare knees made mine buckle. Sandal-clad, her toenails were painted the same aqua marine as her blouse. My long lost friend Jim Fester once said that you could tell a lot about a woman by her feet. I had to force myself from staring at her near "nekkid" legs to peer into her eyes instead. They were like the ocean, pulling me away in an undertow.

"Well," I stammered, "I think I may have just solved that problem for you." I felt cool giving away what wasn't mine. But it was a huge relief to solve this momentous problem. "Have you ever been inside our compound?"

Tonia gushed, "Oh. I've seen it. It's the best."

Yeah, baby. "If you have some time, we could go have a look now. I have some CHUs empty. You could move in right away." It was like finding a new lead singer. Tonia would eventually sign for everything, even the little palm tree.

Oh, she liked me! We made an appointment for the following morning. The woman was positively giddy. She and her right hand girl were moved into their bungalows by the end of the next day, every day a work day, even Sunday.

Walking back to my office, Tony chimed in again, "Would you make love with that woman if you had the chance?"

"I won't have the chance." I looked at him. "Screw." We gave each other serious glances. "Would I screw her? Use a construction term, Engineer. Tap, nail, drill." He was grinning and shaking his head. Tony was actually a lot thinner than when I knew him in 2004. The skin on his face was sallow and deeply creased now, as if he hadn't been taking care of himself.

"That isn't what I asked." I was smiling too. "She has nice tits. What do you think?"

"You mean huge."

I stripped his gears by asking, "Say, tomorrow is Sunday. After my run, would you like to go to chapel? I'm tired of going alone." It was my normal routine.

"Yeah, sure." Tony was always a good sport. "Is that before you give Tonia whatever she wants? Or after?"

"Before."

Hearing my feet step over gravel, the sound of crunching rocks reminded me of the solitary stride felt in Iraq. Surrounded by people all moving elsewhere.

"Hey, how far are you in building the continuity book for your replacement?" Tony asked. Another major was supposed to show up after the Freedom Bird scooped me up, so as a professional courtesy to someone I'd never meet, a small book with points of contacts, explanations on open projects, and any other information for an officer coming in blind would be invaluable to her or him.

"Shit, Tony. I haven't even grabbed an empty binder yet. I thought you said don't worry about it."

"I didn't say don't do it, dipstick. There's nothing to worry about. You're going home remember? Let's get a start on it this afternoon after lunch. Probably won't take that long."

"OK."

• • •

My screen saver was a picture of The Freedom Bird. Ask anyone who has been to Iraq or Afghanistan about it and you'll see a recollection in their eyes, like they're seeing the mythical Phoenix rising from the ashes unto rebirth. You see, unless you go rogue and try to make it home by yourself through the Turkish border, then hitchhike through Europe and somehow get a flight to the good ol' USA on your own dime, just to be jailed for desertion the next time you have contact with law enforcement, YOU DON'T GO HOME UNTIL UNCLE SUGAR BUYS YOU THE TICKET! The screen saver was a pie chart superimposed over a 747 fuselage flying just over your head. Your days already spent in theater were one section of the pie, and the time remaining was practically a sliver.

I called Fort Benning about my Release from Active Duty (REFRAD) date and was told I should show up a week earlier than I had planned in order to give the system enough time to process me out. Sweet Jesus! The pie chart now showed only fifteen days before I had to begin my individual movement. I called home to tell the girls I'd be back by the end of June. Ellen's response was muted. Tony squeezed my shoulder as we admired the slice of time left, like a pizza you couldn't eat fast enough.

One afternoon a Ghurka guard came to my desk to present me with a small brass representation of Nepal. The language barrier was only breeched through smiles, handshakes, bows, and pats on the back. The next day the Ghurka guards were gone. It was like a dream upon wakening, the comforter kicked onto the floor. I continued to look about for the remembrance now lost through too many travels and moves. The Ghurkas were underutilized security. Now, the compound was wide open to any passersby.

An Air Force Lieutenant Colonel took up residence with us. He was going to work projects with the State Department for the following year. I asked him about having to wear civilian clothes and not being able to have a side arm and he confirmed as much. Uncle Sugar was preparing to build a massive super-structure over the Walmart-sized dining facility to the tune of $20 million dollars. "Good luck with that," I thought. But 30-foot pieces of structural steel were already showing up and staged next to the DFAC. The cover would bear the brunt if a mortar hit the bullseye.

British Convoys halved their personnel and many friends went home with healthy bank accounts. They were the horns and woodwinds. I felt like I was playing a sad guitar peal. Tony said that I was too melodramatic. But it worked for me.

The hand receipt for the tens of thousands of dollars of computer equipment was completely jacked up, and angry words flew between me and a supply Department of the Army civilian from Baghdad. I tried to make sense of it, but gave up.

"You're going home. It's over." Tony coached. I wanted a smooth handoff of projects left undone to the personnel remaining.

The big day of the briefing arrived. Every unit, Aviation, Medical, Transportation, Infantry, Signal, Artillery, Military Police, Air Defense, Quartermaster, Legal, Postal, all the Ash and Trash, and me, Engineers, demonstrated our retrograde planned movement to Kuwait to the Marne Division's Executive Officer. My nerves were frayed as I waited my turn to brief the Major General (two-stars). Commanders spoke about their units' personnel strength, equipment on hand, containers to be trucked south, what they couldn't account for, what they had to leave behind, what they were leaving for the Iraqi Forces that would take over Speicher. They'd rename it to be sure to something like,

"THANKSFORTHEFREESTUFFWE'REGOINGTO SURRENDERASSOONASYOULEAVE Air Station."

But in Arabic it sounds much nicer. Speicher was as ready to be the home of the Iraqi Air Force academy and primary aviation station as it could be.

"No bullshit. Tell the General what you know. Don't guess or he'll have your ass." Tony gave good advice. "There's lots of shit that the Army hasn't figured out, but we still have to get out!"

All personnel had to be accounted for, orders cut. All property had to either be brought back to the US or transferred to the garrison or the Iraqi Air Force. Stuff to leave behind had to be annotated, too. Our plans didn't have to be perfect, but at the end of the day, we didn't want the Iraqis to complain about the mess we left them.

Finally, it was my turn to present with the same secret squirrel Power Point shell. I introduced myself, and quickly stated that unlike all other units leaving Iraq, the Corps of Engineers, "We're staying!"

The soldiers in the auditorium laughed and the General smiled. But it wasn't that far from the truth. I saw Tony chuckle and grab the bridge of his nose. He probably thought, "damned fool." Tony, I mean—not the general. Hopefully, not the general. A small contingency of Americans would remain. The President allowed a force of about 1,000 military personnel to stay and the Engineers still had to complete our open projects. Why not break up the tension with some humor?

I explained about how the State Department was taking over the Engineer compound (Boardwalk and Park Place) and dithered on until the general asked a pointed question about the completion of the Air Traffic Control Tower. I explained that the elevator contractor should have the machine commissioned soon. The humongous simulator room was operational, (it was a 360-degree panoramic exact representation of the control room seven stories above and the only one outside the United

States). Other details about the status of the Raytheon equipment was presented. The bottom line was that the Office Jewel was operational and the training of Iraqi Air Traffic Control Operators had begun. He was satisfied, and made a remark about how pivotal this was in support of their new Air Force. The brief went fine.

• • •

My Turkish contractor friend, Derin, called me one late afternoon telling me quickly that two of his men, including Derya, had been kidnapped at our northern most school, near Mosul.

Unfortunately for my Turkish contractor, Uncle Sugar could do nothing. The chiropractor/contractor from Virginia would have to pay the ransom, or not. The kidnappers had waited until the last school was complete to 99.9% before they took the workers at gunpoint. In a weird irony, I suppose they didn't want the school to be left undone either.

Just before I left, I called Derin one more time, and to my relief his two guys had been released. I was too ashamed at American impotence to ask what was done. Knowing Derin, he probably paid out of his own pocket.

That same morning, I placed the continuity book on the blotter of my desk and was escorted to BIAP to board the Freedom Bird by a skeleton crew of British Convoys. I had four duffle bags filled to the brim, punched down and filled some more.

The stress was gone. Just like that the voice of Tony was gone. Better save those tricks for works of fiction, I thought. I forgot to say goodbye. That was pretty lousy of me. He didn't deserve that. Tony said I shouldn't worry about going home. That was bullshit. But it got me on the plane without cracking up. I should have been more appreciative.

• • •

The Freedom Bird isn't made for comfort. We squeezed as many rows of seats onto a huge jetliner as possible, not worried about the comfort of soldiers and Marines, just cost. The ticket was free and the aircraft flew west, trying to catch the setting sun towards the land of beer and pizza. The tight seating was almost unbearable, as I fought for the armrest with the other big guy next to me, my knees up against the seat in front. If the soldier reclined, I was going to lose my mind.

After eighteen hours of feeling imprisoned, overfed, and sticky, with a layover in Ireland, somewhere near the eastern seaboard the cockpit announced that we were now in American airspace and would be in Atlanta in about forty-five minutes. Muffled cheers softly reverberated in the darkened cabin. Heroes about to be zeros remained silent. The lucky entered above the sea to shore asleep.

In a warehouse we emptied our duffle bags and turned in gear gratefully unused. Chemical suits and cold weather gear spread across tables in the Georgia heat. Everyone motored in second gear as barn fans moved the atmosphere of hurry up and wait. I turned in Uncle Sugar's 9-millimeter Beretta by serial number inventory with a huge sigh of relief, finally unarmed from war, as I moved to the next station. There I wrote a check for about $75 for a parka I swear I never had. It was an easy, yet sweaty transaction. No time to spread my toes between quickly growing grass. We Deployables answered post- deployment medical questionnaires that could mean many different stop signs. Medical Hold meant reuniting with family was delayed indefinitely. Those needing pain management were given handfuls of different colored pills.

I was coming back to Wisconsin with all my fingers and toes, and had a job lined up back at McCoy to train the last units to go to war in Afghanistan; but only after I spent several weeks of paid leave back on the block.

Another plane ride and I got back to Milwaukee after midnight. I slept fitfully for a few hours in a hotel, then walked a few blocks to a field to watch planes descend over my head, wondering who else was on a freedom bird. The appointed time to see my loves, again, came in a gas station parking lot, ingloriously. Kisses and the urge to keep driving on this Sunday morning revived me. I didn't make it to church that day, for that day we were church, putting into remembrance the Lord, pleading together so that we may be justified. A secure hand upon the wheel.

The cock-a-poodle greeted me along with a small sea of dandelions. Few things weren't out of place from old memories. Unpacking was a chore. With two girls in the house, a single shelf in the medicine cabinet was unceremoniously cleared. My presence was like a small stone thrown into a small pond in the summer-time; the algae spread momentarily, then covered back the surface in tension, muting the ripples. The disturbance barely registered but for a fleeting glance and a "plop."

Everyone had moved on. The world doesn't stop just because you go downrange. Sometimes, angry loved ones rained emotional blows upon those walking through concourses for the second, third or maybe fourth time, with silence and standoffishness. Most of these just a few feet tall.

The Deployables came home with a skidding stop, broken and lost in our own beds; wanting and ready in a moment to go back overseas, where we were total pros. Removed from a cauldron, soldiers discovered what tremendous pressures they could bear and what they could not. Families just bore the burden.

We expectantly waited for orders that would never come again.

CHAPTER 28

# ISIS and the Caliphate

The civil war in Syria began after the Arab Spring of 2011 and was violently suppressed by another Ba'athist (like Saddam Hussein), Bashar al-Assad. Al-Qaida in Iraq, which was crushed by the USA, morphed into ISIS (Islamic State of Syria and Iraq). The regular bombings killing dozens of people in Baghdad didn't register with American media anymore. The US turned its face away. The freely elected Shia leaders allied with Iran. Civil war seemed imminent in Iraq, too.

I was one of the last mobilized Reservists at Fort McCoy during the wars in Iraq and Afghanistan. Having restored my "street cred" by freshly returning from war was wonderful. Through an administrative glitch, I got only a nine-month mobilization instead of the usual twelve. I thought I had hit the rest button on feeding from the government trough inside the USA. But the fat money was soon to end in an uncertain future. The Army promoted me to Lieutenant Colonel. I finally realized that I wasn't in the Army, but in small part, was the Army, responsible for the lives of those around me and what we, as an organization, would become. Apparently, I'm a slow learner. I thought about telling the Army story my way, but as yet hadn't listened to the new voice whistling in my head.

A National Guard Infantry Brigade from Minnesota trained through Fort McCoy in 2012. But the pace of training units slowed to a trickle as the wars wound down. I worked in Operations. Few units were available to train on the snowy roads and the hip tall drifts in the great frozen tundra of northern Wisconsin.

I called my tribe looking for another gig. I had a job in 15 minutes, as I was volunteering to go back to war, my provenance superb. I heard that Afghanistan was lovely and wanted to see it on America's dime. There was no plan "B." After leaving Active Duty once again, I had several months of paid leave and fought the dandelions mightily. My obsession with curb appeal and constant maintenance eventually profited me one half of the proceeds of the house's sale. My family time was OK. At least I had lots of money in the bank. I'd drink a beer (or many beers) beneath the backyard silver maples, on the deck I had just built, and thanked God for the beauty of it all, and for all my fingers and toes. No PSTD (Post Traumatic Stress Disorder) for me. I was normal like the setting on a washing machine.

Two months into holiday I called USACE to check on my new orders, and I was informed that the position of Area Officer in Charge had been eliminated. I had been a lock, but it was time for America to downsize there, too. This time the President left a residual force of 10,000 troopers, ostensibly to keep the Taliban from immediately overrunning the country. It was a good thing that I had followed up on my orders, because the Engineers had decided that I was no longer in its future, but had neglected to inform me. The good news was I wasn't going to Afghanistan. The bad news was I wasn't going to Afghanistan. The thought of finding another course of employment filled me with dread, like a civilian imagining going to war. The finding-a-job world was about to chew me up and spit me out; bad jobs with bad bosses.

My fears continued to play out for a year, until in an epiphany, I decided to come back to my roots and bend nails as a union carpenter in Milwaukee. I didn't think I could do it physically, but I had underestimated both my stamina and skill set, flooded in doubt about my ability to provide for my girls' hobbies and general maintenance of home. A mighty pull upon my blue collar and my finances stopped hemorrhaging.

• • •

After their occupation of Fallujah, 1,500 motivated uniformed ISIS fighters attacked Mosul in early June of 2014. Sleeper cells detonated their homicide bombs at police stations and checkpoints. Thirty thousand Iraqi soldiers and thirty thousand Federal Police resisted half-heartedly, then melted away, some joining the ISIS advance. In six days, Mosul was captured. One-half million civilians had the black flag's version of Sharia law imposed upon them. Christians, homosexuals, women, those who opposed were robbed, thrown from roofs, raped, then covered and silenced, made to flee.

Attack helicopters were abandoned at the city's airport as well as hundreds of armored vehicles, thousands of rifles, and millions of rounds of ammunition. Captured Iraqi soldiers were hanged or crucified for the viewing public. Four thousand prisoners were murdered and lay in ditches. The Iraqi Republic suffered 2,500 killed in action. In Mosul, ISIS provided only 150 fighters to the butcher's bill.

The black flag pressed its advantage and surged south towards Tikrit and the home of the Iraqi Air Force Academy, chasing the retreating and the few army units who dared to oppose them. Officers, who would not stand, fled instead, toward the state-of-the-art air traffic control tower I had called the Office Jewel. ISIS fighters enveloped, then occupied facilities they could never master nor maintain.

The capitulation repeated itself as officers abandoned their commands. The last orders to their soldiers was merely to lay down their arms, change out of their uniforms, and find their own way home, trying to blend into the fleeing population. Some poured from the formerly named FOB Speicher and were swooped up into buses and promised safe passage. But they were taken to Saddam's former palaces to be tortured and beheaded, videotaped for recruiting drives. Hundreds more were marched into the western desert, in sight of the Office Jewel, to be shot in the back of their heads, rows upon rows, left unburied for tomorrow's unhurried heat. Leaderless, 800 cadets and support personnel were murdered.

• • •

I got hired as a carpenter to do blocking in a hotel alongside an Indian casino in Milwaukee. Where there are pictures, toilet paper holders, mounted TVs, towel bars, etcetera, before the arrival of the Mexican drywall crew, I screwed 2x8s between the studs so there was backing to screw to when it came to mounting things. After three months, the man who hired me came up asking if I wanted to go to Cali and run work. "I didn't hire you to do blocking." I was stunned. I was just grateful to earn a paycheck at the time. So, I pondered and asked the wife what she thought about my leaving again to make more money. It seemed like a no-brainer, since she was the parent and I was the paycheck, anyway. It was equally my fault, and sacrifice and loneliness repeated itself for some. Kids don't get to vote when grownups have to accept rare opportunities the next day.

My project was to remodel the ballrooms and meeting rooms in a big hotel in San Francisco. My primary contractor slept little, washed little, and drank a lot. I know because my nose knew his morning cologne. It was like marriage counseling, with lots of crying, hugging, yelling, and anger. The project manager cut nearly a month from the schedule in mid-stream. Eventually we remodeled the guest rooms, corridors, lobby, re-roofed the hotel, stamped concrete around the porte cochere, paved the parking lot, etcetera. I was relieved when the divorce was final. The Iraqi contractors were much sharper, much more on the ball. Ghulam Faruq would have demanded to get paid more for the accelerated pace.

I found a job in the Army Reserve for the last four years of my military career, establishing the internal training program for an Army Reserve Division stationed out of Fort McCoy, Wisconsin. I worked one weekend a month, with two weeks of Annual Training a year. It continued to grow, having over 500 soldiers assigned to it, when I blessedly retired after 30 years working for Auntie and Uncle Sugar. No break in service. I was toast, burnt out, exhausted at the finish line, just like you should be. I wrote down all my adventures, acquiescing to the characters popping into my brain.

I wonder why people correspond with terrorist recruiters, send cash, or actually join ISIS to kill the "other" in a foreign land. At their center, they must have loneliness and lack. Perhaps they listen to voices churning out hate on the internet, or an evil presence they invite into their heads or imagine for themselves. Defeating ideas like that will be a pretty neat trick.

Not like my pal Tony. Very, very different.

# Glossary of US Army Acronyms

| | |
|---|---|
| AAR | After Action Review |
| AO | Area of Operations |
| AD | Armored Division |
| BIAP | Baghdad International Airport |
| BN | Battalion |
| CO | Company |
| DFAC | Dining Facility |
| ECP | Entry Control Point |
| FOB | Forward Operating Base |
| GI | General Issue ((Soldiers) |
| GP | General Purpose |
| HHC | Headquarters and Headquarters Company |
| HMFIC | Head Mother Fucker in Charge |
| HQ | Headquarters |
| IED | Improvised Explosive Device |
| IBU | Itty Bitty Unit (Laundry, Postal, Water Purification, etc.) |
| ISIS | Islamic State of Iraq and Syria |
| KIA | Killed in Action |
| KBR | Kellogg, Brown and Root |
| LSA | Life Support Area |
| LT | Lieutenant |
| MEDIVAC | Medical Evacuation |
| MP | Military Police |

| | |
|---|---|
| MRAP | Mine-Resistant Ambush Protected |
| MRE | Meals Ready to Eat |
| MWR | Morale, Welfare and Recreation |
| NCIS | Naval Criminal Investigative Service |
| NCO | Non-Commissioned Officer |
| NFL | National Football League |
| NET | Network Electronic Technologies |
| OD | Olive Drab |
| PMCS | Preventive Maintenance Checks and Services |
| PTSD | Post-Traumatic Stress Disorder |
| PX | Post Exchange |
| PT | Physical Training. Uniform (shorts and T-shirt) |
| QRF | Quick Reaction Force |
| RPG | Rocket Propelled Grenade |
| SP | Start Point (or time to leave the wire) |
| TOC | Tactical Operations Center |
| USACE | United States Corps of Engineers |
| UXO | Unexploded Ordinance |
| VBIED | Vehicle Borne Improvised Explosive Device |
| XO | Executive Officer |

# US Army Rank Structure

| Enlisted | Officer |
|---|---|
| Private | Second Lieutenant (Kenny in 1991) |
| Private Second Class | First Lieutenant (Kenny in 1994) |
| Private First Class (Kenny in 1987) | Captain (Kenny in 1999) |
| Specialist | Major (Kenny in 2005) |
| Corporal | Lieutenant Colonel (Kenny in 2011) |
| Sergeant | Colonel |
| Staff Sergeant | Brigadier General |
| Sergeant First Class | Major General |
| Master Sergeant | Lieutenant General |
| First Sergeant | General |
| Sergeant Major | General Of the Army |
| Command Sergeant Major | |
| Sergeant Major of the Army | |

# About the Author

Lieutenant Colonel Kenny Dupar at retirement July, 2017.
Bronze De Fluery award for career contribution to the
US Army Engineer Regiment.

**K**enny Dupar: I was raised in Milwaukee and attended the party school of the University of Wisconsin. "After drinking too much beer and studying too little I fell into academic probation. I realized I needed structure, like joining the ROTC (Reserve Officer Training Corps). I was adopted by the Army family.

All the squared away cadets were prior service, so naturally I enlisted and became Private First Class Dupar. Two summers at

Fort Knox were miserable but the most valuable military training I ever received. Graduating with a degree in Political Science (emphasis on American Foreign Policy and Economics) qualified me to cut grass or go to law school, so I enthusiastically requested Active Duty instead. But the Army downsized after the Persian Gulf War in 1991 and didn't need as many brand new officers, so I was commissioned as a Second Lieutenant in the Army Reserve. I was living in Milwaukee again when I was referred to an Engineer outfit. In a short interview, the Battalion Commander said he could change my branch from Infantry. Now I had already learned in my short career that competing with other men on toughness was like watching lions eat their young, eventually I'd be on the menu. It was far wiser to cross the retirement finish line in one piece and NOT jump out of airplanes or hump it on my back. The US Army Corps of Engineers became my tribe and I learned the basics of project management, road building, demolitions and timber frame construction.

A few short stories and metered poems, a few creative writing classes had given me flashes of joy but the craft became like a musical instrument never picked back up. Subject matter seemed stuck in the pathetic genre of not being able to get laid. Circumstances raced ahead of playfulness and my creative dreams drowned. A bewildering and crushing career path ensued in the civilian world. After a being fired as a rental car agent, I began a Carpentry Apprenticeship to compliment my ad hoc military career.

In 1999, I got married, procreated a honeymoon baby, was promoted to Captain, given a Company Command of over a hundred Soldiers and went into heart failure all in the span of three months. Thank you, modern pharmaceuticals for keeping me alive.

A year after 9/11, I was mobilized under Operation Enduring Freedom. They promised me a year's vacation in Iraq but at the last moment the Army became concerned about my health. The irony of sending me to war but being worried about my well-being was lost in regulations. How I got on the airplane will forever be shrouded in mystery.

The war changed me. You bet. More mature, more vulnerable. Seeing people living in garbage dumps and slums, seeing people get hurt; you can experience that in the US, but the scale is much greater in a war.

Being a smart ass doesn't mean that I don't care. I just prefer to laugh, shake it out, rather than concentrate on the awful bits.

I deployed to Iraq at the start of the war and again at the end, in between training others in Counter Insurgency doctrine. I became a SME (subject matter expert) and retired as a Lieutenant Colonel after 30 years of service in the Army Reserve, eight of those on Active Duty. According to Military courtesy, I should be addressed as, "Colonel, or Sir." Colonel Kenny. That has a nice ring to it.

If you've ever met a person astonished to still be alive, that's me.

CPSIA information can be obtained
at www.ICGtesting.com
Printed in the USA
BVHW072342260720
584565BV00003B/17